THE QUEEN AT 90

ST JAMES'S HOUSE

St James's House, Regal Press Limited,
298 Regents Park Road, London N3 2SZ, UK

www.stjamess.org

Typeset in Avenir.
Printed by Graphicom on 150g GardaMatt.
This paper has been independently certified according
to the rules of the Forest Stewardship Council (FSC).

A catalogue record for this publication is
available from the British Library

ISBN 978–1–906670–39–9

In September of last year, The Queen became the longest serving British monarch, and this year Her Majesty will be 90 years old. It is in recognition of these two memorable moments that this celebration is being held in the private grounds of Home Park Private, Windsor Castle.

The Queen, one of the most respected heads of state in the world, has made a major contribution to her country, its cultural and business interests, and indeed to the Commonwealth as a whole. It is for this reason that we have had so much support for this event from a myriad of business and other interests to thank Her Majesty and recognise her amazing achievements.

Not only will this unique event, which will feature more than 900 horses, the Armed Forces, actors and artists, together with representatives from the Commonwealth, be a memorable "thank you" to The Queen but also it is expected to generate a significant surplus, which will be distributed to a number of her sponsored charities.

The event will be televised live around the world on Sunday 15 May when The Queen will attend.

We hope that you enjoy this spectacular occasion.

With best wishes

Sir Mike Rake
Chairman
The Queen's 90th Birthday Celebration Advisory Committee

"I am looking forward to a busy 2016, though I have been warned I may have Happy Birthday sung to me more than once or twice"

Her Majesty The Queen,
Christmas Message, Christmas Day 2015

Contents

LONG LIVE
OUR NOBLE
QUEEN

The young princess

The early years

There is nothing unusual in the story of a 90-year-old who was born in a house that later gave way to an office block, who performed in pantomimes as a teenager, who trained as a car mechanic and who used ration coupons to pay for a wedding outfit. Except this is no ordinary nonagenarian, which explains why the then Home Secretary rushed to 17 Bruton Street, Mayfair in the middle of the night to attend her birth.

Sir William Joynson-Hicks certainly had other pressing concerns at the time, as a wage-related stand off with coal miners would lead to Britain's first ever general strike within a fortnight. However, tradition dictated that the Home Secretary should witness all royal births, and that of Elizabeth Alexandra Mary, daughter of The Duke and Duchess of York, who was born at the home of her maternal grandparents at 2.40 am on 21 April 1926, was no exception.

The age-old custom of verifying each royal birth in this way is said to have started when rumours were spread in 1688 that a baby passed off as King James II's son had been smuggled into the bedchamber in a warming pan because there had been no actual pregnancy. Understandably, Princess Elizabeth's paternal grandmother, Queen Mary, was less than thrilled about the Court Circular announcing that Sir William "was present in the house at the time of the birth", writing in a letter: "We did not approve of that stupid announcement, all on account of the 'confounded' etiquette. We tried to stop it but it was too late."

Since the Duke's older brother, The Prince of Wales, was the heir apparent, Princess Elizabeth didn't have the pressure of being a future monarch. Nevertheless, the public took a huge interest in the royal baby, who was third in line

PRINCESS ELIZABETH, AGED 9, WITH HER MOTHER AND YOUNGER SISTER. OPPOSITE: THE DUKE AND DUCHESS OF YORK POSE WITH THE PRINCESS AT HER CHRISTENING CEREMONY ALONGSIDE KING GEORGE V AND QUEEN MARY

to the throne, with crowds gathering outside the Bruton Street address even six weeks after her birth.

For her christening at Buckingham Palace at the end of May 1926, the Princess wore a white satin robe that had been made for the baptism of Queen Victoria's eldest daughter in 1841. But her mother generally insisted on dressing Elizabeth and her younger sister Margaret (born in 1930) in a simple way that implied a sensible upbringing. Likewise, as a toddler the Princess was allowed to play with only a single toy at a time despite the fact that, at the age of one, she had already received three tons of toys from well-wishers. "I don't think any child could be more sensiblybrought up," Queen Mary later remarked.

In fact, although a part of Antarctica was named after the young Princess and a wax model of her exhibited at Madame Tussaud's, she was apparently blissfully unaware of her own exalted status. Relatives, staff and the press all insisted that her childhood was "normal", despite members of the public peering through the railings outside the family home near Green Park in central London just to catch a glimpse of the blond-haired, blue-eyed girl playing on the lawn.

During the first year of her life, Elizabeth spent six months with her paternal grandparents at Buckingham Palace while her parents went on a tour of Australia. As a result, she grew very close to the ailing King George V. The public revelled in the

fact that Elizabeth apparently called him "Grandpa England",
and was particularly touched when, in the winter of 1928/29,
her daily visits raised his spirits so much as to help him recover
from a near-fatal illness. Just over a year later, the King gave
"Lilibet", as she came to be known, a pony for her fourth
birthday. By that point, she had already developed her lifelong
passion for horses and dogs, though she only received the
first of her famous corgis for her 18th birthday.

The Princess's life was transformed when, following the
death of her grandfather in January 1936, his successor, her
uncle, abdicated in December of that year and her father
became King. Aged 10, she was suddenly first in line to the
throne and therefore subject to even greater public interest.

Nevertheless, the desire for her to have a "normal
childhood" remained. In 1937, as well as attending her father's
coronation at Westminster Abbey, Elizabeth became a Girl
Guide, and several years later she joined the Sea Rangers.

OPPOSITE: THE WEDDING OF
PRINCESS ELIZABETH AND THE
DUKE OF EDINBURGH. RIGHT:
THE PRINCESS WITH HER FIRST
CHILD, PRINCE CHARLES

In 1939, she travelled on the London Underground for the first time and, having been moved to Windsor during the Blitz, she, Princess Margaret and the children of staff members put on Christmas-time pantomime performances there. In addition, having joined the Auxiliary Territorial Service in early 1945, Princess Elizabeth learnt how to drive and passed a car-maintenance course, thereby reportedly becoming the only British monarch able to change a spark plug!

And yet she also made her first radio broadcast aged 14, was appointed Colonel-in-Chief of the Grenadier Guards in early 1942, inspected a regiment on her 16th birthday and started carrying out some of the duties of Head of State in 1944. Having turned 21 during her first state visit (a tour of southern Africa) in 1947, she went on to marry Philip Mountbatten, who was made The Duke of Edinburgh on the morning of the ceremony, at Westminster Abbey later that same year, using ration coupons to pay for her wedding dress, in keeping with the spirit of post-war austerity.

In November 1948, Princess Elizabeth gave birth to Prince Charles, the first of her four children. Mercifully for her, the Home Secretary was no longer required to attend the birth of members of the Royal Family.

The new Queen

The 1950s

Between 1949 and 1951, the newlywed Princess Elizabeth spent much time in Malta. It was here that her new husband, The Duke of Edinburgh, was serving on HMS *Chequers* with the Royal Navy's Mediterranean fleet. In the August of 1950 she returned home to Clarence House to give birth to her eldest daughter, Princess Anne.

However, by the early 1950s, King George VI's health had started to deteriorate to the point that Princess Elizabeth would often stand in for him at public events, including numerous visits around the UK and the decoration of servicemen on the Royal Yacht *Britannia*. In 1951, she toured Canada and met with President Truman in Washington DC.

In January 1952, she embarked upon a Commonwealth tour, starting in Kenya. It was an ordinary Wednesday afternoon on 6 February 1952 – as she and The Duke of Edinburgh travelled from the Treetops Hotel to the Sagana Lodge, near Nyeri – when the 25-year-old Princess was informed that her father had died earlier that day at Sandringham. Having left Britain a princess, she was to return as Queen.

The Commonwealth tour was cancelled and the royal party flew back to Britain, arriving at London Airport the next day after a 4,600-mile journey. The new Queen was met by Prime Minister Winston Churchill and Foreign Secretary Anthony Eden, and immediately ordered a 16-week period of official mourning.

The coronation of Her Majesty Queen Elizabeth II took place in Westminster Abbey on 2 June 1953, after 16 months of intense preparations, with the ceremony conducted by Dr Geoffrey Fisher, Archbishop of Canterbury. Representatives of the Lords, the Commons and all the great public interests in Britain, prime ministers and leading citizens of the other Commonwealth countries, as well as representatives of foreign states, were present.

Crowds of people viewed the procession all along the route from Buckingham Palace to the abbey, despite heavy rain. The ceremony was also broadcast on radio around the world and on television for the first time. It was The Queen who requested the television broadcast, overriding her prime

PREVIOUS PAGES: THE
QUEEN'S CORONATION
(LEFT); AND HER OFFICIAL
CORONATION PORTRAIT
(RIGHT). OPPOSITE: THE
ROYAL COUPLE WITH A
YOUNG PRINCE CHARLES AND
PRINCESS ANNE. RIGHT: THE
QUEEN AND THE DUKE OF
EDINBURGH IN 1953 DURING
THE COMMONWEALTH TOUR

minister, and nearly 20 million people tuned in. Television brought the splendour of the coronation into the homes of hundreds of thousands of people around the Commonwealth in a way never before possible.

Political duties began at once for The Queen, from the State Opening of Parliament to weekly audiences with her first prime minister, Winston Churchill. Early in her reign, The Queen had occasion to exercise her royal prerogative when she appointed Harold Macmillan as Prime Minister in 1957. Anthony Eden had resigned following the Suez Crisis and, at that time, the Conservative Party did not have any formal electoral machinery for choosing a new leader, so The Queen acted on the advice of government ministers. It was a duty she would perform again in 1963.

Following Macmillan's appointment, life peers were admitted to the House of Lords for the first time. Appointed for their lifetime only, these Lords' titles are not passed on to their children. The Queen formally appoints life peers on the advice and recommendation of the prime minister.

National events impacted on The Queen's royal duties at times. In 1955, a national rail strike forced the cancellation of Trooping the Colour, the military parade marking her official birthday each June. It was the only time in her entire reign that The Queen has not taken the salute at the ceremony.

Taking her role as monarch of the entire UK seriously, The Queen began a wide-ranging programme of visits throughout every part of the country. Her first regional tour was a three-day visit to Northern Ireland. In the same decade, she travelled north, south, east and west, from Shetland to the Isles of Scilly, and from Swansea to Holy Island.

In this first decade of her reign, The Queen saw the ongoing transformation of the British Empire into the Commonwealth of Nations. She embarked on a series of overseas visits

LEFT: THE QUEEN DURING HER
VISIT TO PORTUGAL IN 1957.
OPPOSITE: INSPECTING A
NAVAL GUARD OF HONOUR
IN NEW ZEALAND IN 1953

including some long tours. Indeed, within the first few years of her reign, The Queen travelled to parts of the Commonwealth never visited by her predecessors. She also represented Britain on state visits to countries including Norway, Sweden, Portugal, France, Denmark, the USA and the Netherlands.

Her first Commonwealth tour began in November 1953 and was the longest ever undertaken, covering a total distance of 43,618 miles (70,196 km), and lasting six months. As a result, her 1953 Christmas message was broadcast live from New Zealand.

As part of the tour, she visited Australia and New Zealand – the first reigning monarch to do so. The Royal Yacht *Britannia*, built at the start of her reign, was first used by The Queen on the final stage of the Commonwealth tour. She boarded the ship for the first time with the Duke of Edinburgh on 1 May 1954, at Tobruk in Libya.

Another first saw The Queen address the UN General Assembly in October 1957. She spoke of "people's devotion to the pursuit of those great ideals" including world peace and justice.

There were attempts to modernise the monarchy during this first decade of her reign. In 1958, the practice of presenting debutantes (upper-class ladies who have come of age) to court at the start of the social season came to an end. At the same time, the number of royal garden parties at Buckingham Palace, held as a way of rewarding public service from across the social spectrum, was increased from three to four a year. Over the course of The Queen's reign, around 1.1 million people have attended garden parties at Buckingham Palace or the Palace of Holyroodhouse in Edinburgh. This demonstrates The Queen's determination to ensure that she meets a wide variety of people, not just officials and dignitaries.

The Queen and the Duke of Edinburgh also introduced small, informal lunch parties at Buckingham Palace to meet distinguished people from all professions, trades and vocations. The first was held on 11 May 1956, and the tradition continues to this day.

Her first televised Christmas broadcast in 1957 reflected the surge in TV sales since the Coronation. The Queen was to embrace such technological advances throughout her reign, enabling her to reach a far wider audience.

A modern monarch

The 1960s

As she entered the 1960s, Her Majesty The Queen not only had a crucial official role to play as sovereign, but also had a family life to maintain and two young children to care for. When Prince Andrew was born in February 1960, The Queen became the first reigning sovereign to have a child since Queen Victoria in 1857.

Her ability to juggle her official duties with those of a mother proved impressive. On only two occasions was The Queen unable to open Parliament throughout her reign (in 1959 and 1963, when she was expecting Prince Andrew and Prince Edward, respectively). The first pre-recorded Christmas Queen's Speech was broadcast around the world in 1960.

In May of that year, The Queen and the nation celebrated the marriage of Princess Margaret, The Queen's sister, to Antony Armstrong Jones. It was the first royal wedding to be broadcast on television. Eighteen months later, The Queen became an aunt with the birth of the couple's son, David.

The 1960s saw The Queen had put international relations to the fore as she undertook tours to Gambia, Ghana, India, Iran, Italy, Liberia, Nepal, Pakistan, Sierra Leone and the Vatican City. She had also welcomed US President John F Kennedy and his wife to Buckingham Palace.

This was the era of advances in space exploration, with the Soviet Union beating the USA in the race to get the first man into space. But there were other milestones. The first woman in space was Valentina Tereschkova, who was received by The Queen in February 1964. A "micro-filmed" message from The Queen was deposited by America's Apollo 11 astronauts when they made the first moon landing on 21 July 1969. Later that year, the Apollo

PREVIOUS PAGES: THE QUEEN
AND THE DUKE OF EDINBURGH
WITH PRINCESS ANNE,
PRINCE ANDREW AND PRINCE
CHARLES AT BALMORAL.
LEFT: HER MAJESTY DURING
HER VISIT TO BERLIN IN 1965.
OPPOSITE: THE WEDDING OF
PRINCESS MARGARET AND
TONY ARMSTRONG-JONES

11 crew was received at Buckingham Palace, where they presented The Queen with a replica of the silicon disc carrying her congratulatory words, which had been left on the moon in a metal container.

The Queen made several historic overseas visits in the 1960s, including the first by a monarch since the war to West Germany in 1965. In the divided city of Berlin, The Queen surveyed the Berlin Wall, which was perhaps the defining symbol of the "Cold War" between East and West. Other members of the Royal Family attended the independence ceremonies of several countries as they left the British Empire. Many states became members of the Empire's successor, the Commonwealth, a network of nations sharing friendship across the globe. During her 1963 visit to Australia, The Queen made a unique broadcast to people in remote communities over the flying doctor network in Alice Springs.

During the 1966 tour of the Caribbean, The Queen stopped off in Jamaica, the second visit of her reign. Other destinations on the tour included the islands of St Christopher (more commonly known as St Kitts) and Nevis, where The Queen and The Duke of Edinburgh attended an investiture at Government House, followed by a fireworks display.

Several world leaders visited the UK as guests of The Queen at Buckingham Palace during this decade. They included King Olav V of Norway (1962), King Paul I and Queen Frederika of Greece (1963), President Ferik Ibrahim Abbood of Sudan (1964) and King Faisal of Saudi Arabia (1967).

In 1962, a new gallery was opened at Buckingham Palace to display items from the Royal Collection. The brainchild of The Duke of Edinburgh, the new Queen's Gallery occupied the space of the palace's bomb-damaged private chapel. It was the first time that parts of the palace had been opened to the general public, and proved very popular.

RIGHT: THE QUEEN AND
THE DUKE OF EDINBURGH
RECEIVE PRESIDENT KENNEDY
AND JACKIE KENNEDY AT
BUCKINGHAM PALACE IN 1961

In 1965, Prime Minister Harold Wilson invited The Duke
of Edinburgh to chair a committee to formulate a scheme
to reward industrial and export achievement. The result was
the Queen's Awards for Enterprise, which are given in the
categories of industry, export and environmental achievement.

In politics, the issue of The Queen's royal prerogative
arose again in 1963, as it had done in 1957. Following the
retirement of Harold Macmillan, The Queen acted on his advice
in appointing Lord Home as Prime Minister and leader of the
Conservative Party. The choice caused some controversy, and
in 1965 the Conservatives instituted an electoral procedure by
which to decide the party's leadership in the future. The Queen
has played no subsequent role in the election of Conservative
Party leaders.

The assassination of John F Kennedy, the President of the
USA, in 1963 shocked the world. As a tribute to his life from the
British people, The Queen dedicated a memorial jointly with his
widow Jacqueline Kennedy at the historic site of Runnymede
in Surrey. Those present at the ceremony in May 1965 included
the late president's children, John Jr and Caroline.

The 1960s were a time of great change, both politically
and socially. Women campaigned for greater equality with
men, both at home and in the workplace. The Queen

acknowledged these changes in her 1966 Christmas message when she spoke about the important role of women in society. "In the modern world," said The Queen, "the opportunities for women to give something of value to the human family are greater than ever, because, through their own efforts, they are now beginning to play their full part in public life."

The Queen acknowledged other changes taking place in the 1960s, including the importance of pop culture to young people. In 1965, she presented The Beatles with MBEs at Buckingham Palace in recognition of their contribution to the world of entertainment.

The Queen and The Duke of Edinburgh also had a new addition to their family with a fourth child, Prince Edward, born at Buckingham Palace in 1964. In addition, The Queen's older children, Prince Charles and Princess Anne, began to undertake their first duties in support of their parents' work.

The media were also allowed greater access and insight into the lives of the members of the Royal Family during this decade. In 1969, the first television film about the family life of the royals was shown. The 23 million viewers who watched *Royal Family* saw footage of the off-duty activities of The Queen and her family.

The programme was broadcast on the eve of the investiture of Prince Charles as Prince of Wales in a ceremony at Caernarfon Castle in Wales – an occasion that was watched by some 200 million people worldwide. The Queen had made her eldest son Prince of Wales when he was just nine years old, but later let it be known that the investiture would not be officially held until the Prince was old enough to understand its significance fully.

Silver service

The 1970s

Between March and May of 1970, Her Majesty The Queen and The Duke of Edinburgh embarked on a lengthy tour of Australia and New Zealand. A new practice called the "walkabout" was initiated during this visit. These informal strolls allowed The Queen to meet members of the public, as well as officials and dignitaries. Here the royal couple joined in the celebrations marking Captain Cook's discovery of Australia 200 years earlier. They were accompanied on this occasion for the first time by Princess Anne and, for part of the time, by the Prince of Wales. The Australasian tour was followed by a visit to Canada in July for the centenary celebrations of the North West Territories and Manitoba.

The year 1971 opened with The Queen welcoming a whole new set of likenesses of herself on notes and coins as the UK switched to a decimal currency. Foreign tours in

this year to Canada and Turkey were interspersed with visits to Buckingham Palace by Emperor Hirohito of Japan – his first state visit since the Second World War – and King Mohammed Zaher Shah of Afghanistan.

The 1970s also included a number of milestone events for the Royal Family, providing cause for both public and private celebration. In June 1970, The Queen's eldest son, The Prince of Wales, became the first heir to the throne to gain a degree, graduating in History at Trinity College, Cambridge.

The Queen and The Duke of Edinburgh celebrated 25 years of marriage in November 1972 with a service of thanksgiving at Westminster Abbey. The same venue hosted the wedding of Princess Anne to Captain Mark Phillips on 14 November 1973, a cause for widespread public rejoicing that was watched by an estimated global audience of 100

PREVIOUS PAGES: THE QUEEN, THE DUKE OF EDINBURGH AND THE PRINCE OF WALES ARRIVE AT ST PAUL'S CATHEDRAL TO CELEBRATE THE SILVER JUBILEE (LEFT); AND POSE WITH THEIR FOUR CHILDREN FOR THEIR SILVER WEDDING ANNIVERSARY (RIGHT). LEFT: THE WEDDING OF PRINCESS ANNE AND CAPTAIN MARK PHILLIPS IN 1973. OPPOSITE: THE QUEEN AND THE DUKE OF EDINBURGH ON BOARD THE ROYAL TRAIN

million. Exactly five years to the day after the wedding, in November 1977, the couple welcomed their first child, Peter Phillips – The Queen's first grandchild.

In 1977, The Queen marked 25 years as sovereign. The Silver Jubilee was celebrated with a nationwide tour, Commonwealth visits and festivities at every level. The Queen and The Duke of Edinburgh travelled 56,000 miles (90,000 km) in total to mark the occasion in as many parts of the UK and the Commonwealth as possible.

The actual anniversary of The Queen's accession, on 6 February 1952, was commemorated in church services throughout the country. The Queen spent the anniversary weekend at Windsor with her family and the full jubilee celebrations began in the summer of 1977.

On 4 May, at the Palace of Westminster, both Houses of Parliament presented loyal addresses to The Queen. In her reply, she stressed that the keynote of the jubilee was to be the unity of the nation.

The Queen embarked on a large-scale tour. No other sovereign had visited so much of Britain in the course of just three months – the six jubilee tours of the UK taking in some 36 counties. The home tours began in Glasgow on 17 May, with greater crowds than the city had ever seen before. The Queen continued on throughout England and Wales – in Lancashire more than a million people turned out on one day – before finishing her jubilee odyssey in Northern Ireland.

The climax of the national celebrations came in early June when The Queen lit a bonfire beacon at Windsor – the signal for the lighting of a chain of beacons across the country. On Tuesday 7 June, vast crowds saw The Queen drive in the Gold State Coach to St Paul's Cathedral for a Service of Thanksgiving attended by heads of state from around the world and former prime ministers of the UK.

The Royal Train was used extensively during the Silver Jubilee. The carriages began life in 1972 as prototypes for the standard Inter-City Mark III passenger carriage and were later

LEFT: THE QUEEN ON THE
NORTH EAST LEG OF HER
SILVER JUBILEE TOUR

fitted out for their royal role at Wolverton Works. In 1978, a
Rolls-Royce Phantom VI was presented to The Queen by the
Society of Motor Manufacturers and Traders to mark the jubilee.

The decade also had its share of personal grief.
The Queen's uncle, The Duke of Windsor and former King
Edward VIII, died in Paris on 28 May 1972, at the age of 77.
The Queen's 30-year-old-cousin, Prince William of Gloucester,
was killed in 1972 in a flying accident on 28 August, as a
result of which The Queen cancelled her visit to the Munich
Olympics. And in 1979, Earl Mountbatten of Burma was
assassinated by an IRA bomb blast while fishing in County
Sligo in the Republic of Ireland. Second cousin once removed
to The Queen and uncle to the Duke of Edinburgh, Earl
Mountbatten had formerly served as First Sea Lord and
Chief of the Defence Staff. He had also been the last
Viceroy of India before independence.

The Queen's political duties continued as usual. In 1974,
she had to fly back from an Australian tour when a general
election was suddenly called – the only time she has had to
do so. She rejoined the tour in Indonesia.

Following the general election in February, no one party
had a clear majority in the House of Commons. The question
arose as to whether The Queen should endorse a coalition
between the Conservative and the Liberal parties without first

LEFT: THE QUEEN VISITS NEW ZEALAND IN 1977. OPPOSITE: THE FUNERAL OF EARL MOUNTBATTEN OF BURMA

giving Labour, the largest party, a chance to form a government. In the end, the Tories and Liberals were unable to arrange a coalition, and Harold Wilson returned to power as prime minister. Later in the decade, The Queen received the first female prime minister at Buckingham Palace when Margaret Thatcher replaced James Callaghan as prime minister in 1979.

On the international stage, too, there were several "firsts". The Queen paid a historic visit to communist Yugoslavia in 1972 and travelled to Japan as the guest of Emperor Hirohito in 1975. She also made overseas state visits to meet the leaders of countries she had never visited before, including Turkey (1971), Thailand (1972), France (1972), Indonesia (1974), Mexico (1975) and Saudi Arabia (1979).

Back home, The Queen welcomed King Carl Gustaf of Sweden (1975), President Giscard d'Estaing of France (1976) and President António Ramalho Eanes of Portugal (1978) on state visits to the UK.

The Commonwealth went from strength to strength. The Queen, Head of the Commonwealth, visited Ottawa for the Commonwealth Heads of Government Meeting in 1973. Since then, she has been present in the host country for every such meeting, in Britain or abroad, to demonstrate

her commitment to the organisation and its principles. These included visits to Jamaica in 1975 and Zambia in 1979.

In 1973, The Queen opened the landmark Sydney Opera House, an event that attracted worldwide attention. Australia also figured prominently in The Queen's Silver Jubilee celebrations in 1977, with The Queen visiting every state during a three-week tour.

Restoration work began on the fabric of Westminster Abbey in 1973, a project that would take until 1997 to complete. The Duke of Edinburgh was chairman of the Westminster Abbey Trust, which raised the money for, and supervised, the restoration. The trust decided to fill vacant niches above the abbey's Great West Door with figures of "modern saints" – one of those selected was The Grand Duchess Elizabeth of Russia, the Duke's great-aunt, who left the imperial family to become a nun, nursing the poor of Russia. She was executed by the Bolsheviks following the Russian Revolution.

The Queen's children continued to expand their duties. In 1975, The Prince of Wales took over from The Duke of Edinburgh as Colonel of the Welsh Guards and, in 1976, as Chancellor of the University of Wales.

A global presence

The 1980s

This decade started with a series of visits. As well as a Commonwealth tour to Australia and state visits to Switzerland, Italy and three North African countries – Tunisia, Algeria and Morocco – Her Majesty The Queen visited Pope John Paul II in the Vatican, in October 1980. Not only was this the first British state visit to the papacy, but also it was the first time a British monarch had met with a Pope since Henry VIII broke with Rome in 1534. It was seen as a significant step towards forging relations between the Church of England and Roman Catholicism. Pope John Paul II, in turn, visited Britain in 1982, the first pope to do so for 450 years. The Queen, as head of the Church of England, received him at Buckingham Palace. His six-day tour of the UK was extensive, with crowds turning out to catch a glimpse of him in his "popemobile", a modified Range Rover.

The following year witnessed one of the UK's biggest national celebrations in decades with the marriage of The Prince of Wales to Lady Diana Spencer, which took place at St Paul's Cathedral on 29 July 1981. The celebrations welcomed international royalty and heads of states from around the world, and the service was watched by an estimated global television audience of 750 million.

The vital dedication of the Her Majesty's Armed Forces came to the fore during the Falklands conflict. British troops travelled to the South Atlantic in April 1982 to recover the Falkland Islands and South Georgia. As Head of the Armed Forces, The Queen showed her usual concern for the men and women fighting overseas. In addition, with Prince Andrew seeing active service as the pilot of a Royal Navy Sea King helicopter during the war she shared the anxiety of many other mothers of men and women serving in the conflict.

Ties with the Commonwealth were reinforced through visits to Australia, New Zealand, Canada and the Caribbean, as well as to some less accessible outposts where The Queen is recognised as Head of State. The 11,000 inhabitants of the islands of Tuvalu (the former Ellice Islands) welcomed The Queen on her only visit to the tiny independent nation in the South Pacific in 1982.

As Head of the Commonwealth, The Queen participated in key moments of many member states. For instance, she opened the Jamaican Parliament in February 1983 – the country's 21st anniversary year of independence. The Queen also opened the parliament in Grenada two years later, and

went on to attend an investiture and cultural presentation on the Caribbean island.

In 1982, The Queen was in Ottawa for the patriation of the Canadian Constitution, the ceremony that finally brought the constitution fully and formally within the control of the Canadian Government. The Queen and The Duke of Edinburgh also revisited Papua New Guinea that same year. In addition, there was a trip to New Zealand, where The Queen spent time at the Commonwealth Games, which were opened by her youngest son, Prince Edward.

In 1985, there were several more overseas visits. The Queen travelled to Nassau in the Bahamas for the Commonwealth Heads of

PREVIOUS PAGES: THE QUEEN MEETS POPE JOHN PAUL II ON HIS VISIT TO THE UK. LEFT: THE PRINCE AND PRINCESS OF WALES ON THE BALCONY AT BUCKINGHAM PALACE AFTER THEIR MARRIAGE CEREMONY. OPPOSITE: THE QUEEN WELCOMES PRINCE ANDREW BACK FROM THE FALKLANDS WAR IN 1982

THE QUEEN AND CHINESE
PRESIDENT LI XIANNIAN
REVIEW A GUARD OF
HONOUR IN BEIJING, 1986

Government meeting, and to St Lucia where she laid a foundation stone for a new Red Cross headquarters. She and The Duke of Edinburgh visited Belize where the couple were welcomed by the mayor and given the key to Belize City. They also went to St Vincent and the Grenadines where they attended the Independence Anniversary Parade. The Duke of Edinburgh presented the Duke of Edinburgh's Award Scheme gold awards to local Vincentians during a ceremony at Government House. The royal couple also revisited St Kitts and Nevis where the royal yacht *Britannia* was the venue for a reception.

This Caribbean trip was followed by an historic visit to China in 1986 by The Queen and The Duke of Edinburgh, the first time in history that a British monarch had visited the country. Highlights of the six-day trip included a tour of the Great Wall of China.

In 1988, The Queen marked Australia's bicentenary with a speech at the opening of the new Parliament House in Canberra. The same year, The Prince and Princess of Wales, and The Princess Royal also visited the country.

The Queen and The Duke of Edinburgh welcomed more grandchildren during the 1980s with the births of Prince William (in 1982) and Prince Harry (in 1984) to The Prince and Princess of Wales. Prince William was christened by the Archbishop of Canterbury in the Music Room of Buckingham Palace, as his father had been before him. The Duke and Duchess of York, who married in 1986, had two daughters, Princess Beatrice (in 1988) and Princess Eugenie (in 1990), swelling the new generation of young royals.

Members of the Royal Family continued to support the work of The Queen in raising the profile of a wide range of charities and organisations, and travelled widely as her representatives abroad.

The tradition of The Queen sending congratulatory messages to those reaching their 100th birthdays – or above – continued. In December 1984, a Canadian man aged 116 became the oldest person ever to receive such a message.

The Great Storm of 1987 caused widespread devastation across the country. Around 15 million trees were destroyed and a massive clear-up operation was needed. The Queen experienced first-hand the devastation when the hurricane-force winds blew down most of an old avenue of lime trees in Windsor's Home Park. The avenue was later replanted by The Duke of Edinburgh.

In the same year, The Queen also conferred the title of Princess Royal on her daughter, Princess Anne, in recognition of her "devotion to duty and to public service". The year 1987 also marked the passing of time in another way. It was the first occasion when The Queen received the salute at Trooping the Colour from a carriage. In all previous years she had attended the ceremony on horseback.

A dutiful sovereign

The 1990s

By the start of the 1990s, despite Her Majesty The Queen being well past the official age of retirement, there was little reduction of her duties, or in the workload of The Duke of Edinburgh. The Queen continued to exercise her constitutional role as Head of State – for example, by opening each session of parliament, holding audiences with the prime minister and other ministers, and receiving ambassadors.

The decade started with The Queen leading the commemoration of the 50th anniversary of The Battle of Britain, where tributes were paid to those who had fought and sacrificed their lives for their country during the Second World War. Not long later – in January 1991 – British forces travelled to the Gulf in the Middle East to assist with the Allied action to drive out the Iraqi armies from Kuwait. On 24 February, The Queen made a broadcast to the nation in which she said she prayed that the recapture of Kuwait would be "as swift as it is certain, and that it may be achieved with as small a cost of human life and suffering as possible".

That same year, The Queen undertook a state visit to the USA where she addressed a meeting of the US Congress, the first time a British monarch had done so. Later in 1992, at the Gulf War Welcome Home Parade, The Queen reviewed the march-past of military personnel who had participated in the war.

Political changes in this decade – particularly the collapse of the Soviet Union – meant The Queen could visit places never previously accessible to her. These included such former countries of the Eastern Bloc as Hungary

PREVIOUS PAGES:
THE QUEEN WITH SOUTH
AFRICAN PRESIDENT NELSON
MANDELA. ABOVE: THE QUEEN
PUTS HER SIGNATURE TO THE
NEW RELATIONSHIP BETWEEN
WESTMINSTER AND WALES IN
1999. OPPOSITE: A SMILING
QUEEN IS WELCOMED BY
CHILDREN DURING HER
VISIT TO RUSSIA IN 1994

(1993), Russia (1994), Poland (1996) and the Czech Republic (1996). During the 1990s, she continued her tradition of travelling to countries that no other British monarch had visited, as exemplified by her tours to Brunei and Malaysia in 1998, and South Korea in 1999.

History was made by the reciprocal state visits of The Queen and President Nelson Mandela of South Africa. The Queen's six-day visit to South Africa in April 1995, following the end of apartheid, was her first since 1947. The final trip by the Royal Yacht *Britannia* took place in 1997 when The Queen paid an official visit to the Isle of Arran; the ship was decommissioned a few months later.

The decade saw history made in the UK as new devolved constitutional bodies for Scotland and Wales were created. In May 1999, The Queen opened the National Assembly for Wales at Cardiff, welcoming it as "a bridge into the future". In July of the same year, she also opened the Scottish Parliament in Edinburgh. It was a day of ceremony and celebration marking, in her own words, "the threshold of a new constitutional age".

New technology brought the world within easy reach. The launch of the British Monarchy website in 1997 enabled a global audience to learn about the role and work of The Queen and the Royal Family. Buckingham Palace also opened its doors to the public for the first time in 1993. The State Rooms of the Palace can now be visited during an eight-week summer period – usually in August and September – while The Queen is not in residence.

In the same year, the Royal Collection Trust was set up under the chairmanship of The Prince of Wales. The Royal Collection includes paintings and sculptures dating back more than 500 years and the trust's aim is to increase public access to, and understanding of, these historic treasures.

In 1998, The Queen introduced "theme days" to promote and celebrate aspects of British culture. The first was "City Day" focusing on financial institutions. Others have included "Young Achievers", "British Design" and "Pioneers".

OPPOSITE: THE 1992 FIRE AT
WINDSOR CASTLE. RIGHT, THE
PRINCE OF WALES, PRINCE
HARRY AND PRINCE WILLIAM
LOOK AT FLORAL TRIBUTES TO
DIANA, PRINCESS OF WALES AT
KENSINGTON PALACE IN 1997

On the political scene, most hereditary peers – including The Royal Dukes of Edinburgh, York, Gloucester and Kent – were removed from the House of Lords in 1999. This meant the dukes could now, in theory, vote in elections and even stand for election. However, the Royal Family is expected to be politically neutral, so these rights have never been exercised.

The decade had its share of sadness too, including the fire that caused significant damage at Windsor Castle in November 1992. It began in the private chapel, when a spotlight came into contact with a curtain and ignited the material. It took 15 hours and one-and-a-half million gallons of water to put out the blaze. Approximately one-fifth of the castle area was destroyed.

A few days later, The Queen gave a speech at London's Guildhall for the 40th anniversary of her accession in which she referred to recent events – which also included divorce or separation for three of her four children – as part of an "annus horribilis".

Windsor Castle was restored to its former glory over the next five years. It proved to be the greatest historic building project of the 20th century in the UK, and helped to revive many traditional crafts.

The restoration was completed six months ahead of schedule in November 1997 at a cost of £37 million, which was £3 million below budget. Much of the necessary revenue was raised from opening Buckingham Palace's State Rooms to visitors. To mark the completion, The Queen and The Duke of Edinburgh held a "thank you" reception in the restored rooms for 1,500 contractors.

Throughout the 1990s, the Royal Household continued to work on reducing its energy consumption. This was achieved by new initiatives such as a computerised building management system, which was installed to control heating and power systems around Buckingham Palace. Staff were able to review and adjust these systems to run at maximum efficiency. In 1991, Buckingham Palace started recycling 99 per cent of green waste on site. This waste includes grass cuttings, twigs, branches and cuttings from St James's Palace and Kensington Palace.

The death of Diana, Princess of Wales, was cause for widespread public mourning in 1997. The Queen made a broadcast to the nation on the eve of the Princess's funeral, paying tribute to her life and work. She described the Princess as "an exceptional and gifted human being".

There were also happier times. The Queen led the nation in celebrations for the 50th anniversary of the end of the Second World War in Europe (1995), the wedding of Prince Edward and Sophie Rhys-Jones (1999), and the arrival of the new millennium (1999).

THE EARL AND COUNTESS OF
WESSEX WAVE FROM AN OPEN-
TOP CARRIAGE FOLLOWING
THEIR WEDDING SERVICE

Our gracious Queen

The 2000s

Her Majesty The Queen saw in the new millennium with a service at St Paul's Cathedral and a party at the Millennium Dome. Two months later, in March 2000, she paid her 13th visit to Australia. It followed a referendum in November 1999 in which a majority of the Australian public voted to retain her as Head of State. A more personal landmark for the Royal Family came in August 2000 with the 100th birthday of The Queen Mother, for which The Queen sent her mother an official birthday greeting.

In December of 2000, The Queen received US President Bill Clinton for the third time. The following July she welcomed Clinton's successor, President George W Bush, to Buckingham Palace during his first official visit to the UK. It was only a few months later, in September 2001, that the 9/11 terrorist attacks

in the USA saw the destruction of the Twin Towers in New York and an attack on the Pentagon in Washington. It brought widespread condemnation and outrage: a statement issued by Buckingham Palace said The Queen had watched developments in "growing disbelief and total shock". The Queen later led the mourning at a service of remembrance at St Paul's Cathedral.

London too became the target of a terrorist attack on 7 July 2005, when 52 people were killed. The day after the atrocity, The Queen met staff at the Royal London Hospital in Whitechapel. She also made a substantial donation to the London Bombings Relief Charitable Fund to help the victims and their families. At other times of crisis and natural disaster, The Queen again showed her concern, for example after the floods of 2007 and 2009. She also sent messages of

support to countries hit by earthquakes and floods, including New Zealand, Japan and Haiti.

In July 2001, The Queen approved a new "Great Seal of the Realm", an official seal matrix, which she uses to approve official documents. The previous seal had worn out through use. Such official procedures maintain a link with centuries of royal tradition, but the Royal Household did a good job in keeping up with advances in technology over the decade, in an increasingly computerised and connected age. The Royal Channel was launched on YouTube in 2007 to showcase both archive and modern video footage of The Queen, the lives of other members of the Royal Family and royal events. As the official channel of the British Monarchy, this has proved hugely popular with more than 35 million viewings to date.

Other innovative highlights included The Queen emailing young people across the world to celebrate 60 years of the Commonwealth (2009), the launch of the British Monarchy page on Facebook (2010) and the opening of a royal photograph account online. The Flickr page showcases

masterpieces of early British photography collected by Queen Victoria and Prince Albert, as well as current images of royal engagements.

Changes to The Queen's Christmas Broadcast again illustrated The Queen's willingness to keep pace with the modern world. Her Christmas Day message was posted for the first time on YouTube in 2007 and Sky News was invited to produce the broadcast in 2011. Previously, the BBC and ITV had been the only television channels to have taken part.

The environment was another continuing theme over the decade. Buckingham Palace started recycling computers in 2005, since when more than 500 items of technology have either been reused in developing countries or sent to waste-management depots.

The marriage of The Prince of Wales and Camilla Parker Bowles at Windsor Guildhall in April 2005 was cause for celebration. Significant milestones during this decade included The Queen's Golden Jubilee in 2002, which was celebrated with public events and street parties, as well as visits by The

OPPOSITE: THE WEDDING OF
THE PRINCE OF WALES AND
CAMILLA PARKER BOWLES.
RIGHT: THE QUEEN AND THE
DUKE OF EDINBURGH ATTEND
A PARTY TO CELEBRATE HER
MAJESTY'S 80TH BIRTHDAY

Queen and The Duke of Edinburgh around the UK and throughout the Commonwealth. And on her 80th birthday in 2006, The Queen received nearly 40,000 messages from well-wishers through the post.

The royal couple's diamond wedding anniversary (2007) was marked by a Service of Celebration at Westminster Abbey. This made The Queen the first British monarch to reach the 60-year marital milestone. The service was attended by some 2,000 guests, including 30 members of the Royal Family and Prime Minister Gordon Brown – as well as his predecessors Tony Blair, John Major and Baroness Thatcher.

Dame Judi Dench read out a poem entitled Diamond Wedding, which had been written for the occasion by the poet laureate Andrew Motion. Afterwards, the royal couple unveiled a new "panoramic panel" in the abbey square, which explains landmarks on the London skyline. And later in the week, The Queen and The Duke of Edinburgh travelled to Malta, where they had lived as a young couple in 1949–51 when Prince Philip was stationed there as a naval officer. By the end of 2007, The Queen had surpassed her great-great-grandmother, Queen Victoria, to become the longest-lived British monarch.

There was sadness as well, however, with the deaths in 2002 of Princess Margaret (in February, aged 71) and The Queen Mother (in March, aged 101). More than 200,000 people paid their respects as The Queen Mother lay in state in Westminster Hall. The life of Princess Margaret was celebrated with a special sonnet by the poet laureate.

THE QUEEN MEETS BRITISH
VETERANS IN NORMANDY
IN 2004 AT A CEREMONY TO
MARK THE 60TH ANNIVERSARY
OF THE D-DAY LANDINGS

Throughout the decade, The Queen's diary was as busy as ever, with visits both at home and abroad. There were state visits to many former Eastern Bloc countries – Lithuania, Latvia, Estonia, Slovenia, Slovakia – and a lengthy visit to the USA in 2007 where she was received by George W Bush. The Queen also visited Rome, Norway, France, Germany, Belgium, the Netherlands, Turkey, Australia, Jamaica, New Zealand, Canada, Nigeria, Singapore, Uganda, and Trinidad and Tobago. In 2009, she and The Duke of Edinburgh marked the 400th Anniversary of Bermuda with a tour of the British Overseas Territory.

The Queen joined veterans in commemorating the 60th anniversary of the Normandy Landings in 2004 with a Ceremony of Remembrance at the Juno Beach Centre at Courseulles-sur-Mer. During the event, The Queen laid a wreath on behalf of the Commonwealth and met Canadian veterans. To mark the 200th anniversary, on 21 October 2005, of the Battle of Trafalgar, The Queen attended a special dinner on board HMS *Victory* at the invitation of the First Sea Lord, Admiral Sir Alan West.

Dedicated anew

The 2010s

In politics, Her Majesty The Queen saw her first change of government for 13 years in May 2010, when she accepted the resignation of Gordon Brown, the Labour leader, and invited David Cameron, the Conservative leader, to form a government (the Conservatives and Liberal Democrats having agreed to form a coalition). Twelve prime ministers have been appointed during The Queen's reign, second only to King George III's record of 14.

History was made on 6 July 2010, when The Queen addressed the United Nations General Assembly in New York, in her capacity as Head of the Commonwealth. The speech, her first there since 1957, praised the UN for its work in reducing conflict, offering humanitarian assistance and tackling the effects of poverty. She also laid a wreath at the site of the World Trade Center for the victims of the terror attacks of 11 September 2001.

A public holiday on 29 April 2011 marked the wedding day of Prince William to Kate Middleton – a televised event that attracted an even bigger global audience than the wedding of the Prince's parents 30 years earlier – and, later that year, Zara Phillips married the rugby player Mike Tindall. The year's celebrations also included The Duke of Edinburgh's 90th birthday. To honour her husband, The Queen made him Lord High Admiral, a significant gesture as she had been titular head of the Navy since 1964.

If 1992 was The Queen's "annus horribilis", then 2012 could be described as her "annus mirabilis". To mark this Diamond Jubilee year, Buckingham Palace announced a programme of events throughout the UK and across the Commonwealth, including a pageant on the River Thames. The official emblem for the Jubilee was designed by 10-year-old Katherine Dewar from Chester, the schoolgirl

LEFT: THE DUKE AND DUCHESS
OF CAMBRIDGE RECEIVE A
RAPTUROUS RECEPTION FROM
THE PUBLIC FOLLOWING THEIR
WEDDING CEREMONY AT
WESTMINSTER ABBEY

whose artwork won a national competition held by the
BBC's *Blue Peter* programme.

"In this special year, as I dedicate myself anew to
your service, I hope we will all be reminded of the power of
togetherness and the convening strength of family, friendship
and good neighbourliness," announced The Queen on 2 June,
Accession Day. "I hope also that this Jubilee year will be a
time to give thanks for the great advances that have been
made since 1952 and to look forward to the future with clear
head and warm heart." On 4 June, Jubilee beacons were lit
around the world. The Queen and The Duke of Edinburgh
embarked on an extensive tour of the UK, while her children
and grandchildren toured many Commonwealth countries on
her behalf. As the year came to a close, in December 2012,
she became the first British monarch to attend a peacetime
cabinet meeting since King George III in 1781.

In July 2012, she opened the 2012 Olympic Games
in London and the Paralympics a month later. This meant
that The Queen – who had also opened the 1976 games in

Montreal – became the first head of state to open two Olympic Games in two different countries. For the Olympics opening ceremony, she played herself in a short film – directed by Oscar-winner Danny Boyle – alongside Daniel Craig. The 007 star described her as "incredibly game" during the filming, which started with The Queen at a writing desk in Buckingham Palace, surrounded by corgis, and ended with her appearing to parachute into the Olympic Stadium in East London, then arriving in the arena to take her seat. The gesture was greeted with huge cheers and applause, and became one of the most memorable moments of a rapturously received opening ceremony. The following year, on receiving an honorary BAFTA for her patronage of the film industry, Sir Kenneth Branagh described The Queen as "the most memorable Bond girl yet" at the award ceremony.

Despite becoming the longest-serving British monarch on 9 September 2015, The Queen remains continually busy.

Ties between the UK and other countries have been strengthened by visits from world leaders such as South African President Jacob Zuma in 2010, the US President Barack Obama in 2011 and the President of Turkey in the same year, while The Queen visited Oman, the UAE and Canada in 2010, and Australia in 2011. In 2014 came a state visit to meet the Pope in the Vatican (her third) and trips to Italy and France; a year later came a trip to three cities in Germany. In November 2015, en route to a Commonwealth summit in Uganda, The Queen and The Duke of Edinburgh chose to spend three days on a state visit to Malta, where they had spent many happy days as newlyweds.

One of The Queen's most significant state visits in recent years was to the Republic of Ireland in 2011, the first visit by a British monarch since that country's independence in 1921. This historic event was welcomed warmly by the Irish people and gained much praise from people from all sides of the political divide, both north and south of the border.

The Coronation

1953

Princess Elizabeth ascended to the throne on 6 February 1952, upon the death of her father, King George VI, and was proclaimed Queen shortly afterwards by assorted privy councils and executives. However, there would be a lengthy gap of 16 months between her accession and the Coronation.

This delay was partly due to the tradition that the celebratory nature of a coronation is inappropriate during the mourning period that follows the death of a monarch. Queen Victoria, for example, became monarch on the death of King William IV on 20 June 1837 but was not crowned until the following June, and other Hanoverian coronations observed this custom. The exception was Her Majesty The Queen's father, King George VI, as his predecessor King Edward VIII did not die but abdicated. Princess Elizabeth watched that coronation, on 12 May 1937, as an 11-year-old girl.

However, in a country that was still recovering from the devastating effects of war, the delay provided time to organise a suitably grand ceremony. A Coronation Commission was set up in April 1952, chaired by The Duke of Edinburgh, while the Coronation Joint Committee was established to coordinate foreign visits. The event was organised by The Duke of Norfolk, Bernard Fitzalan-Howard, who was also in charge of King George VI's coronation, and would go on to organise Sir Winston Churchill's funeral in 1965 and Prince Charles's investiture in 1969.

The Coronation took place in Westminster Abbey on 2 June 1953. It was a dignified ceremony conducted by Dr Geoffrey Fisher, Archbishop

PREVIOUS PAGES: THE
CORONATION CEREMONY IN
WESTMINSTER ABBEY, 1953.
LEFT: LONDONERS CELEBRATE
THE HISTORIC OCCASION.
OPPOSITE: THE QUEEN AND THE
DUKE OF EDINBURGH TRAVEL
IN THE GOLD STATE COACH

of Canterbury, which began at 11.15 am and concluded at 2 pm. The service was divided into six parts – the recognition, the oath, the anointing, the investiture (which included the crowning), the enthronement and the homage. The anointing had a particular significance, using an anointing liquid made from the oils of orange, rose, cinnamon, musk and ambergris.

During the investiture, The Queen put on a robe of cloth of gold (the Dalmatic, which was used by King George VI) and was presented with golden spurs, a jewelled sword and golden bracelets. Finally, she put on the Imperial Mantle and received the Orb, the Coronation Ring, the Coronation Glove and two sceptres. Music, directed by abbey organist William McKie and performed by 480 musicians and singers, included settings of Handel's "Zadok the Priest" and Hubert Parry's "I Was Glad" and new compositions by Ralph Vaughan Williams, Arnold Bax, William Walton and the Canadian composer Healy Willan.

A total of 8,251 guests were present, the youngest being the four-and-a-half-year-old Prince Charles. Prime Minister Winston Churchill – who had started his second spell in Downing Street in 1951 – was joined by representatives of 129 countries, with Commonwealth prime ministers including India's Jawaharlal Nehru, Australia's Robert Menzies, Canada's Louis Saint-Laurent, Pakistan's Muhammad Ali Bogra and South Africa's D F Malan.

The Queen, with The Duke of Edinburgh, was then driven back from Westminster Abbey to Buckingham Palace in the Gold State Coach, which was pulled by eight grey geldings: Cunningham, Tovey, Noah, Tedder, Eisenhower, Snow White, Tipperary and McCreery.

The two-hour return procession took a deliberately convoluted five-mile route – via

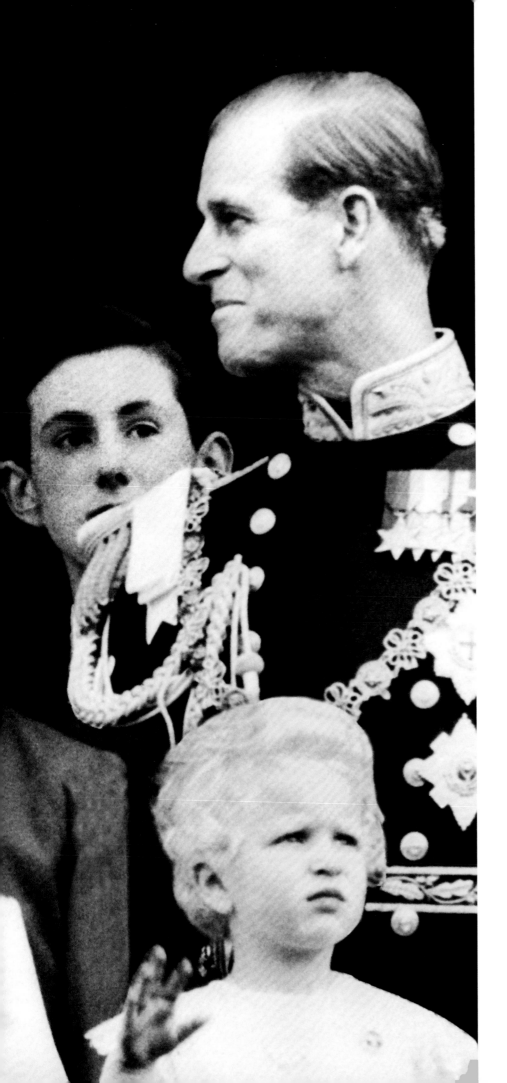

Whitehall, Trafalgar Square, Pall Mall, Hyde Park Corner, Marble Arch and Oxford Circus – and was lined by 29,000 troops from Britain and the Commonwealth. Hundreds of thousands of people viewed the procession all along the route, despite heavy rain. Many even camped for two days in prime positions in order to get a good view. One Australian family had sailed all the way to London in a ketch to witness the spectacle.

The ceremony was also broadcast on radio around the world and, at The Queen's request, on television for the first time – a breakthrough in outside broadcasting. Many people bought their first television sets to watch the event, and dozens crowded around each set to watch. Given that the population of the UK was around 36 million at the time, it's estimated that 27 million watched the event on television, and a further 11 million listened on the radio. More than 2,000 journalists and 500 photographers from around the world covered the event – including one Jacqueline Bouvier, later to be First Lady Jackie Kennedy, then a correspondent for the *Washington Times-Herald*.

On the day of the Coronation, the Royal Family also received the news that New Zealand-born mountaineer Edmund Hillary and the Nepalese Sherpa Tenzing Norgay had become the first people to reach the summit of Mount Everest, an achievement that was described as the ultimate coronation gift to The Queen.

The Silver Jubilee

1977

In her Christmas broadcast of 1976, on the brink of her Silver Jubilee year, Her Majesty The Queen said: "The gift I would most value next year is that reconciliation should be found wherever it is needed, a reconciliation which would bring peace and security to families and neighbours at present suffering and torn apart."

In the spirit of this message, she paid a unique visit to Northern Ireland under conditions of intense security. She also celebrated her jubilee by visiting numerous other parts of the UK – covering 36 counties on six separate tours – and undertaking several important overseas tours. With visits to countries including Western Samoa, Tonga, Fiji, New Zealand, Australia and Papua New Guinea in February and March of 1977, The Queen and The Duke of Edinburgh clocked up more than 56,000 miles throughout the year. In May, she went to Westminster Hall to receive addresses from the Houses of Parliament, and she entertained seven world leaders, including US President Jimmy Carter.

The following month, the main celebrations began. The Queen went to The Copper Horse statue in Windsor Great Park to light the first of a chain of bonfires that spread the length of Britain, echoing the chain of bonfires that had heralded the approaching Spanish Armada in 1588. She went in procession to St Paul's Cathedral, travelling there with The Duke of Edinburgh in the Gold State Coach, last used for her coronation in 1953. Other celebrations included a river procession, fireworks on the Thames, a North London and South London drive, and the Services Silver Jubilee Musical Pageant.

PREVIOUS PAGES: THE QUEEN
WITH THE LORD MAYOR
OF LONDON ON SILVER
JUBILEE DAY. OPPOSITE:
THE QUEEN AND THE DUKE
OF EDINBURGH WAVE TO
THE CROWD FOLLOWING
A THANKSGIVING SERVICE
IN ST PAUL'S CATHEDRAL.
RIGHT: COSTUMED REVELLERS
PREPARE TO LIGHT ONE OF
THE MANY JUBILEE BEACONS

Although all these celebrations appeared to happen effortlessly and to achieve the desired effect, there had been a time when there was uncertainty as to whether the Silver Jubilee would be celebrated at all. Some argued that no money should be spent on it. But many entrepreneurs realised that here was an opportunity not to be missed, so London took its own initiative. Sir Reg Goodwin, Leader of the Greater London Council, said he knew Londoners well enough to know that, if they were seen not to support the jubilee, there would be trouble. An independent committee was therefore created, called the London Celebrations Committee for The Queen's Silver Jubilee. It received the blessing of the Home Office, but no money. Sir Arthur Peterson, the Permanent Under Secretary at the Home

Office, told the committee that there were two precepts they should bear in mind:

"You must not bore the Public.
You must not kill The Queen."

The emphasis was on locally organised celebrations, with relatively few official jubilee events. But there was also a strong move to create environmental changes that would last and make London a better place for the future. Trees were planted and 40,000 acres of neglected land were put to good use, for instance by being converted into urban farms, notably at Newham, which is still flourishing today. There are many other examples, too, such as the Jubilee Gardens on the South Bank, near the London Eye.

In addition, the Silver Jubilee Walkway was created. Now called the Jubilee Walkway, it was originally a ruse to get pedestrians over the bridges to the South Bank, stretching, as it did, from Leicester Square, via Parliament Square, over Lambeth Bridge, along the South Bank and back over Tower Bridge to the Tower of London. It now loops all over Central London and has panoramic panels in key spots to enlighten visitors about neighbouring landmarks.

If there had been fears that the Silver Jubilee would not grip the public imagination, they proved unfounded. As the occasion approached, the festive mood took hold and ran well into the summer, with tens of thousands of street parties and other celebrations held up and down the country and throughout the Commonwealth. More than 4,000 street parties were organised in London alone.

At the end of the year, a television channel broadcast a kaleidoscope of images showing The Queen receiving a mass of flowers from children all over the country. To accompany this montage, they played 1977's most unlikely hit single, "The Floral Dance" from the Brighouse and Rastrick Brass Band.

ONE OF THOUSANDS OF
SILVER JUBILEE STREET
PARTIES THAT TOOK PLACE
ACROSS THE COUNTRY.
OPPOSITE: THE QUEEN ON
A WALKABOUT IN GLASGOW
DURING HER SILVER JUBILEE
TOUR OF SCOTLAND

THE GOLDEN JUBILEE
THANKSGIVING SERVICE
IN ST PAUL'S CATHEDRAL.
OPPOSITE: THE QUEEN AND
THE DUKE OF EDINBURGH
WAVE TO THE CROWD FROM
THE GOLD STATE COACH

The Golden Jubilee

2002

The emphasis of the Golden Jubilee was different from that of the Silver Jubilee 25 years earlier. If, in a sense, the nation thanked Her Majesty The Queen in 1977, then in 2002 The Queen wanted to thank the nation. While the focus was firmly on the young people of the country, and particularly those in schools, there were six key themes that shaped the events: celebration, community, service, past and future, giving thanks and Commonwealth.

The festivities lasted from February to October, and once again The Queen travelled the length and breadth of the UK and also visited Commonwealth countries around the world. Her first trip, to Jamaica in February, came just over a week after her sister, Princess Margaret, had died. And when The Queen Mother also passed away the following month, the festivities were in danger of becoming a solemn affair. However, that didn't turn out to be the case, as the jubilee was marked by many memorable events.

The main celebrations took place on Jubilee Weekend, which started on Saturday 1 June and ended on Tuesday 4 June. They were watched by a million people on The Mall and included spectacular fireworks from the roof of Buckingham Palace, a parade involving 20,000 participants and the first appearance of the Gold State Coach since the Silver Jubilee. Echoing the bonfires of 1977, a chain of 2,006 beacons was also lit across the world on 3 June, from the Arctic to Antarctica. The Queen lit the National Beacon on The Mall that evening in front of the Queen Victoria Memorial, which produced a flame nine metres high.

PREVIOUS PAGES: THE ROYAL
PROCESSION SETS OFF
FROM BUCKINGHAM PALACE.
OPPOSITE: HUGE CROWDS
GATHER ALONG THE MALL.
ABOVE: THE ROYAL FAMILY
GATHER ON THE PALACE
BALCONY FOR TROOPING
THE COLOUR

At 76 years of age, The Queen was the oldest British monarch to celebrate a Golden Jubilee. She also became the first member of the Royal Family to receive a gold disc from the recording industry when the CD of Party at the Palace – a pop concert at Buckingham Palace Gardens that was watched by around 200 million people worldwide – sold 100,000 copies within a week of its release.

Buckingham Palace Gardens were also the scene of three themed parties over the course of the year. They were held for people who were born on 6 February 1952, the day The Queen ascended the throne; young people who'd been born since the Silver Jubilee; and charities under the patronage of The Queen or The Duke of Edinburgh.

As well as being an occasion for celebrations and for giving to charity in the name of The Queen, the Golden Jubilee was also a chance for Britain to take stock. The country looked at the changes that had occurred during her reign, when, as she'd declared upon succeeding as monarch, she had always worked to "uphold the constitutional government and to advance the happiness and prosperity of my peoples".

The Diamond Jubilee

2012

The Diamond Jubilee of 2012 took place in a new age of austerity and, according to a senior adviser, Her Majesty The Queen set two guidelines for the celebrations – that the use of public funds be minimised and that people should not "be forced to celebrate". As it happened, millions were only too happy to do so.

The first large-scale event of the celebrations took place in the grounds of Windsor Castle on 10–13 May. The Diamond Jubilee Pageant saw a cavalcade of 550 horses and 1,100 performers from around the world pay homage to The Queen's tireless sense of duty – having visited more than 250 countries during her reign – as well as her renowned passion for horses.

Back in January 2010, the Labour government's Business Secretary, Lord Mandelson, had announced that the traditional May Day holiday would be moved to June and that there would be two bank holidays in honour of the Diamond Jubilee, taking place on Monday 4 June and Tuesday 5 June. This four-day

weekend became a focal point for celebrations around the UK and the Commonwealth, with more than 10,000 street parties held in the UK alone.

The extended weekend's celebrations started on the Saturday, with The Queen attending the Epsom Derby. The following day witnessed one of the biggest royal events in history, the Thames Diamond Jubilee Pageant, in which 700 boats – the largest flotilla ever assembled on the Thames – sailed down the river from Battersea Bridge to Tower Bridge. At their head was the royal row-barge *Gloriana*, an elegant, hand-built, 88-ft barge powered by 18 oarsmen, based on an 18th-century craft depicted by Canaletto.

In the "royal section" The Queen and The Duke of Edinburgh led the way in a Thames cruiser with baroque red and gold decorations, garlands of flowers and a new 25-ft prow in the shape of "Old Father Thames" – the royal cruiser was heralded by trumpeters from the Royal Marines as it passed

PREVIOUS PAGES: THE
QUEEN ABOARD THE ROYAL
CRUISER DURING THE THAMES
DIAMOND JUBILEE PAGEANT
(LEFT); FIREWORKS EXPLODE
OVER BUCKINGHAM PALACE
FOLLOWING THE JUBILEE
CONCERT (RIGHT). RIGHT: THE
ROYAL FAMILY AT THE THAMES
DIAMOND JUBILEE PAGEANT

under each bridge. It was followed by assorted vessels, which
carried some 30,000 members of the public and numerous
members of the armed forces and the emergency services.
Despite the poor weather, more than a million people crowded
by the banks of the Thames to watch the historic spectacle
and celebrate at the Jubilee Festival in Battersea Park.

On the Monday, the weather had improved for the
star-studded Jubilee Concert, put together by Gary Barlow and
the BBC, and featuring the likes of Stevie Wonder, Elton John,
Paul McCartney, Madness, Grace Jones, Shirley Bassey and
Robbie Williams. Around 10,000 free tickets were distributed
by public ballot for people to watch the event live on the Mall,
while thousands more witnessed it on big screens in Green Park
and St James's Park. That night, a giant network of more than
4,000 "jubilee beacons" was lit across the UK and in many
Commonwealth countries. Sixty beacons alone illuminated
Hadrian's Wall.

On the following day, The Queen and other members
of the Royal Family – including The Duke and Duchess of
Cambridge – attended a Service of Thanksgiving at St Paul's
Cathedral, conducted by the Archbishop of Canterbury,
Rowan Williams. It was followed by a Diamond Jubilee lunch
at Westminster Hall, and a procession along Whitehall and

LEFT: THE QUEEN ATTENDS THE SERVICE OF THANKSGIVING. OPPOSITE: THE DIAMOND JUBILEE PAGEANT IN THE GROUNDS OF WINDSOR CASTLE

the Mall to Buckingham Palace, with horse-drawn royal carriages, military bands, a 60-gun salute and an RAF fly-past from the Red Arrows and several historic aircraft, including the last airworthy Lancaster bomber.

In addition to this long weekend, the jubilee was heralded by other events. On the day of her accession, 6 February, a 62-gun salute was mounted near the Tower of London. Later that month came a multi-faith reception at Lambeth Palace. On 20 March, The Queen addressed both houses of parliament, and on 19 May there was a Diamond Jubilee Armed Forces Parade and Muster near Windsor Castle.

As part of the Diamond Jubilee celebrations, The Queen and The Duke of Edinburgh visited every part of Britain between March and July of 2013. Throughout 2012 other members of the family visited Commonwealth nations – The Prince of Wales and The Duchess of Cornwall visited Australia, New Zealand, Canada and Papua New Guinea; The Duke and Duchess of Cambridge went to Malaysia, Singapore, the Solomon Islands and Tuvalu; Prince Harry and The Earl and Countess of Wessex together visited different Caribbean islands; The Princess Royal visited Mozambique and Zambia; while The Duke of York went to India.

To mark The Queen's 60 years of service, the "Jubilee Hour" invited people to devote 60 minutes of time to voluntary work. More than two million hours of community work were pledged by individuals, organisations and businesses throughout Britain and the Commonwealth. Buckingham Palace welcomed the initiative. "It was The Queen's hope that her Diamond Jubilee would provide an opportunity for communities, groups and individuals to come together in a way that they would not otherwise be able to do," the Palace said in a statement. "There is no doubt that the Jubilee Hour has made a notable contribution to achieving this ambition."

Party of a lifetime

The Queen's 90th Birthday Celebration

It is fitting that Her Majesty The Queen's 90th Birthday Celebration should take place in the private grounds of Home Park Private, Windsor Castle – a location that has been so dear to The Queen since childhood. It is also only appropriate that the four days of celebration will reflect some of Her Majesty's greatest private and public interests – her love of horses, her dedication to the Commonwealth and international affairs, and her deep involvement with the Armed Forces.

Set against the striking backdrop of Windsor Castle, Royal Windsor Horse Show, which takes place during the daytime, will play host to the evenings' celebrations. The Horse Show dates back to 1943, when Count Robert Orssich and Geoffrey Cross organised a horse and dog show to raise money for the war effort. The first shows were well attended by members of the Royal Family, including King George VI, Queen Elizabeth, and Princess Elizabeth and Princess Margaret. At the 1945 show, the princesses won the private turnout (driving) class, and The Queen has regularly entered home-bred horses and ponies ever since, while The Duke of Edinburgh was, up until 2003, a regular competitor in the International Driving Grand Prix.

Held in the same purpose-built arena that will play venue to the Horse Show, the evenings' celebrations will be a suitably grand yet inclusive affair. Each evening will tell the story of The Queen's 90 years over the course of 90 minutes – charting her remarkable life from her birth in 1926, through the Second World War, to her Coronation in 1953 and a reign that spans more than 60 years.

Some of the biggest stars from the world of entertainment
will perform alongside a full orchestra, 900 horses and 1,500
participants. On the fourth evening The Queen will attend the
event with other members of the Royal Family. That evening
will be broadcast live by ITV and singers will include Gary
Barlow, James Blunt and Jess Glynne, along with operatic
stars Alfie Boe and Katherine Jenkins.

Commonwealth acts include the New Zealand Army
Band, the Royal Canadian Mounted Police, the South
Australian Police Band and the Fiji Armed Forces Band.
From the wider world come the Oman Royal Cavalry,
Chilean Huasos and Dancers, Dancers and Djigitovka
horses and riders from Azerbaijan, Mongolian Tumblers
and the celebrated "horse-whisperer" Jean-Francois
Pignon. The British military will be well represented by

THE ROYAL CANADIAN
MOUNTED POLICE

the likes of the Household Cavalry Mounted Regiment,
the King's Troop Royal Horse Artillery, Chelsea Pensioners
and a host of Pipes & Drums.

The equestrian section of proceedings will feature
Shetland ponies, racehorses and polo ponies, and other
animals, including gun dogs and cattle, will be included
in the "Quintessentially British" component of the show.
This segment will also feature caber tossing, bargemen,
swan uppers, Scottish dancers, ghillies and stalkers, and
even a tug of war.

All told, The Queen's 90th Birthday Celebration will
be a unique spectacle, recognising a remarkable milestone
in the life of a remarkable monarch.

A CELEBRATION OF 90 YEARS

Abroad appeal

The Queen's overseas tours and visits

Foreign trips are seen as one of Her Majesty The Queen's most important duties as Head of State. Her life and reign have coincided with a tremendous growth in global travel, enabling The Queen to travel farther, more widely and more frequently than any British sovereign before her. Indeed, by the end of her first decade on the throne, she had already racked up more international miles than any of her predecessors, helping to strengthen diplomatic bonds and cultivate new connections around the globe.

Her first official overseas visit came in 1947, before she was Queen, when she travelled to South Africa. And it was while performing her duties in Kenya in 1952 that she learned of her father's death and her own accession to the throne.

The Queen regularly tours the 15 realms where she is Head of State (in addition to the UK), as well as other Commonwealth countries. She also normally undertakes two or three state visits each year – as trips to countries that are not part of the Commonwealth are known.

Something of a pioneer in international relations, The Queen was the first reigning British monarch to visit China (in 1986), Russia (in 1994), Brunei and Malaysia (in 1998), and South Korea (in 1999). And in 1995, she revisited South Africa for the first time since 1947 and the end of the apartheid system. More recently, in 2011, Her Majesty became the first British monarch to visit the area that is now the Republic of Ireland since her grandfather King George V toured there in 1911.

ABOVE: THE QUEEN AND THE
DUKE OF EDINBURGH WAVE
TO THE CROWDS ON THEIR
ARRIVAL IN NASSAU, BAHAMAS
DURING THE ROYAL VISIT TO
THE CARIBBEAN IN 1966

ABOVE: THE QUEEN ON TOUR IN
TUVALU IN THE SOUTH PACIFIC,
1982. OPPOSITE: THE QUEEN
AND THE DUKE OF EDINBURGH
ARE JOINED BY THE AGONG
OF MALAYSIA DURING THE
WELCOMING CEREMONY IN
KUALA LUMPUR, 1989

ABOVE: THE QUEEN IS
JOINED BY PRESIDENT IVAN
GASPAROVIC DURING HER TWO-
DAY VISIT TO SLOVAKIA IN 2008.
OPPOSITE: IN CONVERSATION
WITH SHEIKH KHALIFA BIN
ZAYED AL NAHYAN, THE
PRESIDENT OF THE UAE,
IN ABU DHABI, 2010

Jewel identity

Boodles

Michael Wainwright knows the value of strong relationships. His family's business – the luxury jewellers Boodles – was established in Liverpool in 1798. It was passed down from generation to generation until Wainwright took the helm nearly 200 years later in 1992, alongside his brother, Nicholas; his nephews Jody and James joined more recently.

Today, Boodles is a world-renowned jeweller, with five boutiques in London, including a flagship store on Bond Street, three stores in north-west England and one in Dublin. "Any success we've had is largely down to our friendly, family approach," says Wainwright. "It allows relationships to blossom between ourselves, our staff and our customers."

Of course, exquisite jewellery helps. The company uses beautiful gems and hand-selects fine craftspeople to create key pieces from its London headquarters. "We pay huge attention to quality," says Wainwright. "Our style is feminine, wearable, not over-ostentatious – and there's often a sense of humour." Boodles also has royal connections: in 1947, it branched out from jewellery to design and make a solid silver cake stand for the wedding of the future Queen and Prince Philip.

Nowadays, Boodles' designs are a favourite on the red carpet, adorning the likes of Kate Winslet, Emma Thompson, Emma Watson and Dame Helen Mirren. The company was the subject of the 2014 Channel 4 documentary "The Million Pound Necklace: Inside Boodles", watched by a global audience of over two million. Its iconic Raindance ring was selected by the Victoria and Albert Museum for permanent display as an outstanding example of contemporary jewellery. One of Boodles' Icon Collections, 'Raindance', also incorporates engagement rings and exclusive one-of-a-kind pieces.

"People often buy engagement rings as their first item of fine jewellery," says Wainwright of the Boodles bridal collection. "So that purchase can be the start of a relationship that lasts for many years." And what about its one-of-a-kind pieces? "Jody, our gemstone buyer, has been extremely bold with the stones he's sourced recently," says Wainwright. "We're using some rare and very beautiful coloured diamonds in a new range." Completing the jewellers' offering are watches by Patek Philippe, with whom Boodles has maintained a very close relationship for the past 25 years.

Boodles is about more than jewellery alone. "Events are a big part of our DNA and we see ourselves as being in the hospitality business," says Wainwright. "My family loves to entertain, and we look after our VIP clients pretty well." The Boodles Tennis is a case in point. "It's a garden party with a spot of world-class tennis in the background," says Wainwright. "And by world-class, I mean Djokovic and Murray in recent years, Sampras and Agassi in previous years." Launched in 2001, Boodles hosts the event, entertaining

700 of its clients over five days every June. "Guests enjoy a sumptuous lunch in the beautiful surroundings of Stoke Park Hotel in Buckinghamshire, where we have a pop-up shop."

Self-confessed sports fanatics themselves, Michael and Nicholas Wainwright also sponsor the leading jockey at Cheltenham Festival, the May Chester Meeting ("the Ascot of the North West") and the Boodles Boxing Ball, a biannual society event that sprung to prominence in 2006 when Prince William and Kate Middleton attended as a couple. "There had been a block on photographing them while they were at university," Michael recalls. "And the first event they attended after they left was the Boodles Boxing Ball, so the pictures were all over the newspapers."

Boodles' latest partnership began in 2014. "We decided that we wanted to collaborate in the cultural sector," says Wainwright. "Several conversations later, we became the Royal Ballet's principle jewellery partner. They are wonderful people to work with!"

This meant that Boodles was given special access to the Royal Ballet's costume archive. "There was so much to be inspired by!" says Boodles' Design Director Rebecca Hawkins. "I was drawn to the connection between two dancers in a *pas de deux*; the way they were in tune with each other and had the ability to mirror each other." Her resulting jewellery is angular and elegant with a harmony and dynamism representative of dance.

For Marketing Director James Amos, the collaboration was a meeting of minds. "The jeweller and the ballet performer are both trying to tell a story and make an emotional connection with their audience. A high degree of skill is required to get started in both worlds, and many years of training are required. To be the best, you need the ability to focus and pay huge attention to detail. In ballet and jewellery, you won't get anywhere unless there's a real passion and desire to be the best." Wainwright adds: "Boodles and the Royal Ballet are both British to the core, and the collaboration has taught Boodles that a great many of our customers love the arts."

Everything comes back to customer service. "We work with successful people," says Wainwright. "They can shop anywhere they want – and we want them to stay shopping with us. So everything has to be right. It's not just the jewellery, it's about being personal, charismatic and always friendly."

Part of the Wainwrights' pride in what they've achieved comes down to Boodles' roots as a family business. Michael Wainwright has worked for the company for 32 years; Nicholas, now Chairman, for 47 years. "We have a totally different feel from a big plc," says Michael Wainwright, noting Boodles' loyal, long-standing staff and personal friendships with clients. "My brother and I make it our goal to get to know our customers, and our events and shops give us a great chance to do that." Employees follow suit: "One of our team had a beautiful wedding in Rome a couple of years ago, with 70 or so friends and family. I was one guest, and around 20 others were customers."

This illustrates perfectly how Boodles is defined not only by exceptionally well-designed and beautifully crafted jewellery, but also by relationships. It is a quintessentially British family business that understands the importance of strong, close connections both with its customers and external partners. "We go to the end of the world to achieve that," Wainwright concludes.

A heritage of style

DAKS

As catwalk models in London and Milan parade the latest womens- and menswear collections from DAKS, the effect is less shock of the new than an intuitive and beautifully tailored nod to the archive designs of the luxury British clothing brand. "DAKS is a prestigious brand with a great heritage," says Creative Director Filippo Scuffi. "My goal is to present it as contemporary and relevant, but always to maintain the highest-quality fabrics and design."

DAKS was founded more than a century ago, which gives Filippo an unrivalled archive catalogue. The signature DAKS check of black, vicuna and camel, which has lined classic trenchcoats and has been woven into cashmere scarves, is just one look that has been reinterpreted in new prints and weaves. "I want to give new energy and vitality to DAKS," says Scuffi, "especially with regard to shape and fit, in order to create garments that can appeal to a younger clientele."

Shape and fit have been the firm's stock in trade since founder Simeon Simpson set up shop on Petticoat Lane in 1894. The success of the "Simpson Suit", which applied the standards of bespoke tailoring to ready-to-wear garments, gained Simpson a reputation for quality fabrics and expert finish. "Then as now, we sell the best of ready-to-wear based on the principles of the finest tailoring you will find anywhere," says Deputy Chairman Paul Dimond.

What transformed the company, however, was the invention by Simeon Simpson's son, Alec, of trousers with the iconic DAKS top in 1934. The patented design of an adjustable side-strap waistband and discreet rubber pads to keep shirts tucked in place did away with the need for braces and became a worldwide phenomenon. "The heart of DAKS is in the 1930s, when we became a modern company," says Dimond. DAKS slacks became synonymous with modern, well-tailored dressing. The stylish gentlemen in Max Hoff's distinctive period advertising illustrations, with slogans such as "English elegance for town and country", created an image of easy sophistication that was exported around the world.

In 1956, DAKS received the first of its Royal Warrants, as outfitters to The Duke of Edinburgh. Further warrants were granted by Her Majesty The Queen in 1962 and The Prince of Wales in 1982. Since 1979, DAKS has been privileged to sponsor the DAKS Pony Club Mounted Games Championship at the Royal Windsor Horse Show. "Our tradition is real and very substantial," says Dimond. "We are a fashion company, but we are also very much about heritage."

It is in part this heritage that has established DAKS as a commercial success around the world, selling to some 30 countries with a particularly strong presence across Asia. "Japan is our biggest market," says Dimond. "The Japanese demand absolute quality, which we provide with a strong sense of British identity."

As Scuffi plans the new season's design theme and reaches out to a younger audience, the spirit of innovation and creativity that formed DAKS is alive and well and ready for its catwalk ovation. "It is immensely important to us that we retain our heritage," says Dimond, "but heritage with a twist that keeps it alive."

Shimmering artistry

Nobuko Ishikawa

"Each piece of jewellery has its own life and story, which reflects the identity and beauty of the person who chooses to wear it," says Yoshie Ishikawa, sister of the late Nobuko Ishikawa, a pioneer of jewellery design in Japan. However, she believes that to describe the company's collection as mere jewellery is to do it a disservice. Ishikawa sees its creations more as art.

Ishikawa explains how her sister drew design inspiration from almost anywhere: Greek mythology; Japanese literature; the view from a train window; a subtle ripple of water; a lunar eclipse. "Hanaakari, for instance, is a necklace which represents cherry blossom in full bloom, as if the flowers themselves shone in the twilight," she says. "In another piece, entitled Opening The Window, you can see a medieval courtyard, a noble scene in a royal court." In both cases, Nobuko captured these scenes and used her creative sensibilities to turn them into outstanding pieces of jewellery.

Nobuko's goal was always the same: to create wonderful, luxurious pieces. She started designing jewellery in the 1960s, a time when most people in Japan did not wear jewellery on a day-to-day basis, but rather kept their jewels at home and brought them out only on very special occasions. Her vision was to design wearable jewellery that would afford Japanese women a daily elegance.

In order to achieve her goal, Nobuko set up a studio where designers and craftsmen could bring her ideas to life – a creative space that exists to this day. "Sometimes, it requires more than 100 parts to create one complete piece of jewellery," says Ishikawa. "Our skilled artisans, some of whom have more than 30 years of experience, put the pieces together stage by stage. Sometimes it can take six months to complete a piece."

It's a process that requires a great deal of attention to detail, endurance and meticulous technique. As a result, each piece is a one-of-a-kind treasure, reflecting authentic Japanese craftsmanship. The studio also serves as a critical space for passing on the distinct designs and traditional techniques to the next generation of craftspeople, so they too can produce jewellery of the highest quality. It is hoped that this continuity will ensure that Nobuko's original vision will last long into the future.

Despite its global appeal, the creative process behind Nobuko Ishikawa jewellery is rooted firmly in Japanese culture. Craftspeople employ traditional Japanese techniques and tools for engraving and decorative work. These include the *tagane*, a popular Japanese tool, often used to eliminate surface glaze and to create more texture. Where possible they also use specifically Japanese materials, such as *syakudo*, a composite metal of copper and gold, and *maki-e*, a type of gold or silver lacquer.

This cultural sensibility has become a big part of Nobuko's appeal. Nobuko hoped that her jewellery pieces would become timeless items, passed down between family members. "Her pieces can be shared between a mother and her daughter, or even a granddaughter," says her sister, "providing happiness for generations."

In 2015, Nobuko Ishikawa was the subject of a major exhibition in France, a show that will also transfer to Madrid, Spain. This is work that transcends not just generations, but national boundaries.

Quiet confidence

REISS

REISS has never gone in for flashy advertising campaigns or Black Monday sales tactics. The privately owned British fashion retailer has prospered through recessions and international expansion thanks to the integrity of its founder's vision and the quality of its product.

So there was a pleasant irony to the unexpected global attention that the company received when Kate Middleton, the future Duchess of Cambridge, wore REISS's Nanette dress for her official engagement photographs by Mario Testino. She then wore REISS's Shola wrap dress in which to meet Barack and Michelle Obama at Buckingham Palace. "She's been a customer for years," says company owner and founder David Reiss. "She's probably the most iconic woman of her generation: everyone loves her. She's a very important part of our identity."

It is typical of the brand that, celebrity endorsements notwithstanding, it allows its menswear and womenswear to speak for itself. "Call it affordable luxury, but people want to feel good in themselves and that is what REISS is all about – everything starts and ends with the product," says the man who has guided the firm from its first outlet in Bishopsgate, London in 1971 to its position as a multi-award-winning British company with glittering flagship stores in major cities around the world.

The traditional men's tailors that Reiss inherited from his father in 1971 was the springboard for the ambitious young entrepreneur. He bought out the barber's shop next door, expanded the shop and began selling Crombie coats and Sta-Prest shirts and trousers. "People were becoming very interested in more modern menswear and I became successful very quickly," recalls Reiss. "I had identified a gap in the market for well-made yet affordable clothes. Reiss is about spending a bit more for clothes that last beyond the latest fashion trend and that make you feel special."

Still only selling menswear, REISS hit its commercial stride in the heady retail climate of King's Road, Chelsea in the 1980s, selling a sophisticated range of imported Italian suits and shirts. The economic shock of the late-1980s recession saw off many competitors, but proved a decisive moment for Reiss. "I have always been reactive to change; it's all about evolution and revolution," he says. "The only way to survive in retail is to have a strong identity, so we created our own label in 1998 with our own in-house design team, based on the same ethos of affordable luxury."

As the menswear shops flourished, Reiss was increasingly being asked why there was no womenswear line. "I have a strong entrepreneurial spirit," he says, "but I also have a level of caution, which could explain why we are one of the few private retail companies still in business after 40 years." Launching a womenswear collection would mean entrusting the brand's carefully defined identity to an outside designer.

In 2000, a capsule collection of womenswear was launched in 15 stores. "It was an absolute disaster," Reiss ruefully admits. Yet, with characteristic resilience, he was quick to turn the situation around. "We had to work together, chip away and make it happen." Within a couple of years, the womenswear collection had become the fashion insider's label of choice.

Then came the British Style Awards in 2003. "We won Fashion Retailer of the Year and all of a sudden everyone was talking about the brand. We were a player. It was great for the whole team. When you put your heart and soul into the business, there is an amazing sense of achievement to win a major award."

Success in the UK was the foundation of Reiss's international expansion plans, which began boldly with a store opening in New York in 2005. The American market, as Reiss comments, has been "the graveyard of many British brands", so Reiss took no chances with getting the concept and look of the store right, taking his architect and his designer to Tokyo to gain inspiration. "Our stores do our marketing for us," says Reiss. "It's retail theatre, which means that there has to be a level of excitement when you walk in. The staff have to be 'on brand' and the service has to be exceptional so that customers leave feeling that they have had a real shopping experience."

The preparation paid off, with Retail Week awarding the West Broadway store Best International Retail Interior in 2005. In 2006, Drapers named REISS Smaller Fashion Multiple Retailer of the Year – tellingly, by 2010 it had won Drapers' Larger Fashion Multiple Retailer of the Year. Also in New York, the REISS shop-in-shop in Bloomingdales is consistently the number-one performing international brand in the department store.

From his striking headquarters in Picton Place in central London, which houses the design team and an atelier complete with pattern cutters, Reiss is pushing forward an expansive programme of openings, with 45 stores as well as shops-in-shops opening in 2016 alone, from Hong Kong to Hamburg. At the same time, online sales were up 35 per cent in 2015, with the click-and-collect service proving extremely popular. "Every time I come into the office, it's like an adventure for me," says Reiss with a smile. "There is so much opportunity at the moment. There is a real clarity of purpose, a point of view, a sense of determination at REISS, and that reverberates right the way through the business."

Over the past 40 or so years, Reiss admits to being so driven he has had no time for reflection, yet the media frenzy that broke when Kate Middleton became his most famous customer gave even him pause for thought. "I was invited to Buckingham Palace and I got a great sense of satisfaction that everyone now knew the brand. I did think my dad would be proud if he could have seen this."

Stone love

Sharon Khazzam

"Usually, the idea comes first," says jewellery designer Sharon Khazzam. "Something will pop into my head and, wherever I am, I'll stop what I'm doing and draw it. But sometimes, I find an incredible stone and think 'Wow – what am I going to do with this?'"

The answer to that question is never the same twice. Every Sharon Khazzam piece is unique; individualised and collectable. Like its creator, Khazzam's jewellery has style, strength and personality – and is likely to appeal to women who share those characteristics.

Khazzam always knew she wanted to be a designer, but her passion for jewellery took a little longer to manifest itself. "I wanted to study fashion design," she says, "but you needed to know how to sew, which wasn't something I thought I would enjoy. So I switched my major to jewellery design and just fell in love."

That passion was obvious to all, including the management of Asprey in New York, who took the new graduate on as their sole in-house jewellery designer. Her Asprey pieces include the Sunflower Collection; she also won the prestigious Diamonds Today competition while working for the company. The relationship went from strength to strength, and when she branched out on her own, in 1993, her very first collection was showcased at Asprey.

Khazzam, who has recently been inducted into the Council of Fashion Designers of America, remains an innovator, always in search of the next great idea. Her current obsession is a type of tourmaline – a startling electric blue stone from very old mines in Brazil. "Any vibrant, natural,

strong colour makes me happy," she says. "Even if it's not one I'm going to turn into jewellery, I just like to look at these stones and hold them." Given her love of bright colours and stones that make a statement, it's little surprise that she's the jeweller of choice for the kind of strong, confident woman who likes to make a statement herself.

"I think my collection speaks to women who are confident and secure, whether they have their own businesses or excel in another field," she says. "These are women who can come and purchase jewellery without needing someone else to tell them if they should or shouldn't. My customer base is extensive, though, and also includes men who want to purchase a beautiful gift for their partners."

This resemblance between creator and collector compels Khazzam to make the purchase of a piece of her jewellery a truly personal experience. Every item is catalogued, and she often creates a book documenting its creation as a gift for the buyer. Each jewel is an original, a heritage piece to pass on to a daughter or grandchild, and Khazzam wants everything about it to reflect that. "It's such an unusual field, constantly changing – I never have a chance to get bored," she says. "There are always new stones being mined, new ideas bubbling up. As you evolve as a woman, the jewellery you desire also changes to reflect that."

Jewellery, after all, is wearable art. Just as an art collector is buying an individual vision of the world, so a Khazzam collector is opting to wear a celebration of female strength and creativity, in colours as bright as the future.

Time honoured

Rolex

From its earliest days, Rolex has been synonymous with Swiss quality – and, specifically, Switzerland's luxury watch industry. What few people know, however, is that Rolex also has strong roots in the UK.

Rolex's founder, Hans Wilsdorf, moved to London to pursue his interest in watches, founding the firm Wilsdorf & Davis in Hatton Garden in 1905. The far-sighted Wilsdorf was one of the first to recognise the potential of a robust, precise and reliable wristwatch and quickly launched models around the Empire. By the time that he registered the brand name "Rolex" in 1908, Wilsdorf & Davis was one of the leading firms in the British watch trade and London became the worldwide export centre for Rolex watches.

Above all, accuracy was key for Wilsdorf. The foundations of the legendary precision of Rolex watches were built on the first chronometer certificate for a wristwatch obtained in 1910 in Switzerland and, four years later, a "Class A" precision certificate, a hallmark of excellence, from Kew Observatory near London. These were world firsts for a wristwatch.

Wilsdorf kept his ties with Britain after he moved the company to Geneva in 1919. Today, the UK remains one of Rolex's most thriving markets and a model for its world-class servicing through its state-of-the-art Kings Hill service centre in Kent and its elegant headquarters in St James's Square, London.

Rolex's inextricable connection with the UK is replicated in its partnerships with iconic cultural institutions. The brand is the official timepiece of the Royal Opera House, and Welsh bass-baritone Bryn Terfel, a Rolex Testimonee, joins the panoply of great British artists with whom the company has been associated. In the company's philanthropic programmes,

the Rolex Mentor and Protégé Arts Initiative have included theatre director Sir Peter Hall and artist David Hockney. Over the 40-year history of the Rolex Awards for Enterprise, several distinguished international jury members have come from Britain. Rolex has also fostered its connection with exploration and science as Corporate Benefactor to the Royal Geographical Society.

But the brand's affinity for human achievement is perhaps best manifest in its support of prestigious British sporting events. The Wimbledon tennis championship has been a partner since 1978, when Rolex became the tournament's Official Timekeeper. Through its historic partnership with the Royal & Ancient Golf Club of St Andrews, Rolex is Official Timekeeper of the Open Championship. The brand is also associated with the Royal Yacht Squadron in Cowes and, in motor sports, with the Goodwood Revival.

For over 50 years, Rolex has cultivated a privileged relationship with equestrian sports, beginning with British show jumper Pat Smythe in 1957 – the first Rolex Testimonee in equestrianism – and continuing today with Zara Phillips, among other international champions. The Rolex Grand Slam of Show Jumping brings together three seminal events on the international show jumping calendar: in 2015, young Briton Scott Brash was the first rider ever to win it. Rolex is also the Official Timepiece at Badminton and Burghley, each part of the Rolex Grand Slam of Eventing.

Rolex is delighted to perpetuate this bond with the UK through its support for the Royal Windsor Horse Show and is honoured to take part in the 90th birthday celebrations for Her Majesty The Queen as Official Partner.

Elegant intimacy

La Perla

"The concept of intimacy is at the root of La Perla," says Chairman Silvio Scaglia. "Intimate in the extended sense: we make clothing for all the occasions where somebody is really at ease with themselves: on holiday, at parties, at home, with friends, travelling."

While La Perla is known for its sophisticated lingerie, it's the company's ability to apply this elegance and comfort to all the intimate moments in life which has transformed it into one of the world's leading luxury brands. And today's collections go far beyond La Perla's original handcrafted corsetry, which first captured women's attention more than 60 years ago.

"We are expanding La Perla's traditional range into the concept of loungewear, and that is rooted in intimacy," says Scaglia. "Loungewear is what you wear for yourself: you are not dressing for other people. There's still the elegance, the preciousness that you enjoy, but first of all it has to be comfortable."

This ethos goes back even further than the company's own founding in Bologna in 1954, to Her Majesty The Queen's great-grandfather, King Edward VII. As The Prince of Wales, he's credited with transforming the functional smoking jacket into a more stylish piece worn to host friends and later as outerwear in the form of the tuxedo. It's an attitude that's at the heart of La Perla's approach to loungewear. "This is exactly the definition we are giving," says Scaglia. "You like it, you find it comfortable but it is beautiful and elegant and you can use it in any public occasion."

Over the course of six decades, La Perla have added nightwear, beachwear, legwear and fragrances to the lingerie which still forms its main collections. Intricate embroidery and Leavers lace combine with sensual natural silks, satins, chiffon, organza and georgette, plus innovative new-generation fabrics such as neoprene.

Craftsmanship and heritage are always at the heart of the company's creations, even if the way they're worn now has changed dramatically. Today, lingerie and sleepwear inspires evening looks, while some of the most exclusive bras feature a small sleeve to cover the hooks and allow the back to be worn on show. From the beachwear range, bikinis and swimsuits match with cover-ups that wouldn't look out of place on a yacht or at a pool party. The company even presented its first Atelier Collection during the 2015 Haute Couture week in Paris.

"The key attributes are sensuality, elegance and preciousness," says Scaglia. Even the company's name was inspired by precious gems, with boxes lined in red velvet used to present founder Ada Masotti's first creations.

This foundation of artisan heritage, a corsetiere's intimate knowledge of the female body, a timeless mix of innovation and tradition, and a touch of Italian style, still influences the company today, in particular the exclusive Made to Measure service in flagship stores. Sewn entirely by hand, using gold thread and Swarovski crystals, it offers the chance to customise a select number of La Perla's luxurious creations to ensure they are instantly one of a kind.

"That is the peak of La Perla's production, for the most iconic designs," says Scaglia. "We can do the colours a client wants, we can adjust to the size and shape of each body. It's a line we launched nearly two years ago and it's very successful all over the world, in Europe, the USA and especially in Asia."

To ensure comfort is never compromised, La Perla has developed new fabrics in which gold thread is integrated into the embroidery of the lace. The finished material is smooth rather than metallic to the touch, making it as easy to wear as it is elegant. Less overtly eye-catching, the "impossible lace" used in other creations is uniquely luxurious in its own way.

After a scrap of fabric dating to the early 1900s was rediscovered at a vintage market in Paris, a maître dentellier in Calais put his mastery of lace-making techniques to the test to attempt the seemingly impossible: reproducing the elaborate design of this fabric. A traditional wooden loom had to be specially modified to create the complex patterns without compromising the softness and lightness of the antique lace, resulting in a spectacular, ethereal fabric used in ready-to-wear garments. It's this dedicated attention to detail and determination to create the highest quality which sets La Perla apart.

"Lace is something which is core for us," says Scaglia. "As a company, we probably know more than anyone else about lace. We wanted to continue to push this frontier in terms of design, in terms of technology, in terms of heritage. In this case, using a century-old loom as any modern loom would have made the lace too stiff, losing the charm of it."

Alongside lace, only silk occupies such an essential position for the company, featuring across La Perla's collections from lingerie to loungewear, sporty pieces and men's ranges. "Silk has fantastic qualities," says Scaglia, "in terms of temperature control, breathability, but its beauty and elegance is unmatchable."

"The developments now are in being able to combine new materials and new technologies with the traditional, the lace and silk, to constantly improve the comfort and elegance. New materials are based on silk, for example, but are also elastic, offering an element of comfort that goes beyond what was done traditionally."

First comes La Perla's new accessories line, which will feature shoes and handbags, and will be launched in time for summer 2016. "We're always following this concept of extended intimacy," says Scaglia. "Something which is very practical and comfortable but still extremely elegant and sophisticated."

More flagship stores are planned, while a sophisticated and stylish refitting of the existing boutiques will reflect La Perla's luxury heritage as it takes inspiration from Italian architecture. And with more than six decades of heritage and history to draw on, the company has big plans for its coming years as well.

"La Perla is elegance, preciousness, sensuality – with an element of surprise," says Scaglia. "The future is to build a complete lifestyle around La Perla, which stems from the original know-how and craftsmanship, following both women and men in all their intimate moments in life."

Forever summer

Babajaan

A designer, fashion industry veteran and former architect, Brazilian-born Sandra Moleirinho knows a thing or two about style. When she moved from Milan to London in the 2000s, Moleirinho felt that Britain was the perfect place to launch her own sun-drenched line of beach and resort wear, Babajaan. The London weather can present something of a challenge, but Moleirinho delights in drawing influence from the capital's creative community.

"There is something genuine about the UK," says Moleirinho. "It has an energy that I connect to – and as well as its history and tradition, London is always quirky and forward-thinking."

Capturing the celebratory spirit of her native Brazil, Babajaan is a glamorous addition to Britain's fashion portfolio. The simple lines and luxurious touches that feature in the range of one- and two-piece swimsuits, kaftans and authentic Panama hats are a tribute to womanhood, embodying the spontaneity of Brazilian women and offering a slice of summer all year round.

"I'm the Creative Director and, along with my two design assistants, I make sure I'm involved fully with the manufacturing process," says Moleirinho. "From overseeing the topstitching or the addition of a trim, Babajaan and I are always growing and learning."

Moleirinho's inspiration ranges from her love of fashion and vintage fashion photography, to the flora and fauna of Brazil and South America. The bold hues that adorn the feathered samba dancers at carnival offer a bright palette of colours to inspire Babajaan's Signature collection, while vintage Hollywood glamour is referenced in the high-waist bikini briefs in the Black and Nautical collections.

"Our identity is about being natural and true to one's self," says Moleirinho. "Babajaan women have spirit and integrity." The label is available worldwide – from Four Seasons in Maui, Hawaii to Mykonos, and from Modaoperandi.com to St Barth's – and style leaders, such as Gigi Hadid and Jessica Alba, have fallen for Babajaan's simplicity. "I want our pieces to be something that's easy to wear," says Moleirinho, "but also that reminds you of special places and memories."

Designed in the UK, the swimwear is made in Italy and Brazil and all the separates can be made in any of the colours. The beachwear features fine fabrics such as silk, chiffon and georgette, and features tactile embroideries and trims to elevate the styles from day to evening. One of Babajaan's flagship products is the Panama hat.

"All of our hats are developed in London and handmade in Ecuador, the home of the Panama," says Moleirinho. "They incorporate a flavour of the collection, giving the classic shape a twist with new colours, weaving techniques and special luxury details." As well as ensuring authenticity, Moleirinho chose to manufacture in South America for ethical reasons. "We want to give back to each country involved in producing the collection," she adds. "For instance, Babajaan is working on a project to establish support organisations to help children in Brazil, India and Ecuador. It will bring education in order to support a sustainable way of life and future for the community."

Celebrating life, travel, summer and the essence of womanhood, Babajaan's capsule collections capture the spirit of endless summer and happy memories – a must-have for any traveller.

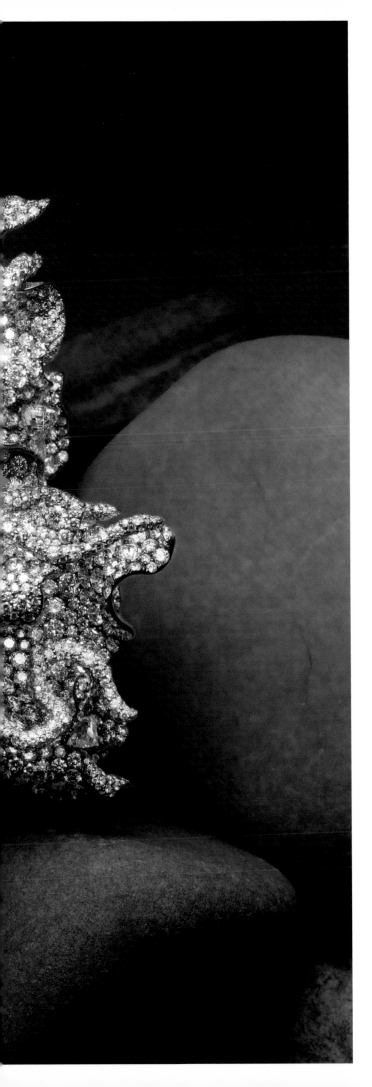

The art of jewellery

Cindy Chao

The work of Hong Kong-based jewellery designer Cindy Chao is full of dualities. As likely to be seen on the red carpet as they are in a museum, her pieces are both fashion and art, fluid and organic yet made from metal and stone. In the case of her Forest Collection, even the grotesque has been rendered beautiful by Chao's delicate hand. Since she founded Cindy Chao: the Art Jewel in 2004, her work has garnered a dedicated international following of collectors, and her pieces consistently fetch auction prices far above their estimates, with prices rising markedly since 2007.

When it comes to Chao's work, her methods are more artist than designer. "There's no doubt that Cindy is gifted and talented," says Yuting Hung, the company's Marketing Director, "but she has different views on how to create a piece of jewellery." Unlike other designers, Chao starts not with pencil and paper, but with a piece of wax. "Cindy's three-dimensional approach means always beginning with a wax sculpture," says Hung. "This way she can visualise the piece from every angle; and sometimes she'll even place the diamonds or stones to get a feel of how they'll fit." This sculpture acts like a maquette, a miniature mock-up of a work of art. "When it comes to the technical aspects of design," says Hung, "it's almost like mini-architecture."

These two influences on Chao's craft come directly from her family; her sculptor father showed her his techniques in his workshop, and her architect grandfather designed temples all over Taiwan. Although Chao studied at the Gemological Institute of America, it is her artistic soul that sparks the inception of a piece.

"Many people ask me where I get my inspiration," says Chao. "I do not know. I only know that, during the creation process, I devote my spirit, my soul, and my all to the works. The piece takes the form, the life, and the emotions I felt in my heart, and that is what I want to present to the world." This absorption in her craft results in sculptural jewellery with detail visible from every angle. The fluid, organic forms features in her cuffs hint at Chao's love of Spanish architect Antoni Gaudí, while the use of colour and suggestion of light in her brooches owe something to her artistic idol, Vincent van Gogh. "It is important to Cindy to know how to use the gemstone," says Hung, "and, like Michelangelo, she believes that working with the sculpture will release the form and soul within the stone."

Butterflies and flora feature prominently in Chao's signature Black Label Masterpiece collections; and it is these natural forms and her use of unusual stones that make her

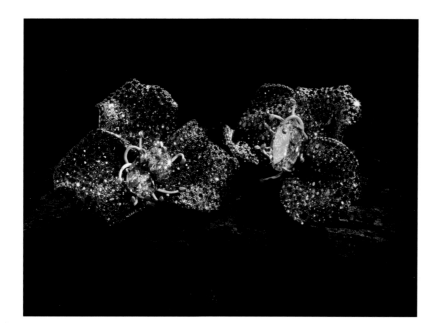

work so contemporary and collectible. A single, intricate piece can take anything from eight months to two years to make, as each one can contain up to 4,000 jewels. "A team of employees collect and select diamonds, and each stone must be of the highest quality and have the very best colour," says Hung. "Cindy uses her knowledge to experiment with new materials and setting techniques, and all the pieces are made in Switzerland and France. It's fusing ancient jewellery-making with a modern touch."

Because these Black Label Masterpieces are so unusual, collectors are often surprised when they visit Cindy Chao: the Art Jewel's private Hong Kong and Taipei showrooms, or auction houses such as Sotheby's and Christies. "Often the organic shapes take collectors by surprise, as they go beyond the imagination," says Hung. "It requires having a different perspective, and our collectors are proud to own something so unique – and that's hard to capture in an auction catalogue."

Since 2008, Chao has crafted a new butterfly-themed masterpiece each year, capturing that fleeting beauty and movement in a different brooch. In 2010, the 2009 Royal Butterfly Masterpiece brooch was inducted into the Smithsonian Museum of Natural History in Washington DC, and sits alongside such well-known treasures like the Hope Diamond and Marie-Louise's diadem. This sophisticated piece features more than 2,300 diamonds in different colours and gradients, sapphires, rubies and tsavorites, weighing almost 77 carats in all. The clever layering of rough and cut gems produces a lifelike, perfectly imperfect representation of a butterfly's asymmetric delicacy. It's this unusual representation of nature that attracted actress and philanthropist Sarah Jessica Parker, with whom

Chao collaborated on the Ballerina Butterfly Brooch to raise funds at Sotheby's for the New York City Ballet in 2014.

Although Chao's White Label collections are described as more "everyday", they're no less exquisite than her Black Label Masterpieces. These White Label collections are more playful in their exploration of Chao's signature Four Seasons theme; or her new Aquatic Collection, inspired by a summer snorkelling trip; or the Forest Collection, inspired by a walk in an autumnal forest. Here, the reference to nature's bounty is evident in the curled leaves and twisted vines of her necklaces; the tiny diamond droplets on a dewy web in her Forest Collection spider earrings; or the multifaceted shimmer on the tail of the puffer fish brooch from the Aquatic collection. "People often ask why the pieces are not more oriental in theme," says Hung. "They wonder why no dragons or lions are featured, even though Cindy is from a Chinese background. But Cindy believes her culture is evident in her actions and her attention to detail, rather than the forms of her creations."

Chao takes great pride in the fact that her work is recognised and revered the world over, whether she's showing at Masterpiece London to celebrate Her Majesty The Queen's Diamond Jubilee in 2012, or at the 2016 Paris Biennale des Antiquaires. From New York to Beijing, Chao's success is remarkable, especially considering her star has only been rising since 2004. Like the butterflies she renders so beautifully with her immense skill and natural artistry, Cindy Chao has transformed with a freedom and passion that will continue to grow and develop like nature itself.

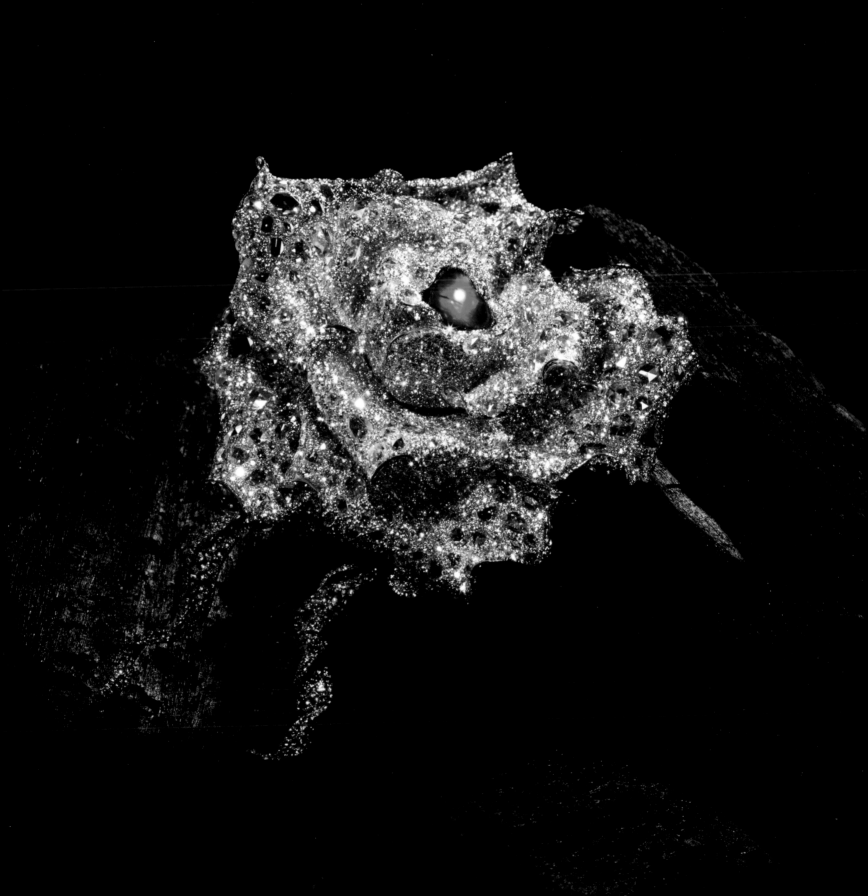

A glittering legacy

Michael Young Jewels

At the time of Her Majesty The Queen's birth, Michael Youssoufian's grandfather was jeweller to the Royal Court of Egypt – an office that he held from the 1920s to the 1950s. It's a regal legacy that informs Youssoufian, the fifth generation in a long line of jewellers, to this day.

With British and Armenian ancestry, Youssoufian has honed his skills in some of the world's greatest centres of jewellery, spending time in Alexandria, London and Geneva. In 1997, he settled in Hong Kong, where he established his own brand – Michael Young Jewels – and his own boutique. It's a place that compels those who walk past to pause and gaze at the pieces in the window. Exquisitely wrought necklaces of diamonds, rubies and emeralds glitter enticingly. Magnificent cluster rings spill over with sparkling stones. Delicate earrings in the art-deco style are finished with tiny, lustrous pearls. Each is a work of art in its own right.

Part of the magnetic allure of these pieces is down to the stones themselves. Like many of the greatest jewellers across the generations, Youssoufian has an innate sense of the qualities possessed by each gem stone he picks up, and an ability to draw designs to suit wide-ranging tastes and requirements from this simple but powerful starting point.

It might be a delicate pendant in which a particular sapphire or ruby will occupy pride of place. Or it might be a thick cuff bracelet, composed of a kaleidoscope of different stones. Whatever the piece and preference, Youssoufian will work closely with each client to produce an end result that fulfils their ideals of beauty and design. "Every request is taken personally," says Youssoufian. "Building lasting friendships with clients is one of the most rewarding aspects of the business."

While many contemporary jewellery brands subscribe to modern trends tending towards the stark and minimal, Youssoufian speaks to a particular kind of shopper who seeks artistic quality in a piece of jewellery. "Art is a form of expression unlike any other," says Youssoufian, who studied at the High School of Fine Arts in Geneva before following his family's footsteps into the field of jewellery. "All forms of art help to shape my ideas."

He gestures towards a cabinet housing an eclectic array of designs marrying multiple influences from across the ages. His appreciation of the classics is always evident, not only in the rare collection of antiques that form part of his collection but also in the touches and techniques that characterise his custom creations.

He now combines his passion for the past with an astute understanding of current markets, translated into a ready-to-wear collection that speaks to a current generation of buyers. The pieces harness the time-transcending quality that have come to characterise Youssoufian's works, capturing the essence of contemporary style in a way that will retain its beauty forever.

For Youssoufian, it has never been about following trends. Instead, he stays true to his initial source of inspiration – the world of fine jewellery, past and present, and his own family heritage of skilfully crafted, exquisite work. "We don't adapt our lines to the markets," he says firmly. "We stamp our own style on the jewellery world with each unique piece."

Sparkling design

Deema Oman

The bespoke tableware that Shadya al-Ismailiya designs serves more than just a practical purpose. Each piece is a work of art and a talking point in its own right. One customer says, "I look for excuses to host dinner parties at my house to show off the chinaware that Shadya designed and made exclusively for me."

Omani culture and heritage are the dominant sources of inspiration for the stylish pieces created by al-Ismailiya for Deema Oman, the company she founded in 2008. Teapot lids inspired by minarets, and artwork that recalls mosque wall mosaic tiles are just some of the features of her recent tableware collections.

These Omani surroundings are also represented in al-Ismailiya's jewellery designs: necklaces are adorned with delicate date palm fronds worked in gold; dolphin pendants dangle from chains; and earrings carry subtle Islamic symbols. Deema Oman is the first luxury jewellery brand to emerge from Oman, which Her Majesty The Queen and The Duke of Edinburgh famously visited in 2010.

Originality is key to the success of the company, and the reason al-Ismailiya has become the designer of choice among royals and fashionistas wanting to look their best. "We believe in originality in whatever we do," says al-Ismailiya, "So we always come up with our own ideas and transform them into designs. That's why there are stories behind most of our jewellery designs, and all our lines are related to Oman in different ways. We draw inspiration from our heritage, nature and architecture as well as from Islamic patterns."

It is the attention to detail that also ensures a Deema Oman creation stands out. Throughout the process, from designing to finishing, al-Ismailiya oversees everything to ensure her customers are delighted with their commissions. This insistence on the highest quality brought her work to the attention of one of the UK's most renowned luxury retailers, who commissioned her to design tableware for its store in what was Deema's first venture in the UK. Al-Ismailiya's dedication and flair have also been recognised with a Women Entrepreneurs Award (Almara) in 2013.

For al-Ismailiya, her satisfaction comes from seeing someone wearing one of her pieces of jewellery or admiring her tableware. For her customers, it comes from knowing they own something that looks stunning and is guaranteed to attract admiring comments.

The perfect tonic

NB Gin

When Johnny Roxburgh – the party architect for the Royal Family – needs a premium gin for the luxury events he hosts, the chances are it will be made by the North Berwick Distillery. Roxburgh describes its flagship product, NB Gin, as "superb", and he's not alone in his love of the drink. NB Gin now finds itself served by the world's most exclusive restaurants and department stores, and has been the gin of choice for the BRIT Awards aftershow party for the past two years.

It's a remarkable success story – and one that has happened in an astonishingly short time-frame. Husband-and-wife team Steve and Vivienne Muir decided to set up a gin distillery, united in their ambition to create the perfect drink. Five years later, an operation that started life with a £1,000 mini-still in their kitchen in North Berwick, near Edinburgh, has become a company that ships thousands of bottles of premier gin around the world every month.

The initial investment was months of experimentation and tasting. For nearly two years the couple tried several botanicals – the natural ingredients that give a gin its unique taste – before settling on the eight that act to produce its smooth and balanced flavour. "Most people tend to wake up to coffee," says Vivienne Muir, the company's CEO. "We would put the still on during the night before and wake up to the smell of gin." As NB Gin started to achieve high ratings against major rivals in blind tastings, the couple decided to invest in a distillery with a still that was custom built in London and installed in North Berwick by the oldest makers in the world, John Dore & Co.

The Muirs launched NB Gin in October 2013 and were taken aback by the strength of demand, selling thousands of bottles within two months. "The feedback we got was absolutely phenomenal," says Muir. "Our business is all about perfection, maintaining that perfection and consistency."

NB Gin has won a host of prizes culminating in being named the 2015 winner of World's Best London Dry Gin at the World Drinks Awards. It is now being sold in the USA, Canada, France, Spain, Germany, Denmark, Belgium and Australia. It will launch in China this year, with strong interest coming from other major territories, including Singapore and Hong Kong. The company aims to be bedded into multiple overseas markets by 2017.

Muir says that 2016 "tipped the scales" for the company. "Because we have had such fast growth and export deals," she says, "this year will be about augmenting those markets and really bedding in the products."

At your service

S2 London

Luxury entrepreneurs Ali Samli and Goran Svilar are committed to offering the very best to their clients. Together they own S2, which boasts a high-end portfolio of luxury businesses, including a concierge service; luxury properties; interior architecture and design; premium wines and spirits; and the ConSept store on the King's Road, London.

Samli, who has a background working with luxury brands, learnt the pivotal importance of customer service while working in the world of fashion. His retail expertise complements Svilar's experience in interior design, property, and buying and selling luxury estates. With their combined talents, the pair are experts in every field that the company covers and are extremely passionate about quality. Their success has won S2 an array of elite VIP and celebrity clients, who rely on the company's concierge, property and shopping services.

Central to S2 is providing its clients with the optimum experience. "That might mean helping them to purchase a property, arranging a holiday or organising a personal shopping experience at ConSept," says Svilar. "Only the best will do."

S2 Concierge London is an invitation-only service available to S2's most high-profile clients, who are looked after by an expert team. "Our concierge team will attend to the client's every need," says Samli, "whether that means booking the most in-demand restaurants, hotels and shows, or sourcing a limited-edition piece of jewellery. Our team is renowned for its excellent level of service and dedication to its loyal clients. We can organise bespoke travel arrangements and tailor-made holidays. We can also book flights

or jets and arrange accommodation, international visas and an array of the best fast-track services to ensure a smoother trip."

The company's clients agree. "S2 London is a silent, smooth operator," says one satisfied client. "They make the unattainable attainable and the impossible possible."

S2 offers design and property services for its VIP clients both in the UK and internationally. With global access to exclusive new and pre-owned assets, and extensive knowledge and experience in the international luxury industry, S2 advises, represents and facilitates deals on behalf of its clients in the utmost confidence. The company also offers business introductions to clients relocating to the UK or overseas, helping them find properties, office spaces or even introducing them to new clients.

A recent addition to the S2 portfolio is ConSept, located on the King's Road in Chelsea. Launched in March 2015, it is already starting to rival the world's most talked-about concept spaces, with a layout and brands that changes every six months. VIP shoppers have been flocking to the store since its inception to purchase limited-edition luxury products from the likes of Hermès, Versace, Baccarat, St Luis and Vistosi. A host of international models, European dignitaries and even Kylie Minogue have been spotted at ConSept.

"What is not available on the shop floor, we can supply via clients' private orders through the shop or our concierge service," says Samli. "I think what differentiates us is not price, but our selection of items. We make sure that we cater for our varied levels of clientele. Everyone has to leave the store with a smile on their face. That's our rule."

Heavenly hosts

Dorchester Collection

Guests who pass through the doors of a Dorchester Collection hotel experience something truly special. They feel it in the way they're greeted; see it in the stunning elegance around them; discover it in the service they receive; and delight in its unique characteristics. It's an impression that stays with them long after they leave.

The difference is in the detail. From captivating style to state-of-the-art facilities and outstanding locations, each hotel embodies the culture of its surroundings. The natural charm and heritage is matched by exceptional service.

Dorchester Collection is a dynamic, luxury brand with an enviable portfolio of famous hotels, each one a historic landmark that captures the culture of its setting. The hotels are situated in exceptional locations and are renowned worldwide as the places people go to see and be seen in – making a stay in one of the group's hotels anything but ordinary.

The current portfolio includes the Dorchester, London (pictured, above); the Beverly Hills Hotel, Beverly Hills, California; Le Meurice, Paris; Hôtel Plaza Athénée, Paris; Hotel Bel-Air, Los Angeles; Coworth Park, Ascot (pictured, opposite); Hotel Principe di Savoia, Milan; 45 Park Lane, London; Le Richemond, Geneva; and Hotel Eden, Rome. These hotels have all hosted their share of royalty, world leaders and celebrities over the years and have thus played a part in major moments of cultural history. Each property has its own individual style and charming stories to tell. Celebrated guests from the past include Elizabeth Taylor at the Dorchester and the Beverly Hills Hotel, Grace Kelly and Marilyn Monroe at Hotel Bel-Air, Christian Dior at Hôtel Plaza Athénée, Federico Fellini at Hotel Eden and Charlie Chaplin at Le Richemond.

The award-winning restaurants and bars of Dorchester Collection are considered by many as the hottest in town. The group has eight Michelin stars across the collection, including three at both Alain Ducasse au Plaza Athénée and Alain Ducasse at the Dorchester, the only London hotel with this prestigious accolade. Relaxation is high on the agenda at Dorchester Collection and nowhere is this more obvious than at its impressive selection of luxury spas. The hotels have teamed with their own exclusive choice of beauty partners, inviting guests into such award-winning spas as Spa Valmont pour Le Meurice; the Dior Institut at Hôtel Plaza Athénée; and La Prairie spas at both the Beverly Hills Hotel and Hotel Bel-Air.

Dorchester Collection constantly invests in its properties and draws inspiration from the idiosyncrasies of each location. Its philosophy is to ensure the hotels remain part of the fabric and culture of their host cities. To realise this ideal it has collaborated with an amazing array of distinguished interior designers including Alexandra Champalimaud, Thierry Despont, Martin Hulbert, Charles Jouffre, Marie-José Pommereau, Philippe and Ara Starck and Adam Tihany. They all specialise in creating private homes and spaces of intimacy and comfort, in blending the contemporary with tradition, and in giving each property its individual and incomparable style.

Island of serenity

Andronis Exclusive

Of Greece's many beautiful islands, only one is a caldera: the largely submerged remains of a volcano that exploded around 3,500 years ago. That one, Santorini, has the good fortune to face the sunset. It is an exceptionally lovely place, with sunshine and beaches, whitewashed villages, superb local wines, great food and a history that stretches back to before the volcanic eruption. The Ancient Greek philosopher Plato claimed that the lost city of Atlantis was sunk within its gracefully curved coastline.

In the south of the island, the Bronze Age settlement at Akrotiri is a favourite destination. Like Pompeii, it was preserved by ash from the volcano's eruption. It is also an important RAF base, which Her Majesty The Queen and The Duke of Edinburgh visited in 1961 on their way to India.

The visitor to Santorini is spoilt for choice; but few hotels can match the elegant luxury of the family-owned Andronis Luxury Suites in beautiful Oia, perched on the sunken caldera's northern tip.

The villas and suites that make up Andronis Exclusive seem to cascade gently down the side of the island. All the rooms have arched ceilings, elegant decor, terraces with views over the caldera, and private hot tubs. Eight have their own swimming pools.

Each suite has been designed, says Managing Director George Filippidis, to be special: "We try to present rooms that respect local tradition but also offer all the comfort and personal service that the contemporary traveller is looking for." Every guest, he says, receives all the care and attention imaginable, from their favourite brand of toiletries and type of pillow to seamlessly organised days out on sailing boats, vineyard tours or trips to monuments.

If they just feel like lounging around, guests at all three of the family's properties can use Andronis Alta Mare's cave pool, built into the hillside, for a swim; or sunbathe on the prime segment of beach Andronis reserves for its guests. Little wonder that this is the escape of choice for celebrities and royalty from Qatar, Saudi Arabia and the UAE.

Everything at Andronis – including the infinity pool – is integrated into the landscape. The beds are raised on stone platforms to give the best possible views of the Aegean. The Lycabettus Restaurant perches on a clifftop. It was named Number One of luxurytravelexpert.com's Top Ten Restaurants With Views That Match the Food.

The cuisine there – and at the larger Lauda Restaurant – relies on delicious locally sourced ingredients. "We are very lucky," says Filippidis. "We have capers, aubergines, great fish, local cheeses and the famous Santorini tomatoes; as well as wonderful white wines made from the Assyrtiko grape."

Santorini actually boasts several of its own grapes, all bravely growing out of the volcanic soil. But the Assyrtiko grape – the vines of which can date back over 100 years – makes an astoundingly good minerally white wine. These grapes, like the luxury resorts offered by Andronis Exclusive, stand out as the best of the bunch.

Up, up and away

Eastern Safaris

The Lonely Planet guide to Myanmar features an image of a hot air balloon flying majestically above temples in the ancient city of Bagan. The balloon is one of a fleet owned by Balloons Over Bagan, operated by Eastern Safaris, and the image conveys not only the popularity of the experience but its significance in a country only recently opened up to international tourism.

"Ballooning is a magical way to explore fragile areas such as Bagan leaving only a minimal footprint," says Eastern Safaris co-founder Khin Omar Win. "In 2015, we flew more than 21,000 people. To do that with so little impact on the environment is incredible."

Win met her husband and business partner Brett Melzer while travelling in Myanmar in 1997. Despite there being no established tourist industry to work with and having no experience of luxury travel, the couple bought a balloon, enlisted a qualified pilot and eight local staff and took to the skies. Now, with 12 balloons and a staff of 190, Balloons Over Bagan is the largest commercial balloon operation in Asia with an impeccable 100 per cent safety record. "It's been an adventure," says Melzer. "We wanted to do something pioneering that would make a difference and have an impact."

Success in Myanmar spurred Win and Melzer to stray still further off the tourist map into Bhutan, where they opened Gangtey (Goenpa) Lodge in 2013. The 12-room boutique hotel, set high above an unspoiled valley, is a refined and discreetly luxurious take on Bhutanese architecture and featured on *Condé Nast Traveller*'s Hot List of Best New Hotels in 2014.

Eastern Safaris isn't just about giving clients memorable experiences in beautiful surroundings. "Commercial success is not an end in itself," says Win. "It's the basis for what we can do within the community." She and Melzer provide donations to health, education and environmental projects in and around Bagan, relying on staff to suggest what is needed and where.

"It has always been important that the needs of people on the ground are expressed, and that it isn't a top-down process," says Win. "When we choose a school to donate to, our team helps us find out how many children there are and what they need from us." At Gangtey Lodge, guests who join morning prayers and blessings at the nearby 17th monastery are invited to donate alms to the monks who study there.

Next on the horizon is Balloons Over Atacama, which takes the Bagan model to Chile's arid interior. "Clients fly over one of the world's driest places – the stunning Valley of the Moon – with rock formations covered in salt and a backdrop of volcanoes," says Win.

"After Bagan, we know intuitively what will work," says Melzer. "You need a passionate team and the right location." With its formula of exhilarating visitor experiences in the air and a collaborative, charitable support operation on the ground, the sky is the limit for Eastern Safaris.

Island idyll

Cape Verde

Cape Verde, the group of islands some 1,500 km south of the Canaries, might have been a Portuguese colony but it has long had links with the UK. Throughout the 19th century, the British Navy used Mindello harbour to store coal while on Bóa Vista Island the Rendall family patriarch settled as First Consul of Queen Victoria in the late 1830s. The last British officials left the islands in 1960 but they left their architecture, English tea, whisky, golf and the dubious combination of khaki shorts paired with white socks.

Nowadays, visitors travel to the islands primarily to enjoy the miles of untouched sandy beaches and their year-round sunshine climate. The Resort Group, a superior quality property developer, first arrived there in 2007, when CEO Rob Jarrett committed to the purchase of a piece of development land on Sal Island, one of the 10 volcanic islands that make up Cape Verde.

"For me it was all about finding the right destination," says Jarrett. "I was immediately struck by the potential of Cape Verde. It was an untouched paradise, pure white sandy beaches and continuous sunshine. There was no hesitation, this was the perfect place." Jarrett's vision was to establish Cape Verde as "the European Caribbean" as it's only six hours from the UK and in an adjacent time zone, which means tourists can get there without any jet lag.

The company's first resort was Melia Tortuga Beach, a five-star establishment that has been consistently popular since it opened in May 2011. This was followed three years later by the Melia Dunas Beach Resort & Spa, which stretches over 1 km in length, making it the largest resort on the African continent. Since opening, both resorts have enjoyed consistent praise and have won certificates for excellence through the World Travel Awards.

The latest addition to the collection is Melia Llana Beach Hotel, while a further six resorts are planned for Boa Vista Island. Once completed, the Resort Group will have delivered more than 6,500 hotel rooms across the Islands. "All our resorts create a truly world-class tourist destination that these islands deserve," says Jarrett. "We are all immensely proud of our achievements to date and will continue to work alongside the Cape Verdean people to ensure that these stunning islands have a prosperous future driven by tourism."

Working alongside the local community is of high importance to the Resort Group, which has established a foundation offering charitable support to many local community projects around the islands. "We wanted to help the local communities with funding and support for key projects and charity work," says Jarrett. "There is a particular emphasis on helping Cape Verde's schools and young children so that they have more opportunities in the future.

"A close working partnership with Cape Verde's government has been crucial in the delivery of all our resorts, as the country continues to extend its UK links," he adds. "This is based on a long and lasting friendship and cooperation between both our countries, and long may it continue."

Refining luxury

Lucknam Park Hotel & Spa

Approached by a magnificent, mile-long double avenue of lime and beech trees, Lucknam Park Hotel & Spa is a stunning mansion, dating back to 1720, that stands within 500 acres of unspoilt parkland and manicured gardens, offering the true luxury of space. Recently awarded Hotel of the Year 2016 by the South-West Tourism Excellence Awards and the Luxury Travel Guide Global Awards, the five red-star hotel and spa is the epitome of British luxury.

While Lucknam is perfectly placed for exploring nearby Bath, the Cotswolds and Wiltshire's wealth of heritage sites, many guests find they never leave the grounds – it is the perfect place to retreat from the real world. "This is country-house living at its best," says Managing Director Claire Randall. "Lucknam is a luxurious home-away-from home that prides itself on its rare level of attention to detail."

Lucknam is effortlessly elegant and full of history. A private home until 1987, the Palladian mansion welcomed Queen Mary as a guest during the war, when airmen from the nearby aerodrome used the trees lining the drive to camouflage their Spitfires. The glorious public rooms are furnished with antiques, sparkling chandeliers, sumptuous fabrics and deep sofas, which guests can sink into and indulge in traditional afternoon tea in front of a log fire. Lucknam combines heritage, grandeur and refined luxury without being stuffy. The Park restaurant, in the elegant former ballroom, has held a Michelin star for 11 years under the award-winning chef Hywel Jones. For contrast, the contemporary Brasserie offers informal, delicious dining.

The hotel's 42 individually designed rooms and suites are antique furnished while offering all the modern comforts, and views from the house over the grounds are breathtaking. Wonderful facilities are balanced with great hospitality, provided by perhaps Lucknam's greatest asset – the personal attention from the 150 staff offering service above and beyond.

For guests of all ages, there is so much in which to indulge, including the impressive cookery school, the sleek, world-class spa offering fabulous facilities, unique treatments, thermal experiences and a well-being house for specialist relaxation and, at the extensive equestrian centre, riding for all levels of experience is available. The use of estate lodges and outbuildings to house these amenities ensured that none of Lucknam's charm was lost when these facilities were added.

"This is a truly special place," says Claire Randall, "where many people come to celebrate landmark moments in their lives and make wonderful memories to take away."

Estate of grace

Luton Hoo

What guests quickly come to realise about Luton Hoo, a Georgian estate in Hertfordshire, is its sheer vastness. At its centre lies a period property dating back to the late 18th century, painstakingly restored to its former glory by Elite Hotels, which re-opened the country house as a five-star hotel in 2007.

"It was a long and involved process that took eight years," says Jayne Alison, Business Development Manager. "We brought in expert stonemasons, historians and the expertise of English Heritage to bring the mansion house back to how it was in 1903. And that's not to mention the recreation of the 1,055 acres of gardens that were originally landscaped by Capability Brown."

Luton Hoo is steeped in history. It was originally built for a prime minister, the first Earl of Bute, and was later owned by diamond magnate Julius Wernher, who used his considerable wealth to fill the rooms with a priceless art collection. The Royal Family also have long associations with the house, with Her Majesty The Queen and The Duke of Edinburgh spending part of their honeymoon there.

It retains the same grandeur today and, indeed, has often been used as a location in many British and Hollywood films to signify aristocratic decadence. The hotel has had to create over ten distinctions of bedroom to preserve their authenticity. All are spacious and luxurious, and bathed in rich colours.

Today the mansion house is joined by the more modern but no less attractive intimate country club in converted stables, as well as a golf course, spa and exclusive conference venue. And, with the Wernher Restaurant, it has an eatery with two AA rosettes. Despite its grandeur, Luton Hoo retains a relaxed atmosphere; staff are welcoming and friendly, professional and efficient, but never stuffy. Some visitors will lounge their weekend away in the oversize sofas, sipping excellent coffee; others might enjoy an afternoon of shooting or walking, or perhaps a visit to the spa. "We like to make everyone feel comfortable," says Alison. "What we offer is a complete country weekend destination." With excellent transport links to major motorways and airports, Luton Hoo also serves as an impressive conference centre. Delegates can enjoy total privacy at Warren Weir, the hotel's self- contained "business bubble".

"Elite Hotels only pick highly individual properties that are steeped in tradition," says Alison. "And there are not many properties that are the size and scale of Luton Hoo. There is simply nothing you can't do here, which is why our guests come back again and again."

The beauty of wood

Dinesen Floors

A deep sense of serenity pervades the Dinesen Home. Passing from room to room, a soothing, holistic vibe hangs softly in the air, washing away any trace of the bustling streets of Copenhagen below. It's something to do with the cool calm of the interiors, the foundations for which were put in place by the British designer Anouska Hempel 10 years ago. Only selected clients of Dinesen Floors are invited to stay here and experience the essence of the Danish family-run company.

When the apartment was remodelled more recently, Hempel's design was incorporated into a fresh vision, using modern Danish influences. The result is a revitalised sense of space, where the scope for movement is enhanced by minimalist use of furnishing – enough to make it feel like home while allowing freedom to move and breathe.

Underpinning this, quite literally, is the flooring. Long, sweeping swathes of wood, each pale plank stretching from one end of the room to the other, establish a clean, harmonious base, creating a sense of continuity throughout. It's a perfect example of using flooring as a key design feature, something that Dinesen achieved by working with numerous international architects and designers to create extraordinary effects.

Among these is prominent British architect John Pawson. "Many years ago, he taught us the important lesson of what floors can do for a space," says Thomas Dinesen, who runs the company along with his wife Heidi Dinesen. This understanding has since proved its worth in many of the company's international collaborations, where the combination of Dinesen's deep-rooted knowledge about wood and the aesthetic input of talented designers has resulted in remarkable solutions.

Dinesen counts a number of exhibition spaces among its clients, which include high-profile museums and galleries, such as the Royal Society of Arts and the Saatchi Gallery in London, with more than 5,000 square metres of long and wide Grand Douglas planks alongside studios and private collection spaces. "Increasingly, there is a focus on the fact that wide floorboards are a fantastic foundation for art and fine furniture," says Dinesen. "Many of our clients have a special interest in art or may even be art collectors, and they appreciate this distinctive yet discreet quality."

The benefits of this are felt across all of Dinesen's projects, which range from private apartments, villas and beach houses to castles, hotels, restaurants and offices. In each of these environments, Dinesen's beautiful wood brings a new dimension to the design, simultaneously harmonising with and enhancing diverse settings, from historic homes and heritage sites to the most avant garde and futuristic spaces.

Dinesen's considerable expertise and experience in creating floors for listed buildings played a central role in the renovation of Frederik VIII's Palace, which is part of Amalienborg Castle in

Copenhagen. A royal residence since the 1700s, the palace underwent a significant restoration to transform the interiors into a contemporary home for the Danish Crown Prince Couple.

The challenge for Dinesen rested in finding new solutions that would befit the creative marriage of old with new that characterised the renovation. Where the existing wooden plank floors could not be reused, new pinewood floors of a quality and appearance suited to the elegant palatial interior were installed. Today, new Dinesen floors of extraordinary quality live their future life alongside the historic floors in Frederik VIII's Palace.

While flooring accounts for the majority of Dinesen's production, the breadth of company's expertise means that it is often called upon to provide other bespoke solutions. "Our experience is so broad that we naturally take on a wider perspective," says Dinesen. "We are often seen as the link between the clients' requests and the possibilities of nature. When a strong and beautiful tree is felled and cut up, it opens a world of bespoke solutions for quality-conscious people, from walls and ceilings to custom-made furniture where the wood becomes a design element."

Respect for wood and a passion for the possibilities it offers are at the heart of all that Dinesen does. In a family business that goes back 118 years, this ethos has guided the company across the generations, resulting in the creation of extraordinary products that have taken wooden floors to new levels and established Dinesen as a leader in the field. The company has also received numerous awards. Dinesen Home won a Wallpaper* Design Award in the category of Best Apartment. Meanwhile, Dinesen's showroom in Copenhagen, created in co-operation with OeO Studio and

praised for its refined take on wood, was Winner of the Iconic Architecture Awards 2015 in the Interior category and also received a German Design Award in 2016.

"Since the company was first established in 1898, high-quality craftsmanship has been our core value," says Dinesen. "Our production of planks is based on 118 years of experience, growth and dedication. My great-grandfather was interested in technology and wood, my grandfather was interested in production and wood, and my father was interested in creativity and wood."

The expertise and achievements of Thomas Dinesen's forebears remain part of the company today. One thing each generation had in common was a desire to use the individual tree with respect. "It is a fascinating and demanding legacy that I feel and live by every day," says Dinesen, emphasising the importance of maintaining a sustainable approach towards production and preserving the forests for future generations.

"As an old family business," he continues, "we are well aware of the importance of planning for the future, and all our suppliers practise sustainable forestry where the consideration of future generations is the key aspect of daily life. Many of the forests, especially in Germany, have been owned and tended by the same family for hundreds of years. Present generations are harvesting the rewards of their fathers and grandfathers and maintaining the forest for their children's children."

It is this sense of longevity and respect for both the past and future that underlies the work that Dinesen does today. The company is laying down exquisite wooden floors that will last generations, retaining their elegance and beauty decade after decade.

Pure pleasure

The White Company

"Getting the shade of white right is critical," says Chrissie Rucker, founder of the White Company. "Whites with blue hues are cold, while yellow hues are like clotted cream. I'm a great believer in that pure warm white."

It's this attention to detail that has seen Rucker's company grow from a 12-page mail-order brochure in 1994 to one of the leading luxury high street brands in the UK. It also earned Rucker an MBE from Her Majesty The Queen in 2010. The company now employs 1,300 people across 56 stores in Britain. Everything still hinges on four core values – plus that passion for white. "Our goal is to create beautiful, simple, stylish designs that are great quality, that really work and are still affordable," says Rucker. Along with this top-quality design, great customer service and a committed team behind the scenes are key.

But unlike other brands, it's not about slavishly following that season's fashion. The White Company's products are a starting point to develop an individual style. "We are really passionate about trying to inspire, so for every issue of the brochure and every online feature, we come up with ideas that are quick and easy to do," says Rucker. "I'd hate anyone to think we were trying to dictate."

The company's distinct approach sprang from Rucker's own experience of decorating her then boyfriend's house. Applying the idea that "simple is best" – one that she had picked up working previously on magazine shoots – Rucker found that the high-quality but well-priced designs that her company now sells simply didn't exist back then. Since its launch, the brand has expanded from homeware into furniture, fragrance, women's clothing, loungewear and the Little White Company for babies and children, launched to fill another niche around the time when Rucker started her own family.

"Our passion is trying to find ways of creating perfect simplicity, taking the everyday and making it extra special," she says. "Everything from a cup of coffee in a lovely mug to having a hot bath and wrapping yourself up in a fluffy towel."

This simplicity makes detail all-important, whether it's sourcing the softest cashmere, cool linen and crisp cotton or ensuring the precise height and width of a glass. And as part of the Ethical Trading Initiative, this focus extends to the way products are made.

To celebrate its 21st birthday, the company launched Chrissie's White Heart Foundation, where 10 per cent of sales from hand-picked products are donated to three charities helping vulnerable women and children. The Prince's Trust, of which Rucker is Silver Patron, supports young people in difficult circumstances and encourages young entrepreneurs. Refuge helps women fleeing domestic violence and a third partnership is set to enable more counselling and mentoring for young children in need.

Next? The world. "Our plan in the next five years is to double the size of the business," says Rucker. "International is on the agenda." Four million brochures are already sent out in the United States, in addition to the 10 million across Britain. "The great thing about white," says Rucker, "is that whoever you are, wherever you live – whether it's sleek and modern or pretty and country – white works."

Local hero

Love-Local.com

"It's easy to forget what's around you," says Liz Oram, director of online gallery and shop, Love Local Shop Ltd, which works with a small team of passionate fellow directors across the south-west of England. "Every day we're delighted by products that are so lovingly made here in the South West and throughout Britain, and we want people to realise that it can be easy to find them."

Featuring renowned brands and small business, Love Local celebrates the wealth of products, art, crafts, food and drink in the region and currently showcases some 2,000 items. Handmade gifts, homeware and artisan products from Devon, Cornwall, Dorset, Somerset and Wiltshire are all available from the website, which celebrates its evolution with a new website in 2016 and expansion throughout the UK and beyond.

"I think that handmade is particularly vibrant in the South West," says Oram. "Because of the rural nature of the counties, the landscape inspires makers and there are some world-class businesses on our doorstep."

Passionate about British-made products, Oram recognised the importance of small businesses when she worked for Business Link and the South West Tourism Board. "There are over 44,000 businesses in the South West, and a huge majority have 10 employees or less," she adds. "People are recognising

that crafts aren't just for the kitchen table, and British-made artisan products are available, as well as more widely-known brands such as Royal Warrant holder Royal Brierley Crystal."

Eschewing mass-produced manufacture, the "Great British" provenance of the products appeals to an international audience as well as those in the UK. "People want to know where their product comes from," says Oram, "and we make sure that each county has a selection of different products so that the makers get exposure."

The new website invites shoppers to connect with designers – introducing more "meet the maker" profiles so that each piece has its own history and personal origin. It is the hope that Love Local captures the spirit of "slow living", encouraging shoppers to understand the time, love and skills that go into the individual and, by nature, unique pieces. The products range from hand-thrown ceramics to silver jewellery, as well as beautifully made kitchens and even handmade, totally organic cosmetics.

The company's plans to expand across England to represent each county, eventually, mean that Love Local celebrates "local" on a global level – encouraging the connection between something that is original and hand-made to people the world over who take pleasure in locally-sourced, quality goods.

Fringe benefits

Margam Jones Tassels

Luxurious thread, Swarovski crystals and soft leather in a range of colours sound like the raw materials for a pair of couture shoes or a piece of statement jewellery. Yet all are used in various creative guises at Margam Jones and Partners, a business in South Wales that produces handmade bespoke tassels and tie-backs.

"Harrods was the very first shop we supplied with tassels," says owner Margam Jones, "which inspired us to create oversized, bejewelled tassels using luxurious materials." Now the tassels add flair to a host of private residences and prestigious property developments across the UK, the USA and the Middle East.

Margam Jones began making tassels for a local interior designer, having left the teaching profession. However, this wasn't just a hobby. She spent three years studying rope and cord making, and became apprenticed to a wood turner to learn how to bring her concepts to life. For her, tassels had become not only a passion but also a business venture.

"I had a never-ending flow of ideas," she says, "and with so many materials, styles and sizes I soon realised I would require the expertise of a whole group of people to produce the pieces in my imagination." She now works with a team of highly skilled tassel-makers, whose creations range from small key tassels to large, embellished pieces. "Each tassel is made by hand," she says. "The beaded ropes alone can take two hours each to thread." Margam Jones sells through leading interior designers, as well as SoFarSoNear in Belgravia. Immaculate craftsmanship is essential. "Our standards are very high," she says. "The team themselves know if something is perfect or not."

A trademark of Margam Jones Tassels is hand-blown glass, used to create tassel tops that could be clear, embellished or silver-lined for a lustrous finish. "We work with a high-skilled team that includes an accomplished glass maker," says Margam Jones. "He is always willing to try new finishes and he inspires us with his beautiful and imaginative creations." The Margam Jones team also includes experts who carve a variety of woods and varnish them with burnished lacquers. "Having all these skills in-house enables us to create bespoke finishes to match a sample of fabric," she says.

Margam Jones and her team work amid spools of coloured thread in more than 2,000 shades, boxes of crystal and glass beads. These couturiers of the well-dressed window patiently create the interior designer's antidote to minimalist restraint: tassels and tie-backs of bejewelled flair and brilliance.

Crystal-clear ambition

William Yeoward

"At William Yeoward, we like to think that we are leading rather than following," says the company's eponymous owner, William Yeoward, who has been creating a distinctive blend of luxurious and liveable English products for the home for the past 30 years.

Since opening his first shop on King's Road, Chelsea in 1987, Yeoward has used his love of antiques to reinterpret furniture, crystal, home accessories and fabrics with colourful originality. His impulse to design and innovate is as keen as ever, and has earned him an international clientele. "There are very few people who produce the breadth of products that we do," he says, "and the joy today is as strong as it was when I started."

For someone consummately at ease in his field, Yeoward acknowledges that his early success was born out of the frustration of not finding the particular pieces he was searching for to furnish his own home. "I could see that there are talented people everywhere," he says. "The thing to do is find people who can make things for me."

In 1995, Yeoward met third-generation crystal designer and maker Timothy Jenkins, who immediately realised that they shared the same passions and aspirations and William Yeoward Crystal was born. William Yeoward Crystal has been granted a Royal Warrant of Appointment as suppliers of crystal glass to The Prince of Wales. American *Elle Décor* wrote in 1996 that William Yeoward Crystal epitomised "a zenith in crystal making", helping

to fire the brand's success in the USA and subsequently worldwide. "It is only because the product is so marvellous that people know about it," says Yeoward.

Yeoward's breadth of creative interest doesn't stop at glassware, however. Teaming up with Tricia Guild he has produced collections of wallpaper and fabrics, taking inspiration from vintage prints and fabrics he finds on his travels. "I keep my eyes open," he says. "I used a heavy linen Chinese tie-dyed skirt, for example, as the source for a fabric that I thought would make a wonderful Roman blind. It's not reproduction, but reinterpreting an original pattern and making it suitable for use today."

The search for sympathetically made 'old–new' furniture led Yeoward to a partnership with Jonathan Sowter of Jonathan Charles Fine Furniture. "Furniture is the hardest thing to get right," says Yeoward, "but Jonathan not only gets the proportions spot on, but creates details that speak for themselves. Our drawers, for instance, are lined with hand-inlaid marquetry polka dots."

William Yeoward is a great believer that you cannot please everyone, so it is best simply to please yourself. Luckily, his taste and keen eye for beautiful designs and fine craftsmanship turn out to please a lot of discerning customers, too. "If you have one foot in yesterday and one in tomorrow," he says, "somewhere in the middle you will find the spirit of today." Spoken like a true style leader.

A floral tribute

Moorcroft Pottery

When Hugh Edwards, Chairman of Moorcroft Pottery in Staffordshire, found himself in conversation with Her Majesty The Queen at an official occasion in 1999, talk turned to how, as a young woman, white was Her Majesty's favourite colour, as exemplified by her choice of white orchids in her bridal bouquet. It's only natural, then, that when it came to designing a vase in honour of The Queen's 90th birthday, Edwards' encounter served as inspiration, and thus the Buckingham Orchid was born. Established in 1897, Moorcroft held a Royal Warrant between 1928 and 1978 and has permission to use The Queen's "E II R" cypher on the Buckingham Orchid. It continues the company's long-standing and noble royal association.

Quilty pleasures

Quilts by Lisa Watson

"We are a fantastic nation with a brilliant textile heritage that I wish to celebrate," says Lisa Watson, the namesake founder of Quilts by Lisa Watson. "The materials used in my quilts are all sourced from British manufacturers. The thread comes from a mill in Lancashire, my ribbon is from Cheshire and the Harris Tweed from Scotland. I aim for my quilts to be 100 per cent British made."

Based in Manchester, the heart of the UK's historic textile production, Lisa's company was launched in 2013. But her quilts, which often take inspiration from art galleries or historic designs, are investment pieces that are stitched to last.

With a background in art and design, including a degree in Fine Art Textiles, making her limited-edition quilts has been a way for Watson to combine her love of fabric, textures and patterns. "I am also passionate about the quality, integrity and authenticity of Made in Britain products," she says.

From Colefax & Fowler prints to Berisford ribbon, it's the combinations of materials that really set Watson's creations apart, such as the contrast of British velvet with Harris tweed, supplied by just two producers in the Scottish Isles. Protected by the Orb trade mark, the tweed has long

been a favourite of the Royal Family, ever since it was adopted by Queen Victoria's inner circle.

Based on traditional utilitarian patterns from northeast Scotland, each Harris Tweed strip design takes at least 10 hours to create. And Watson's bespoke commissions – a stylish update on quilting's original use of scraps, bedding and uniforms – have incorporated wedding dress materials as well as baby clothes.

"I really enjoy the challenge of one-off quilt commissions," she explains. "It is great to be able to work with a client and their cherished fabric to create a unique personalised quilt. In these days of fast fashion, it's nice to have something with a story woven into the fabric to pass on as a cherished heirloom. A quilt will warm your body and comfort your soul."

Watson's inspirations come from her knowledge of historic and contemporary art and design, plus an eye for everyday beauty. Those striking colour combinations, meanwhile, owe much to the influences of her own Scottish heritage.

"People buy my quilts because they want something that is unique," says Watson, "as well as something that is really well made, British and bursting at the seams with quality."

The seal of approval

Taking care of business

Like any family, the Royal Family needs to buy goods and services to go about its everyday business. Unlike most families, however, it is in the unique position of being able to use that engagement to actively encourage and promote British businesses and promote excellence. Today, it does this using three mechanisms – the Royal Warrant, the Royal Charter and the Queen's Awards for Enterprise.

For centuries, the Royal Family has used its patronage to help promote organisations that it deems worthy of support by the awarding of a Royal Warrant by Appointment. The winemakers Berry Bros & Rudd and the whisky blenders J&B (Justerini & Brooks) have both been supplying the Royal Family since King George III; while the tailors Gieves & Hawkes, tea merchants Twinings and gun makers James Purdey & Sons have warrants that date back to the Victorian era. Other companies – such as Samsung and Scan Computers – have been granted Royal Warrant status in the past few years, reflecting changes in the kind of technology used in royal households.

All these companies have to prove that they have been supplying a royal household for five of the past seven years

and have an ongoing trading arrangement. This gives them permission to use a royal crest on their product's labels and promotional materials, together with the phrase "By Appointment to Her Majesty The Queen", "By Appointment to HRH The Duke of Edinburgh" or "By Appointment to HRH The Prince of Wales". There are currently around 800 Royal Warrant holders.

One key rule for the Royal Warrant Association is that its awards have always been for tradespeople who provide goods and services, rather than professions. The likes of doctors, lawyers, teachers, architects or schools are represented by a different mechanism – the Royal Charter.

Originally used to establish towns and cities, the Royal Charter is still the mechanism by which a British town is elevated to city status. However, there are now more than 900 organisations with Royal Charter status. These include some of the UK's most venerable institutions – including the BBC, the Bank of England, the Royal Mint, the British Armed Forces, the Royal Academy, the Royal Shakespeare Company, the RSPCA and the Royal Opera House. The list also includes most British universities created before 1993, many of the

ancient City of London guilds (from the Worshipful Company of Basketmakers to the Worshipful Company of Mercers) and dozens of professional institutions – from the Institute of Actuaries to the Chartered Institute of Taxation.

Over the course of The Queen's reign, the Royal Family has become more active in its promotion of British businesses. One key innovation came in 1965 with the establishment of the Queen's Award to Industry. At the inaugural ceremony in April 1966, the award was given to 115 organisations. In 1975, it was renamed the Queen's Awards for Export and Technology, with separate awards in each category; by 1992 it had added a Queen's Award for Environmental Achievement. Following a 1999 review, chaired by The Prince of Wales, it was renamed the Queen's Awards for Enterprise, with awards under three broad categories: International Trade, Innovation and Sustainable Development.

In 2005, the Queen's Award for Enterprise Promotion (QAEP) was added, honouring individuals who make outstanding contributions to enterprise culture in the UK. The QAEP is equivalent to an MBE and is made by The Queen on the advice of the prime minister; who, in turn, is advised by an Enterprise Promotion Assessment Committee, which includes representatives of government departments as well as entrepreneurs and business leaders. A maximum of 10 QAEPs are awarded each year.

The Queen's Awards for Enterprise are administered by the Department of Business, Innovation and Skills, and awarded on behalf of The Queen and the prime minister. They are supported by an advisory committee, chaired by the head of the civil service and comprising representatives of government, the private sector and the trade unions.

The awards process is rigorous and competitive, with somewhere between 100 and 200 businesses reaching the tough criteria each year – that's around 20 per cent of those that enter. The International Trade award, for instance, requires a company to show a substantial and sustained increase in export earnings over three consecutive 12-month periods, to a level that is outstanding for the size of the organisation and the products and services concerned. To qualify for the Sustainable Development category a company needs to make detailed submissions addressing the "pillars of sustainable development", including environmental issues, management approaches and contributions to the local community.

The awards are open to any UK-based business that has a minimum of two full-time employees and a track record of outstanding commercial success. Some Queen's Award winners employ thousands, such as Jaguar Land Rover and Anglian Water (both winners of Sustainable Development awards in 2015). Others might have just a handful of staff: 116 of the 2015 winners had fewer than 250 full-time employees; and 17 of them employed fewer than 10.

Winners receive a workplace presentation from a royal representative and an invitation to a reception at Buckingham Palace hosted by The Queen. They are given an engraved crystal bowl and a hand-signed scroll, but – beyond these physical awards – the benefits are often far-reaching. Winning companies often enjoy a boost in sales, an increase in publicity and invariably notice a hugely improved staff morale. They can also use the prestigious "award emblem" on company stationery, websites, on goods and in advertising, granting them an edge over competitors.

A Queen's Award is a real feather in the cap for any business. Like a Royal Warrant or a Royal Charter, it brings with it a huge overseas clout and a high degree of credibility.

Singled out for success

Gordon & MacPhail

Gordon & MacPhail has long been revered as the custodian of the world's greatest single malts. However, during his time as a pupil at Gordonstoun school in the 1960s, Prince Charles associated this iconic Scottish company with a very different type of product.

"When he opened our Benromach Distillery in 1998, he recalled with great fondness how a Gordon & MacPhail van used to sell confectionery at Gordonstoun," says Stephen Rankin. "But His Royal Highness also knew a great deal about the whiskies we've produced over the years."

Rankin is Gordon & MacPhail's UK Sales Director and part of the fourth generation now working for the family business. "It all started when James Gordon and John Alexander MacPhail set up a grocers in Elgin on Speyside in 1895," he says. "The shop stocked teas, coffees, high-quality groceries, wine and spirits. However, from the beginning there was a strong leaning towards whisky, and Gordon & MacPhail would send empty casks that once contained fortified wines to distilleries throughout Speyside to fill with new spirit for creating house blends and malts. Aged 15, my great-grandfather John Urquhart was one of their first employees and soon started working on the whisky side of the business, which also involved selecting and buying malts to create house blends."

The Speyside region is home to around half of Scotland's whisky distilleries, so Urquhart couldn't have chosen a better spot for his career. When Gordon & MacPhail started bottling under licence for local distillers such as Glenlivet, Glen Grant and Mortlach, it set the scene for John Urquhart – and eventually his son George – to utterly transform the business and the whisky industry as a whole.

When MacPhail retired in March 1915 and Gordon died two weeks later, John Urquhart became senior partner. Over the next few years, he experimented by maturing whiskies for much longer than was common at the time, and his son George – who joined the company in 1933, also aged 15 – took this innovative approach even further.

"They both went very much against the grain," says Rankin, "and, in the 1960s, George helped lay the foundations for the single-malt industry by launching a range called Connoisseurs Choice. Back then, very few distillers actually bottled their own malts as singles. Nowadays Gordon & MacPhail is custodian to some of the world's finest and rarest single malt whiskies. And, with Connoisseurs Choice, George drew attention to many lesser-known distillers, many of which are today household names." As a result, noted whisky writer Michael Jackson commented on George's passing in 2001: "I believe that single-malt whisky would simply not be available today were it not for the work of George Urquhart. When others knew nothing of malt whisky, he was one of the handful of people who understood this great Scottish contribution to the pleasures of food and drink."

One cask filled by George Urquhart in February 1952 was later emptied and bottled to celebrate Her Majesty The Queen's Diamond Jubilee. In 2012 it was released by Gordon & MacPhail as 85 uniquely numbered crystal decanters of Glen Grant 60 Years Old. "That single malt exemplified our philosophy to mature whisky for a very long time," says Rankin. "Where others simply bottle it, we draw on more than 120 years of experience in observing how different malts mature in different types of casks and warehouses, which enables us to carefully match spirit, oak and environment to create complex yet perfectly balanced and subtle whiskies of the highest quality."

Gordon & MacPhail's exclusive Generations collection was launched in 2010 and comprises some of the world's rarest single malts. The initial release was a 70-year-old Mortlach, then the world's oldest whisky, and the company was invited to present the first bottle to The Queen, who donated it to the National Museum of Scotland in Edinburgh. The following year in March, a bottle of 70-year-old Glenlivet was auctioned off for £15,000 to help the tsunami relief effort in Japan, where Gordon & MacPhail's then Managing Director, George Urquhart's son Michael, had been due to fly that month.

The royal seal of approval and a desire to support its communities both characterise Gordon & MacPhail. During the Second World War, the company sold large quantities of whiskies to the US to earn money for the war effort, while, during the difficult 1940s and 1950s, it frequently placed substantial orders with Speyside distilleries to provide them with much-needed financial support.

"As well as maturing other distillers' single malts to perfection, it had been our ambition since the days of John Urquhart to make our own whisky," says Rankin. "We finally achieved it when we bought the Benromach Distillery, which was officially opened by The Prince of Wales in 1998. He was supposed to stay for only 45 minutes but ended up spending two and a half hours chatting to our staff and finding out about the distilling process. He even signed the first cask, which is now on display for our visitors." More recently, the business has received visits from other members of the Royal Family. For instance, The Princess Royal came to Elgin in 2013 to present the company's second Queen's Award for Enterprise in the International Trade category.

Prince Charles attended Gordonstoun at around the same time as Stephen's uncles, George Urquhart's sons Ian, David and Michael, who, like his mother Rosemary, have all worked for Gordon & MacPhail. Today Stephen, his sister Suzy Bearne, and his cousins Neil, Stuart and Richard Urquhart, all work for Gordon & MacPhail. Like generations of Urquharts before them, all five are custodians of Gordon & MacPhail's "liquid library of distilleries and age profiles", as Rankin puts it, to bring some remarkably ancient single malts to market.

In 2015, Gordon & MacPhail launched the latest addition to its luxury Generations range, a 75-year-old Mortlach, the world's most exclusive whisky. Only 100 handcrafted crystal decanters have been produced, and they come with a specially commissioned book written by acclaimed whisky writer Charles Maclean and bestselling author Alexander McCall Smith.

This extraordinary spirit is yet another triumph for the pioneers of single malts. For whatever The Prince of Wales's earliest memories of the company may be, as whisky writer Michael Jackson said: "To malt lovers, 'bottled by Gordon & MacPhail' is a phrase that resonates around the world."

Store of memories

Waitrose

These days, Waitrose is a familiar name on Britain's high streets. But back in 1904, the grocery chain started with just one shop: at 263 Acton Hill, west London. In those days it was called Waite, Rose & Taylor, after its three owners: Mr Waite did the buying, Mr Rose worked behind the scenes on the accounts, and Mr Taylor was the branch manager. Their aspiration then was one the store still shares today: "To lift the food trade to a higher plane".

Mr Taylor left the business after a few years and Mr Waite and Mr Rose combined their surnames to form the name we all know today. Sadly, Arthur Rose was injured in the First World War and Wallace Wyndham Waite ended up running the company alone. By 1926 it had opened branches from Windsor to Gerrards Cross; and in 1937 it was taken over by the John Lewis Partnership.

It is said that Her Majesty The Queen's reign has coincided with the fastest pace of social and technological change ever known in global history. Supermarkets have been part of that transformation and Waitrose has always been swift to embrace new ways of shopping.

The "self-service" supermarket that arrived in the 1950s was so different from the old-style counter service that staff were positioned on the door to explain to customers that they really could help themselves from the shelves, but they would need to pay before leaving. Change continues with the growth of online shopping, but Waitrose still manages to put personal customer service at its heart.

The store has grown phenomenally since its beginnings. By 1977, Waitrose had expanded to a chain of around 50 shops. Today, there are 348 branches, from Scotland to Cornwall, and 27 outlets at motorway service stations. Yet while Waitrose is one of Britain's major supermarket chains, it is run differently from the rest: the 58,000 people who work for Waitrose are Partners who own the business. The company believes it is this model that makes a difference: not just to its Partners, but to its suppliers and customers too.

The spirit of the partnership runs through everything the store does. It is closer to the supply chain than other supermarkets, as it is the only one to have its own farm: on the Leckford Estate in Hampshire. The farm supplies Waitrose with milk, eggs, mushrooms and apples (pictured, opposite), and even sparkling wine from its own vineyard. This affords the company special insight into growing and producing food; and raises its awareness of the many challenges that farmers face today.

In 2002, Waitrose became the only supermarket ever to be granted The Queen's Royal Warrant, followed by that of The Prince of Wales in 2011. Mr Waite, Mr Rose and Mr Taylor would doubtless have been extremely proud to see the store they started receive these accolades; as honoured, in fact, as Waitrose is today to be an official partner in Her Majesty's hugely special 90th birthday.

State of the art

The Royal Academy of Arts

The Royal Academy of Arts, housed in the Palladian splendour of Burlington House, London, might appear to be a bastion of artistic tradition. However, in recent years, it has become one of Britain's leading contemporary arts venues, staging world-class exhibitions by David Hockney, Anselm Kiefer and Ai Weiwei among others.

"We have almost redefined the scope of the monographic exhibition with an amazing run of major shows," says its President Christopher Le Brun. "The Royal Academy has definitely become more spectacular over the years."

What gives the Royal Academy (RA) its vibrancy is the fact that it was founded for and by painters, sculptors, printmakers and architects who continue to direct its agenda today. There are 80 Royal Academicians who are elected by their peers and re-elect their president annually. The RA is an independent, self-funding charity, which allows it great flexibility, free from government oversight. "That and the fact that we have been electing a younger generation of artists such as Fiona Rae, Grayson Perry, Thomas Heatherwick and Yinka Shonibare has meant we are now more representative than ever of contemporary practice," says Le Brun.

The RA received royal patronage in 1768 from King George III to promote the "arts of design", raising artistic standards by establishing Britain's first art school, the Royal Academy Schools, and providing exhibition space for Britain's leading artists.

"Not many people realise that the RA Schools is still within the Royal Academy, with 50 post-graduate artists working here," says Le Brun. "It gives a very different feeling to a place, to know art is actually being made in it." George III was keenly involved in the business of the RA and that royal patronage continues today. "I personally attend the palace each year to present Her Majesty The Queen with the list of new members of the Royal Academy," says Le Brun, "which she reviews and confirms."

Funding from George III didn't last long, so, says Le Brun, "We became the original self-funding arts institute. We invented the Friends membership scheme, a model now used worldwide." The success of the RA's fundraising and its record visitor numbers have enabled Le Brun and the Royal Academy's governing council to plan an ambitious £50 million expansion programme to coincide with its 250th anniversary in 2018.

The masterplan by Sir David Chipperfield CBE RA will connect Burlington House in Piccadilly with Burlington Gardens to the north and reveal aspects of the Royal Academy which have hitherto been unseen by the public. The expanded two-acre campus will feature a learning centre, a new lecture theatre, refurbished exhibition spaces for Royal Academicians, invited artists and RA Schools students, and a new free display of many treasures from the RA's collection. There will also be an annual architecture exhibition. "It's a key area of interest for us," says Le Brun, "and it is an audience we want to grow."

Against such forward-thinking developments, and in its 248th year, the RA's Summer Exhibition may seem anachronistic. Yet in 2015, with Michael Craig-Martin RA curating, it welcomed 230,000 visitors. "That was the highest number since the RA unveiled the Annigoni portrait of The Queen in 1955," says Le Brun. "The Summer Exhibition is such a flexible, accessible model that it is starting to look rather vibrant and essential." As is the Royal Academy itself, now more than ever in its illustrious history.

Sweet dreams

Harrison Spinks

Few people put as much effort into delivering a good night's sleep as the team at Harrison Spinks. With over 126 years of experience, the Yorkshire-based bed manufacturer even raises its own flock of sheep to ensure the quality of its luxurious mattresses. It's just the kind of creative, environmentally astute approach that, combined with the best of traditional skills, earned the family business two Queen's Awards in 2013 – for Innovation and Sustainable Development – and a nomination for the latest awards in the International Trade category.

Today, around 490 people work for the company, including craftspeople whose skills have been passed down from generation to generation. Producing bed brands such as Somnus and John Lewis's own label, the company has also expanded into upholstery and car seating in recent years.

"We always try to do things traditionally," says Managing Director Simon Spinks. "So we side stitch the edge of the mattresses by hand, a traditional technique where one row can take over an hour to complete. If there isn't a better way to do it, we don't innovate for the sake of it."

While Harrison Spinks is proud of its place in Yorkshire's long heritage of wool and weaving, it's far from old-fashioned. The company has its own testing laboratory, where it experiments with everything from new spring designs to different mattress fillings. Its own ultra-fine titanium alloy wire enables Harrison Spinks to pack 4,000 tiny springs into a single layer of a mattress, using almost eight miles of wire in total. "We also design and build machines to manufacture our unique, patented springs," says Spinks. "We really can say that no one makes springs like us." The company's

award-winning, patented Revolution system places one small spring inside a larger one for extra support and comfort, while its flexible high-density pocket springs adapt to each individual's body shape.

The firm's aim isn't simply to create a luxuriously comfortable product but to maintain this high quality in a more sustainable way. To this end it has replaced petrochemical foams with recyclable springs and natural fibres – the latter being grown on the company's own 300-acre farm, Hornington Manor. There, Texel, Mule, Suffolk and Zwartbles breeds provide the pure-grade wool, while half the farm's acres are dedicated to growing flax and hemp, whose naturally antibacterial fibres are perfect for the mattresses. Even the waste products from producing the fibres are used for biomass fuel, animal bedding and building materials.

Other more exotic natural fibres, from cashmere, mohair, angora and silk to Egyptian cotton, are carefully sourced and blended at the factory. With no pesticides used, the farm helps preserve ancient hedgerows and wildlife too, including 11 threatened bird species that are local to the area.

The fact that it takes a year to grow some of the materials for a single mattress is testament to Harrison Spinks's commitment to sustainability. Its next goal is to replace the existing chemical sprays demanded by British safety regulations with inherently flame-retardant wool-based fabric that the company has woven itself.

"We are working on the next generation of springs too," says Spinks. And with an eye on new international markets for its innovative components, Harrison Spinks won't be caught napping. Unlike its contented customers.

High-pressure performer

Fort Vale

When the prime minister and the chancellor hail Britain's hi-tech industrial potential and highlight the "Northern Powerhouse", they may well be thinking of Fort Vale Engineering Ltd. The Lancashire-based precision-engineering company makes stainless-steel valves and fittings that are essential for the safe transportation of bulk liquids in the tank container, road tanker and rail industries.

The conveyance of gases and liquids by road, rail and sea needs to be done safely. To this end, Fort Vale works with the industry and regulatory bodies, delivering quality design, materials and manufacture that ensure first-class safety is a reality for all.

The company's international success story is one rooted in humble origins. It was founded in 1967 when a 30-year-old engineer named Edward Fort bought two machines – a borer and a grinder – cheaply at an auction of surplus tools. As good fortune would have it he promptly received an order to design and make a 2.5-inch cast-iron three-way flow control valve, which he did from a workshop in his home town of Colne, Lancashire. The first two machines, bought on a whim, were, by chance, perfect for the valve's production. Fort's design swiftly became the leading valve on all the fuel-oil delivery vehicles in the UK.

By 1972, staff still numbered just 13, but in 1975 the firm purchased larger premises in the nearby town of Nelson. Fort Vale now employs 530 people in seven countries, and Her Majesty The Queen recognised Edward Fort's services to industry by awarding him an OBE in 1987. The company's status as a key components supplier for tank containers, bulk containers, road tankers and railway tank cars may be in no doubt, but it has never rested on its laurels.

Pursuing innovation and seeking out new markets has been the bedrock of the company's success for the past 49 years. One of the most important products was the Maxi Highflow pressure-relief valve. Since the year 2000, Fort Vale has made 320,000 of these valves based on the original design.

All Fort Vale products are the result of extensive research, development and testing in order to offer users unparalleled performance predictability. The company's investment in design, R&D and innovation has given it a leading edge over competitors.

Another of its important inventions was the Pressed Manlid, a revolutionary method of constructing a hatch for personal access into a vessel for inspection. Its design has excellent insulation properties, which is important when the vessels are carrying hot products.

As well as being a preferred supplier to equipment manufacturers, the company's goal is to be the premier after-sales supplier for spares. With this mind, Fort Vale also has offices and

stock in Australia, China, Holland, Russia, Singapore and the USA. "We are quite unique as a company to be able to offer that service," says Fort.

The growth of the company has also been based on exports. Fort sold his first overseas order to Ireland in 1971, and by 2014 exports made up 94 per cent of the company's turnover. It has helped Fort Vale to win four Queen's Awards: for Export Achievement in 1981 and 1986, and for International Trade in 2008 and 2013.

International Trade winners are judged on growth of overseas earnings, innovation and sustainable development, including management of resources and people. When it received the accolade, Fort Vale had increased its overseas earnings by an incredible 255 per cent over the previous three years.

The company established its current factory and offices in Simonstone near Burnley in 2006, and in 2014 The Duke of Kent opened its new Research & Development Facility at the site. Wholly self-sufficient, the factory provides Fort Vale with control over all processes from R&D, design, investment casting, pressing, forging, plasma and laser cutting, to assembly, testing and certification.

"It is very state-of-the-art, has the latest machines, and the shop floor acts as our showroom," says Fort, who was born in Colne and has always worked within a 20-mile radius of the Lancashire town, at Rolls-Royce, Lucas Aerospace and Drum Engineering before founding Fort Vale.

From the outset, the company has put a strong emphasis on taking on young people and giving them the training they need to tackle new roles and responsibilities. Around a fifth of the workforce have joined Fort Vale from school, college or university, and the company has taken on apprentices every year over the past four decades.

"I began my engineering career as an apprentice with Rolls-Royce at the age of 15 and personally feel this is the best way to join the profession," says Fort. "I see it as a social responsibility to operate an effective apprenticeship scheme and time has shown that apprentices become core managers and are the future of our company."

The company has 24 apprentices currently going through the four-year course, and usually takes on between six and eight apprentices annually. Former apprentices who have risen up to senior positions at Fort Vale include Chief Engineer and Design Director David Bailey, General Manager of Fort Vale Nuclear Ltd, Quality Director Peter Staveley and Senior Sales Manager Andrew Bishop.

Fort Vale has withstood the highs and lows of the economic cycle over the past five decades. Thanks to its experienced workforce, the management team, led by MD Ian Wilson, and its constantly evolving range of products, the company was in a good position at the outset of the tank container market and its exponential growth. In its latest financial year, it enjoyed a turnover of £48 million – a 9 per cent growth on the previous year.

"The beauty of engineering is that you design products that will have a life for years ahead," says Fort. "If you are an accountant or a banker you may never see what it is you have achieved."

As the company approaches its golden anniversary in 2017, Fort says it is well placed to thrive over the next 50 years. "As night follows day, you get seven years of boom followed by a bit of a downturn. We have been through it before and the world does not stop."

The export experts

Gapuma

When Jack Bardakjian is asked about Gapuma, it's telling that he begins by outlining the company's overarching approach to conducting business. "We believe in working with integrity and honesty," says the company's Group Managing Director. "We don't want a customer-and-supplier relationship. We want to make personal friendships, become part of their family, a trusted partner. It's a very transparent relationship." It's this attitude that helped Gapuma win the Queen's Award for Enterprise.

Gapuma's core business is the trading and distribution of an array of commodities, from steel, polymers, solvents and pharmaceuticals to fertilisers, helping to keep industry moving. "Simply put, we're a customer-focused trading company," explains Bardakjian. "But the added value comes in the detail – the sophisticated and modern logistic supply chain we manage, the quality assurance, the stewardship of the inventory and in delivering goods exactly to the expectation of our partner."

Around 90 per cent of this work takes place in Africa, which Bardakjian identified as a potential emerging market when he founded the company in 1999. "We felt a lot of the market elsewhere had matured and there were limited opportunities for us to penetrate," he says, "and decided Africa was the continent that was up and coming and presented the best opportunity for growth. We now have various warehouses in different African countries for distribution and storage. We operate in around 16 countries on the continent and have been there so long we have established our brand to the extent that we are regularly contacted by other companies looking to enter Africa for advice on the business culture. There are challenges as it's

very diverse culturally from one country to another and there's also a lot of risk. We needed to understand that risk and identify best practice."

The company now employs around 140 people, controlling its international network from the London office that Bardakjian describes as "the nerve centre". From here, it also manages its commitment to Corporate Social Responsibility, working with Rotary Club and Outward Bound alongside children from disadvantaged backgrounds at local community schools, many of whom have African heritage and don't have English as their first language.

"We have a duty of care to Africa, and are involved in a library-building project in Ghana and various other charitable initiatives," says Bardakjian. "We've had a lot of success in Africa, and it's important for us to put something back, both in the area around our headquarters in London and in the markets in which we operate." This is something Bardakjian encourages personally. "I was the founder of the company and still own and manage it, so it's the philosophy and culture I've installed. Most of the people I employ have the same ideology. Winning a Queen's Award is a mantle of responsibility. We have to live up to those standards and the very Britishness of our identity. Integrity, decency, fairness and even-handedness underpin how we trade."

Gapuma has big plans for 2016, even if Bardakjian recognises that it could be a volatile year for industry thanks to falling oil prices and fluctuating stock markets. "We are looking at expanding our distribution channels in Africa and increasing our warehouse capacity. We are also establishing a subsidiary in Holland for purchasing opportunities in Europe. It'll be a challenging year for many industries but we have our eyes open."

Streets ahead

Simulation Systems Ltd

Several of society's most significant discoveries, such as penicillin or X-rays, have come about by way of happy accident. And while those made by Simulation Systems Ltd (SSL) aren't yet mentioned in the same breath as such seismic breakthroughs, many have also been born of unlikely origins but been of great benefit to the common good.

"So many of our innovations came about by sheer luck of being presented with a problem to solve or just having a lightbulb moment," says SSL company owner Louis Chavasse Thompson. Which is somewhat ironic, given that SSL leaves nothing to chance in its efforts to minimise the risks for all of us on the nation's roads.

As well as being the UK's most widely installed supplier of motorway technology, the company has developed large-scale control systems, including the software for one of the world's highest capacity digital CCTV surveillance systems (commissioned by Transport for London for the 2012 Olympics). SSL designs and manufactures some of the most sophisticated long-range CCTV surveillance equipment as well as small, simple electronic devices that enable blind people to cross the road in safety. Years of these advances led to the company being invited to Buckingham Palace to receive a Queen's Award for Enterprise in the innovation category.

"After graduating from Newcastle University in 1986, I joined SSL and at the time the company consisted of the original owner," says Thompson. "I was initially taken on to develop a complex mathematical simulation package used by structural design engineers. At around that time, the government started farming out projects to small enterprise and we were tasked to provide a trial system that was to become the first automatic incident detection and signalling system in the world. The trial requirements grew substantially and ultimately led to a 100 km high-reliability system on the M1. This became the groundbreaking Motorway Incident Detection and Automatic Signalling (MIDAS) system, which is the backbone of the new SMART Motorways today."

Three decades later SSL has grown significantly and employs around 160 people, though its pioneering spirit remains unchanged. The company is still based in Yatton, North Somerset, and its eclectic output still has the key characteristic of benefitting the public in an innovative way.

SSL's "BlueTruth" traffic information system was another world first. Based on an idea by Thompson, it uses a long-range sensitive antennae system to detect in-car Bluetooth

equipment travelling at speed on the road. It offers a far lower cost approach than the existing automatic numberplate-recognition systems.

"Our BlueTruth readers can be quickly and easily installed along the highway: on, for instance, camera poles or traffic lights," says Thompson. "They pick up anonymous signals from Bluetooth equipment in vehicles. The data is processed to assess traffic conditions. The SSL BlueTruth hardware can also serve as an information publication stream and we can ping messages to devices in the cars to provide journey information and alerts. We deployed the first Bluetooth-based journey time system in the UK for Somerset County Council for the 2009 Glastonbury Festival. Seven years later, the product has been acclaimed and installed widely all over the UK. It was shortlisted for the 2016 Lloyds Bank National Business Awards, where I was delighted to meet Buzz Aldrin at the awards ceremony."

Defying perceived wisdom, the company developed CCTV cameras that produce a clear image even in zero-light conditions over a long range. "For safety reasons," says Thompson, "Highways England issued a requirement for 100 per cent CCTV coverage on the new sections of the motorway where all lanes are used and there is no hard shoulder. The concern of Highways England was that if, say, a motorbike crashed at night on an unlit section of the motorway, all that would be seen with standard CCTV cameras would be headlights and tail-lights of passing cars and the rest of the scene would be invisible. To fulfil the

new performance requirements and meet the associated deadlines, we came up with a good solution in record time."

The odds were stacked against SSL to the point that a respected consultancy panicked and erroneously "blew the whistle" and attempted to advise Highways England that SSL's system could never work. "But we proved them wrong," says Thompson. "The system fulfilled and exceeded all hopes. As a further benefit, the 300-watt CCTV camera systems actually save the government money because each of them can identify incidents over 1.5 km of unlit motorway. By contrast, lighting that same stretch to motorway standard would consume about 15 kilowatts per hour. If you add that up across the country, the savings are enormous."

This fact led to SSL being presented with a Highways England Supplier Award in 2015 for "Driving Down Cost". 2016 has seen SSL provide other specialist innovative products, including a unique CCTV-based system which detects HGVs which are carrying dangerous goods.

"Our skills are very transferable," says Thompson. "We have an extraordinarily talented bunch of people here, with 12 PhDs in the team, so we seek customer requirements that are ambitious enough to differentiate us, whether it's working for governments or private organisations. Customers generally tender for technology they know is easily achievable, but – for us – the tougher the challenge, the more likely we are to win the work and show what we can really do."

Excellence in architecture

Royal Institute of British Architects

"I'm so proud to be part of this remarkable institution," says Jane Duncan, President of the Royal Institute of British Architecture (RIBA). "We've been passionate about architecture since 1834 and we'll continue to champion architecture in society for generations to come."

The institute received its Royal Charter in 1837 for the "advancement of civil architecture" and now offers recognition, funding, training and social and professional support for its members and chartered practices. "Our Royal Charter distinguishes us as the authoritative voice on excellence in architecture," says Duncan.

RIBA champions better buildings, both in the UK and internationally, through its vast network of members and practices. "Our ethos is to ensure that architectural standards are the best they can be, whilst embracing new approaches, innovation and encouraging diversity and equality in our profession," says Duncan.

The rich history of the institute and of architecture more widely are celebrated by its world-class architectural collection, the British Architectural Library, which showcases the work of distinguished architects and architectural photographers throughout history and from across the globe. RIBA's galleries dedicated exclusively to architecture are used as important learning and educational resources by architects and to engage the wider public.

RIBA's continued celebration of architecture takes its form in the institute's distinguished awards programme, commending the very finest examples of architectural achievement throughout the world. Queen Victoria inaugurated the first Royal Gold Medal winner in 1848 and this practice is continued today with Her Majesty The Queen approving recipients such as 2016 winner Dame Zaha Hadid. RIBA has been attributing awards for architecture projects for the past 50 years, with the most prestigious prize in architecture, the RIBA Stirling Prize, running since 1996.

In addition to recognition of excellence, RIBA acts as an important force in bringing issues surrounding architecture to the forefront of government and society, to improve the design quality of public buildings, new homes and communities. "As an institute, we are privileged to have so many active members who are engaged with a breadth of issues surrounding architecture," says Duncan. "It is our responsibility to make sure their voices and ideas are encouraged at the highest possible level."

The institute continues to innovate and expand, this year launching a major award, the RIBA International Prize, as a new global standard of architectural achievement. The prize is chaired by a group of internationally recognised architects and the competition is open to practices and buildings from all over the world. "A key objective of the RIBA International Prize is to uncover the world's most innovative and visionary architecture," explains Duncan, "and to spark local and global debates about the positive impact that well-designed buildings and places can have on their communities and environment."

RIBA has been active in society since the nineteenth century, observing unprecedented change in technology and society yet continuing to embrace new ideas, encourage impeccable standards and act as a platform for its members to develop and grow – always with architecture at its heart.

Driven to succeed

Jaguar Land Rover

Embodying the best of British innovation and ingenuity, Jaguar Land Rover is driven to provide its customers with experiences they love for life.

From sports utility vehicles that enable their drivers to go above and beyond their expectations, to sports cars and sedans that excite the senses, Jaguar Land Rover puts it customers first, anticipating and exceeding their needs and desires.

In recognition of this, the company has received many awards and accolades in its 80-year history, but there is one of which it is especially proud. "We are the only car manufacturer in the world to have been awarded all three Royal Warrants – from Her Majesty The Queen, The Duke of Edinburgh and The Prince of Wales," says Chief Executive Dr Ralf Speth. "We are immensely proud of this distinction."

Jaguar Land Rover's first Royal Warrant was awarded by The Queen's father, George VI, in 1951 and the Royal Family has used the company's vehicles ever since, starting with a custom-built Land Rover Series 1. Since then there have been many royal vehicles, the latest being the State Review Range Rover. Developed over 18 months, it was hand-built by the best of British craftsmen with innovation at its heart: a diesel hybrid engine enables it to run at times purely on electric power.

Luxury and performance are only part of the tale. Responsibility runs through the story, too. Land Rover has been associated with the British Red Cross for nearly as long as The Queen has been the charity's president – since 1952 – and with far-reaching impact. Since the first car was donated to the British Red Cross in 1954, Land Rover vehicles have been part of a fleet that has helped bring vital relief during disasters as well as ongoing support to vulnerable communities around the world and in the UK. On what was also Land Rover's 60th anniversary, the company donated 60 vehicles to the British Red Cross, which were used for humanitarian programmes worldwide.

Having received the Queen's Award for Enterprise many times, Jaguar Land Rover was given the award in the category of sustainable development in 2015 in recognition of the cutting-edge policies it employs to protect the environment with its products and manufacturing techniques.

Jaguar Land Rover is a global company but its heart is entirely British. With plants at Solihull, Castle Bromwich, Halewood, Gaydon, Whitley and Wolverhampton it has a workforce of 38,000, and supports almost another 200,000 British jobs through the wider associated industry.

The company is the UK's largest car manufacturer, one that designs, engineers and builds some of the finest premium cars in the world. It is also the biggest investor in automotive research, development and engineering in the country, taking British ingenuity, craftsmanship and innovation to 170 markets worldwide.

The company's ethos is based on five key principles – integrity, understanding, excellence, unity and responsibility. These words sum up the entire approach of Jaguar Land Rover.

A history of innovation

Millers Oils

"Virtually every company claims to be innovative – but Millers Oils has the record to prove it," says Jamie Ryan, the company's Managing Director. Many automotive lubricants that are taken for granted today were actually first developed and launched by Millers Oils.

"In 1967 Millers Oils developed the very first engine oil specifically designed for diesel cars," says Ryan. "In 1979 we developed the first 'extended drain' commercial vehicle oil which is now standard fleet maintenance practice globally."

Millers Oils was founded in 1887, in Brighouse, Yorkshire. It celebrates its 130th anniversary next year but retains the ethos of its founder John Watson Miller, who insisted that "the quality of my oils will always be rigidly adhered to". From local beginnings, primarily supplying the textile industry in Yorkshire, the company has always invested in innovation in lubrication and today sells its multi-award-winning range of high-performance, ultra-low-friction lubricants across the globe.

With talented staff and a cutting-edge research-and-development facility, including a state-of-the-art laboratory, Millers Oils has continued to innovate across industrial, agricultural, automotive and motorsport sectors. This has resulted in multiple innovation awards including the Motorsport Industry Association's Business Excellence Award in 2012 and the World Motorsport Symposium "most Innovative product" in 2009 for its unique, groundbreaking "Nanodrive" ultra-low-friction nanotechnology oils.

Millers Oils was the first UK lubricant company to incorporate nanotechnology in lubricants initially, introducing it into motorsport engine oils, where any increase in performance is vital. "We were able to demonstrate that, even when replacing a top-class conventional lubricant, a Porsche 911 could be power boosted by 5 per cent," says Ryan. The resulting growth led to a Queen's Award for Enterprise (Export) in 2012.

Nanotechnology has since been applied to Millers Oils' "Energy Efficient" range of automotive and commercial vehicle oils and will shortly be available for industrial applications, so all customers can reap the benefit of this groundbreaking technology.

The Millers family connection continues today with Andrew Miller MBE, great-grandson of the firm's founder, still sitting on the board of directors. It is this continued stability and passion for innovation that has allowed the company to thrive and also embrace its three guiding values of "innovation, integrity and inclusiveness".

"The world around us is constantly changing and we want everybody in our business to contribute," says Ryan. "We had some really great people whose talent and potential was untapped. Now we have been able to promote from the shop floor and actively encourage our team to help us develop the best possible technology in lubrication."

Millers remains at the forefront of technology and innovation. "We are proud to continually punch well above our weight," says Ryan. "We have nanotechnology products that are so far ahead of some of the big names it's scary – people have been winning races with our technology for years. In that time, we've made the change from a family-run business to one where everybody is involved and it has been a very rewarding journey."

A pharma pioneer

Norbrook Laboratories Ltd

No description of Norbrook Laboratories would be complete without paying tribute to its late founder, Lord Ballyedmond, who lost his life in a helicopter accident in 2014, aged 70. Born Edward Haughey and ennobled in 2004, Lord Ballyedmond was undoubtedly one of Northern Ireland's, and indeed Great Britain's, most successful entrepreneurs.

He had the unique distinction of sitting both in Ireland's upper house, the Seanad Éireann, and in the House of Lords. He also played an important behind-the-scenes role in the Northern Ireland peace process. He collected an impressive array of honours and doctorates in his lifetime, and was especially proud of his Honorary Fellowship of the Royal Society of Chemistry, bestowed "in recognition of his unparalleled contribution to the chemical sciences".

Norbrook Laboratories, which Lord Ballyedmond founded in 1969, has grown to become one of the world's most significant pharmaceutical companies, specialising in the manufacture of revolutionary veterinary products for farming and domestic animals. He once described the company as catering for "everything from ladies' poodles to the lion".

"The company has received the invitation to Buckingham Palace to accept a Queen's Award no fewer than five times," says Liam Nagle, the company's CEO. "So Her Majesty's 90th birthday celebrations have a special significance for us all at Norbrook."

Based in Newry, the company is a substantial employer throughout the local area. "A lot of the work is skilled and high-calibre," says Nagle.

"Norbrook has 1,800 staff here, and is one of the largest privately owned employers in Northern Ireland. We have a further 500 staff worldwide."

The company also collaborates with Ulster and Queen's Universities in a number of research education programmes. "Most of these are designed to equip our staff with specific skills for use at work," says Nagle. "But they also have an educational value in themselves."

Norbrook takes particular pride in being one of only a few companies in the world which are licensed by the US Food and Drug Administration to manufacture sterile injections for veterinary use and import them for sale within the United States.

Research and development is central to Norbrook's work, and more than 10 per cent of its annual turnover is invested in the development of new products. The latest of its pioneering successes has been the release of the revolutionary Closamectin Pour On solution for large animals. Developed to eliminate parasites such as fluke, it is the only product available in Europe that can be administered by external application to the backs of livestock. This makes its application simple and painless.

After his untimely death, Lord Ballyedmond's family and the Norbrook board resolved to advance his pioneering vision with a renewed vigour and determination, as befits his memory. With the impressive portfolio of new products soon to be released worldwide, Norbrook and the memory of its founder are set to remain at the forefront of pharmaceutical development for many decades to come.

A label of quality

London Tradition

If entrepreneurs are defined by their willingness to take a chance, then Mamun Chowdhury is a great example. Today, the co-founder of luxury outerwear manufacturer and Queen's Award winner London Tradition laughs at his first forays onto the fashion scene.

"I made an audacious attempt at selling shirts from my suitcase to Marks & Spencer in 1992," he says. "I had only been in the UK six months and was unaware of the protocol – of course they wouldn't buy from a bloke just walking into a store!" But that experience cemented Chowdhury's determination to make it. "I was inspired by the story of Michael Marks and Thomas Spencer – immigrants like myself. I see many parallels between their story and mine."

Hailing from Bangladesh, Chowdhury's father and grandfather were businessmen, and he was raised on a diet of deals and negotiations. But the 1971 Independence War destroyed the family businesses and the Chowdhurys lost everything so, in 1991, Mamun came to England hoping to build a business here.

Within a decade, Chowdhury was successfully running a high-end manufacturing business using his own factory in East London to make coats for high-street labels. He met Rob Huson and the pair became close friends as well as colleagues. Chowdhury saw an opportunity to manufacture their own outerwear, designed with a high level of customer involvement and selling wholesale to trade, targeting the sub-couture market. London Tradition was born.

"Quality and skilled craftsmanship rooted in London's heritage and culture are the label's defining features," says Chowdhury, citing state-of-the-art equipment and technology. "Our dedication to detail is relentless and unwavering." Multiple quality checks throughout the manufacturing process ensure consistency. The brand is also proud to offer a fair working environment for its employees.

Today, London Tradition is particularly popular in the Japanese market, and the brand has grown largely by word of mouth. Winning the Queen's Award made a significant difference. "It was a tremendous honour," says Chowdhury, "bringing a huge amount of publicity and interest from new customers."

The company's future looks exciting, including a new high-end fashion label, Churchill of London, and an e-commerce website aimed at the retail market. "We see business planning as a journey," says Chowdhury. "We have a clear strategy to grow organically in existing markets and enter into new ones." No suitcase required.

Engineering excellence

Balmoral Offshore Engineering

The making of equipment to be used at 35,000 ft below sea level comes with its own unique stresses – quite literally. It has to be able to cope with the extremities of temperature and pressure that are characteristic of the deep-water environment.

With access to advanced manufacturing facilities, Balmoral Offshore Engineering (BOE) uses specialist technology to develop products that are able to withstand these harsh conditions. Since its founding in 2006, BOE has grown rapidly and today creates world-leading engineering products for the offshore and deep-water energy industries.

"We have an outstanding engineering team that is always working on something new – this innovative spirit is fundamental to our business," says James Milne CBE, Chairman and Managing Director of parent company Balmoral Group Holdings Ltd. "As a private company, we don't require shareholder approval for research and development, or the introduction of new technology."

Aberdeen-based BOE specialises in buoyancy and insulation products, with 97 per cent of its projects involving deep water. "We are achieving some incredible things, thanks to our technology, our innovative thinking and our continuing investment," says Milne. "This is in spite of the downturn that is affecting the global oil and gas industry at the moment."

In the past ten years, BOE has carried out a number of major offshore projects in various parts of the world, including Angola, the Gulf of Mexico, Brazil, Norway and Ghana. It has also achieved export sales of 95 per cent of turnover – more than three times the industry average.

The company's plans include the launch of a Brazilian division, which will service the South American market from a custom-built manufacturing facility in Vitória. It is this kind of international ambition that has made the company a three-time recipient of the Queen's Award for Enterprise in International Trade in 2010, 2012 and 2015. "It was a genuine thrill to go to Buckingham Palace," says Milne, "both for us and for the other companies that had been successful, especially the young ones that had just broken through."

Characterised by innovation, speed of response and the careful consideration of its customers' needs, BOE plays a vital role in the success of major deep-water projects. "We are the last link in a chain," says Milne. "This means that, if we let our customers down, it can cost them hundreds of millions of pounds. Timing, cost and reliability are extremely important. Our ability to provide all of this boils down to years of experience and a proven track record." It's a mix that makes managing the pressures of the industry just that little bit easier.

Courage and compassion

Royal Orthopaedic Hospital NHS Foundation Trust

The crest of the Royal Orthopaedic Hospital (ROH) depicts a cross surrounded by laurel leaves. The cross represents courage, the leaves compassion. Both these qualities are as relevant today for this NHS trust as when they were chosen more than 100 years ago. "The laurel leaves and the cross are still very much part of our values," says Jo Chambers, Chief Executive of the Birmingham-based hospital. "They're at the heart of what we do here along with respect, excellence, pride, openness and innovation."

Granted a Royal Charter in 1888 by Queen Victoria, the ROH has consistently been at the forefront of providing orthopaedic care for patients and pioneering new surgical techniques. It is the largest specialist centre in Europe for the diagnosis and treatment of benign and malignant tumours of bone and soft tissue. Since it was founded in 1817, the hospital has always led the way in the research of rare bone cancers; and patients are referred here from across the country to benefit from the expertise of its doctors. The ROH cancer team is recognised worldwide in the field of oncology.

The ROH's strong heritage of innovation is still being built on to this day by the hospital's experts. They include Professor Lee Jeys, who has been using computer technology to help remove bone tumours. The ROH also plays host to a network of specialists who can guide patients through treatment options for Ewing's sarcoma and other rare cancers. Patients also stand to gain from the pioneering work ROH specialists are

carrying out on bone, joint and spinal infections. The ROH's dedicated bone infection unit was highly commended by the Nursing Times Awards 2012 and a finalist in 2015. "This is a hugely important area of work," says Chambers. "We are one of the leading places in the country where patients are referred. Many improvements have been made in terms of the length of hospital stay. It used to be six weeks for a bone infection but now it averages just two."

As well as doing its best for patients, the ROH is dedicated to investing in its staff. From healthcare assistants to business administrators, the trust is committed to providing apprenticeships, which Chambers is confident will enable this specialist teaching hospital to "grow our own team members with the kinds of skills and values we need".

Those who have benefited include Emily Harris, a healthcare assistant who completed a clinical apprenticeship in 2010/11. Now studying for a nursing degree, Emily plans to return to ROH as a registered nurse. Long-service awards and recognition are among the benefits for the employees of this hospital, which in 2015 was rated by the Health Service Journal and NHS Employers as one of the best places to work in the NHS.

The ROH is unafraid to push boundaries to make sure it delivers the best care possible. It is this quality, along with the care and understanding of its remarkable staff, which will see the hospital celebrate its bicentenary in 2017 and ensure it has a long future ahead.

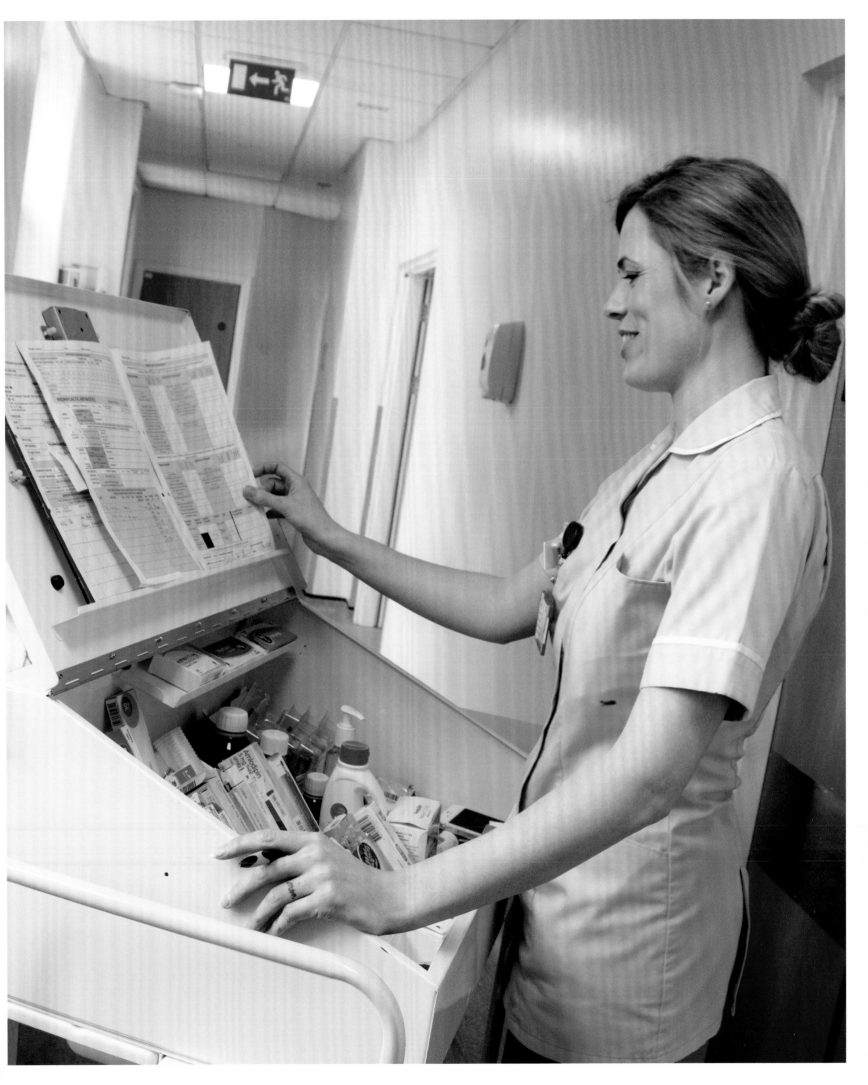

Patent genius

Minesoft

In business, there would be no progress without innovation and no innovation without the security offered by patents. For over 15 years, London's Minesoft has allowed companies to navigate the complicated world of patents thanks to its pioneering software, which allows firms to search patent documents in a variety of ways, regions and languages. Its easy and effective service has helped the company win two prestigious Queen's Awards for Enterprise.

"We take patent documents as they're published in more than 100 states, and we're adding more all the time as regions become more innovative," says co-founder Ann Chapman. "Patents are critical to business development. It's an issue that often comes up in *Dragons' Den* – what is the intellectual property of the innovation? Anything with a technical, engineering or industrial edge will need a patent to protect it."

Chapman set up Minesoft with her husband Ophir Daniel, a computer programmer. "We knew we could create better products than were available at the start of the internet era," says Chapman. "People were using private data networks with complicated command languages. We decided to produce web browser products that were easier to use but still took in the complex nature of the reports. Patent departments saw the benefits and we are now the world's best repository of science and technology information."

Minesoft counts some of the world's largest firms among its clients. These companies use the software for a variety of reasons, although primarily to protect their own innovations. "With any company, the first thing it has to do before filing a patent is perform a patent search to see if somebody else has come up with a similar idea," says Chapman. "Also, a large company will check patents to see if there's one coming up that infringes its own ideas."

If an innovation is new, a company can apply for a patent; if something similar exists, they may try and license it for their own use. Firms can also use patent information to keep track of their rivals – what Chapman calls "an early warning system" – or even find gaps in the market to explore.

Some clients ask Minesoft to create bespoke software to help them maintain a cutting edge. "Older firms may have done their own cataloguing, creating their own systems," says Chapman. "They may now want it stored in one place to be searched using an internal classification system. We will take their classifications and apply them to the wider world of patents so every week their database will be fed with the latest innovations in their technology."

Minesoft already offers the opportunity to explore patents in different languages, having translated 20 million English-language patent documents into Mandarin in 2014. In 2015, it created Chemical Explorer, a database of chemical information. "We text-mined millions of patent documents," says Chapman, "and extracted the chemical structure information so people can, for the first time, draw a structure and locate it in the patent document."

Such creativity has seen Minesoft grow every year since it was formed – a feat recognised by Queen's Awards for Enterprise in 2009 and 2015. This is quite an accomplishment for the Richmond-based company, which employs around 50 people. "We achieve a lot for our size," says Chapman. "But above all we help companies protect themselves and be innovative."

Flooring the competition

Floortex Group

In 2002, Steve Bull bid farewell to the US floor-protection company he was working for in order to set up his own UK-based firm. With its focus on European customers, it's unlikely that he could have anticipated that, 14 years down the line, the USA would be his biggest market.

Bull had observed that chair mats were a very popular product for protecting work surfaces in homes and offices across the USA. With this in mind he predicted that, if adapted to European markets, they would prove to be a surefire commercial success.

Having started out with a core team of just four employees, Bull's company, Floortex, has since expanded its international workforce to over 50, spread across the UK, Germany and the USA. Over the three years up to 2013, its export sales grew by more than 50 per cent, and it now exports to more than 40 countries worldwide.

This impressive increase earned the company the Queen's Award for Enterprise in the International Trade category in 2015. In July of that year, Steve Bull, the company's CEO, and Financial Director James Bull – Steve's son – attended Her Majesty The Queen's awards reception at Buckingham Palace.

According to Bull, the award has proved more important for the company than even he had expected. "Seven or eight months after we received the award it was still huge news," he says, "especially overseas." The accolade has given Floortex extra exposure in the USA, where there is a strong interest in the Royal Family, and in Commonwealth countries, especially Australia and Canada. "Commercially, it has helped by giving the business even more credibility than it had previously," he adds.

The company's success is, in part, due to its emphasis on innovation. Floortex pioneered a polycarbonate material that is more durable, longer lasting and more environmentally friendly than PVC. It also developed orthophthalate-free PVC chair mats and uses up to 30 per cent renewable energy in the manufacture of all its chair mats.

Another of the company's new developments is Craftex, which it launched earlier this year at a US show aimed at the country's $30 billion arts and crafts market. "The initial response we have had is absolutely unbelievable," says Bull. With total US sales forecast to represent more than 50 per cent of its turnover this year, Floortex can rightly claim to be not just a leading European player, but a global success story.

Manufacturing success

CarnaudMetalbox Engineering

For Andrew Truelove, General Manager of CarnaudMetalbox (CMB) Engineering, Her Majesty The Queen's birthday celebrations have a special meaning. "I was invited with John Crabtree, our Lead Engineer, to a reception at Buckingham Palace in 2014 to celebrate winning a Queen's Award for Enterprise," he says. "This award is the highest honour a UK business can receive, and few manage to make the grade." To have garnered three, as CarnaudMetalbox has done – for Technological Achievement and twice for Enterprise in the International Trade category – is a rare distinction indeed.

Based in Shipley, West Yorkshire, CMB Engineering began life as a textile machinery manufacturer and later became Metal Box in the 1930s. Following a merger with the French manufacturer Carnaud, it became CarnaudMetalbox Engineering, and is now owned by Crown Holdings Inc, one of the world's leading metal-packaging companies. "Just as the name Metal Box is synonymous with metal packaging," says Truelove, "CarnaudMetalBox Engineering is synonymous with the production of high-quality can-making machinery."

For Truelove, the recent success of the business is down to having a happy and engaged workforce, and a management team that values inventiveness. "We actively encourage employees' ideas," says Truelove. "If an idea is good we will endorse it and provide the tools to get on with it."

The company continues its commitment to training via the CMB Academy of Can Making and Seaming. The academy itself is a first in the industry and, as a former CMB apprentice himself, Truelove is well placed to appreciate the value of training. "We place a great deal of value on our apprenticeship scheme," he says. "We believe it is vital that we keep this new talent filtering through our organisation."

The company takes great pride in entering apprentices for the World Skills Competition, regarded as the Olympics of vocational skills. In the two most recent events its apprentices achieved fourth and fifth-placed world rankings respectively, winning medallions of excellence along the way. "It's a true mark of world-class achievement," says Truelove.

The company continues to innovate, launching a number of new machines in recent years. "Throughout the 20th century, the Metal Box name had a fantastic reputation," says Truelove. "We continue to strive every day to maintain the prestige of that name."

In good company

The Fishmongers' Company

Among the treasures collected by the Worshipful Company of Fishmongers over the past eight centuries, Pietro Annigoni's 1954 portrait of Her Majesty The Queen, which hangs in Fishmongers' Hall, affords its members particular pride. The company has long had close ties with the monarchy. The Queen was last an honoured guest at the hall to celebrate the 90th birthday of a former Prime Warden, The Duke of Edinburgh. Soon their daughter, The Princess Royal – the present Renter Warden – will sit in the Prime Warden's chair.

The Fishmongers' Company received its first Royal Charter in 1272 and is one of the City of London's 12 great livery companies. "As a maritime nation, fish stocks and the fishing industry have always been an important part of our heritage," says current Prime Warden, the Hon Michael McLaren QC. "The company's home, Fishmongers' Hall, has been at the head of London Bridge, close to old Billingsgate Market and the Pool of London, since as early as 1434." The current Fishmongers' Hall dates from 1834.

There is, however, a great deal more to the company than its history alone. In contrast to some of the ancient City livery companies, Fishmongers' Company maintains strong links to its original purpose. "The Fishmongers' Company still has an active and valued association with fish and fisheries, particularly in the areas of trade and consumer education, research, awareness and as an independent forum for considered debate," says the Clerk, Major General Colin Boag CB CBE. "Despite our long history, we are continually striving to stay relevant in a rapidly changing world."

The Fishmongers' Company also provides wide-ranging support in the educational and charity sectors, including funding and help for the City and Guilds of London Art School. "Their stone carving students were involved in the restoration at Windsor Castle," says Peter Woodward, Assistant Clerk, "and they were also involved in carving the golden bow on the barge for The Queen's Diamond Jubilee."

Since 1715, the Fishmongers' Company has organised the annual Doggett's Coat and Badge sculling race on the Thames for young watermen. "The Fishmongers' Bargemaster, Bobby Prentice – the record holder since winning the race in the 1970s – is also a Queen's Waterman, with the privilege of rowing the Royal Family on state occasions," adds Major General Boag.

With this rich and productive history, there is good reason to predict that the Fishmongers' Company will still be around and thriving in 700 years' time.

"I know of no single formula
for success. But over the years
I have observed that some attributes
of leadership are universal and
are often about finding ways of
encouraging people to combine their
efforts, their talents, their insights,
their enthusiasm and their
inspiration to work together"

Her Majesty The Queen, address to the UN General Assembly, 6 July 2010

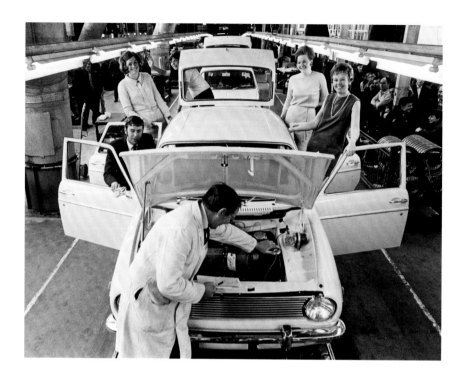

Enterprising times

Ninety years of British business

As well as marking the birth of Her Majesty The Queen, 1926 heralded the onset of a period of significant turmoil for the business community. It was the year the Trades Union Congress called out workers in the rail, transport, printing, docks, ironworks and steelworks in support of 1.5 million coal miners who had been locked out of the pits after rejecting the owners' demands for longer hours and reduced pay.

The nation's first General Strike was unsuccessful but it was the start of bitter relations between businesses and workers that culminated in the 1936 Jarrow Crusade, a march of 200 people in protest against the 70 per cent jobless rate in the north-eastern English town. It was a bitter protest that caught the national mood.

Britain, whose business community was dominated by industries such as textiles and shipbuilding that faced weak global demand and oversupply, suffered from low growth, high unemployment and deflation during most of the second half of the 1920s. In between that first General Strike and the Jarrow Crusade was the Great Depression, certainly the most catastrophic financial crisis to hit Britain in living memory until the 2008/09 global recession.

As with the more recent financial crisis, the 1929 problems started in the USA. On 28 and 29 October 1929 historic falls in the New York stock markets saw billions of pounds wiped off the value of shares across the developed world. British businesses were hit as global trade collapsed amid the financial panic. The burden of an overvalued pound, which had added to the pain for exporters, was relieved in 1931 when the government took sterling off the Gold Standard, a fixed exchange-rate system.

The Bank of England responded by cutting interest rates, stimulating a housebuilding boom, and the economy started to mend. A gradual re-armament programme in the 1930s also delivered a belated fiscal stimulus. In addition, firms started to adopt modern techniques of managerial control, installed cost accounting and professionalised the way that senior managers operated.

After the Second World War, the Labour government of Clement Attlee was elected on a landslide majority and a manifesto of higher taxes, nationalisation of key industries and the creation of a welfare state. Even after wartime leader Winston Churchill returned to Downing Street with the Conservative party after the 1951 election, the terms had been set for an economic

PREVIOUS PAGES: THE
PRODUCTION LINE AT BRITISH
LEYLAND IN COWLEY, 1969 (LEFT);
THE BANK OF ENGLAND (RIGHT).
OPPOSITE: THE JARROW CRUSADE
OF 1936. RIGHT: PRIME MINISTER
HAROLD MACMILLAN PROCLAIMS
AN ERA OF PROSPERITY IN 1957

strategy that, broadly speaking, crossed party lines for the next few decades. "Butskellism" – a portmanteau word combining the names of the successive chancellors of the 1950s, Labour's Hugh Gaitskell and the Conservative's R A Butler – was used to describe this postwar consensus.

Economic growth started to reach unprecedented levels. By 1957, four years after The Queen's Coronation, Prime Minister Harold Macmillan was able to tell fellow Conservatives that "most of our people have never had it so good". Britain's economy remained strong with low unemployment into the 1960s. The structure of British business was also changing, but by the end of the decade the scene was still dominated by a small number of large companies concentrated in traditional activities such as manufacturing and heavy industry. Around two-thirds of firms on the FT30 (the precursor to today's FT100) came from the industrial sector – one third retailers, one-third from the food and drink sector. None came from the worlds of finance or energy, and no one had heard of information technology.

Since then, blue-chip companies such as Leyland Motors, Dunlop Rubber, machinist Alfred Herbert and paint manufacturer Pinchin Johnson & Associates have disappeared from the FT list. The iron and steel industries, which employed

more than a quarter of a million British people when The Queen was born, now employ fewer than 20,000. More than a million people were employed in footwear, textiles and clothing – that figure is now down to less than 100,000. Some 700,000 people worked in agriculture, a number that is now down to less than half a million.

Part of this shift was due to the end of the postwar economic consensus that came with the election of Margaret Thatcher's Conservative government in 1979. Privatisation, deregulation and the reform of trades unions were Thatcher's prime concern, while a monetarist policy reduced public spending and kept a tight control of the money supply to reduce inflation. As a result, competition policy was emphasised over industrial policy, while deindustrialisation and a high level of structural unemployment was more or less accepted.

Such reforms throughout the 1980s ushered in a time of change for Britain's economy. Manufacturing and industry declined, partly replaced by sectors such as finance, IT and telecommunications. The UK started to move into areas that made greater use of high skill levels and innovation. Analysis by the Department of Business, Industry and Skills shows how relatively higher technology-based industries have grown in size while relatively low-tech ones have declined.

In 1926, the economy was filled with unskilled and semi-skilled jobs in industry and manufacturing. Today, a mixture of technology and globalisation has greatly reduced those numbers, with much of the same work either carried out through automation or being farmed out to lower-wage economies in the developing world. The commensurate decline in the number of people working in factories and the increase in office workers has struck a chord with people concerned about the loss of Britain's industrial heritage.

However, to a large degree, these unskilled and semi-skilled jobs have been replaced with high-skilled alternatives, calling for a better qualified workforce to deal with the growth in hi-tech industries such as medical and precision instruments; chemicals, pharmaceuticals and bioscience; and aircraft, rail, marine and motorcycles. Manufacturing has changed, too. While it still includes established industries such as food and drink and automotive, new industries are based around emerging technologies. These include low-carbon and green technologies, biotechnology, nanotechnology, and digital and advanced materials such as composites.

Service industries have also expanded. They make up almost four-fifths of today's economy and include activities from hairdressing to horticulture, with whole swathes of financial services in between. Britain has seen a faster growth in services employment than its international peers. The sector accounts for 83 per cent of jobs – it was less than 50 per cent in 1960 – and registered a trade surplus of almost £58 billion in 2011. It is plainly the engine of growth in the modern British economy, and includes highly skilled activities in which the UK has a global lead, such as architecture, advertising, insurance and legal services.

Britain has realised the future lies in high-value manufacturing, financial services and value-added businesses such as electronics, ICT and biotechnology. The route to success is by ensuring that organisations in the services sector – both public and private – continue to focus on delivering excellent quality in a way that will both attract overseas buyers and deliver affordable solutions to consumers and other businesses.

It's true that Britain is not the industrial superpower it once was. It is, for example, no longer Europe's biggest maker of automobiles and the world's biggest car exporter, as was the case for the first three decades of The Queen's life. However, British people now have access to high-quality vehicles from around the world, and this emphasis on quality and competition has raised the standard for what remains of the UK's car industry.

The British economy has changed massively in the past 90 years. It is leaner, meaner, tighter, and has greater depth and diversity in its business sectors than could possibly have been imagined in the year of The Queen's birth.

The gentle giant

Unilever

There's more than a slim chance that you have a few Unilever products in your kitchen or bathroom. The Anglo-Dutch giant's brands include Persil, Wall's, Marmite, Ben & Jerry's, Cif, Vaseline, Knorr, Dove, Hellmann's, Sure, PG Tips and Flora. Indeed, it's estimated that seven out of ten homes across the world own a Unilever product. The company's brands are household favourites in almost every country in the world, which is quite an achievement. But, with its mission to make sustainable living commonplace, Unilever sees itself as more than just another multinational. According to Dutch Chief Executive Paul Polman, Unilever is "the world's biggest NGO".

Unilever was formed in 1930 following a merger of the UK's Lever Brothers Ltd and Dutch firm Margarine Unie. Lever Brothers made soap, while Margarine Unie made margarine, which meant they used many of the same materials. Bringing the two firms together in one of the biggest industrial amalgamations of its day made sense.

The British strand of the company dates back to 1885. In 1888, Lever Brothers opened a factory on the banks of the Mersey to produce Sunlight soap. The site became known as Port Sunlight, and Her Majesty The Queen visited it on two separate occasions (pictured right, Her Majesty's July 1957 visit). Yet more royal connections exist – a number of the company's brands have a Royal Warrant: Persil, Colman's, Hellmann's and Stork. Others, such as Marmite, have run campaigns for the Golden Jubilee and several Unilever brands are sponsoring The Patron's Lunch, a giant street party in June celebrating The Queen's patronage of more than 600 organisations on the occasion of her 90th birthday.

In December 2015, The Prince of Wales singled out Unilever's work in countering deforestation as a pioneering example of sustainability. This recognition echoed the Prince's words of a few years earlier. "This really is a groundbreaking development, which could make the whole difference to the future of the rainforests," he said. "I can only pray that other companies will follow your determined and principled leadership – this really is corporate responsibility in action."

When Paul Polman was appointed Chief Executive in 2009, he was determined to expand upon a long-standing commitment to corporate sustainability while improving the company's economic health. "I believe the two go hand in hand," he says. "If you want a long-term sustainable business then the foremost priority is to ensure you are in sync with society and its environment." In 2010, the Unilever Sustainable Living Plan was launched in which the company undertook to decouple its growth from environmental impact and improve the health and well-being of more than a billion people.

OI S 47C4JUN 47
The lifetime guardian of health...
LIFEBUOY SOAP
LIFEBUOY
SOAP
LIFEBUOY SOAP
LIFEBUOY
SOAP
AD2334
LEVER BROTHERS (INDIA) LTD.

For Polman, this aligned Unilever with principles held by William Lever in the 1880s. Lever was an industrialist and philanthropist who protected workers' rights and built a model village to house employees alongside his Port Sunlight factory. His products helped to improve the hygiene of the Victorian poor. Lever believed that sleeping outside was conducive to his health whatever the weather and, when Polman joined Unilever, he immersed himself in this legacy to such an extent that he spent a night in Lever's rooftop bed at Port Sunlight. "I was the first CEO from outside the organisation and understood that I needed to be accepted," says Polman. "I committed myself to understanding the company's core. That helped me become accepted and to identify where we needed to make the changes." Polman also authorised multi-million-pound investments in the company's factory and research laboratory at Port Sunlight, contributing to the UK's manufacturing base and intellectual capital.

Unilever's goal, however, is to improve society across the globe, not just in the UK. As well as its work on deforestation, it has attacked waste and improved worker conditions across its supply chain, using its brands to drive change for the consumer. This is at the heart of its business model.

"We use our brands to positively address issues, such as using Domestos to deal with sanitation, Ben & Jerry's for free trade and Dove for women's self-esteem," says Polman. "We want every brand to make a positive contribution." Among these is Lifebuoy, one of William Lever's earliest products, which Unilever sells in Africa and Asia. The brand is reaching millions of people in the developing world with its simple message that handwashing can improve lives and reduce infant mortality.

Polman feels this is the right thing to do for several reasons. "If we truly believe in being around as a company for another 100 years then we have to take care of the planet and of society," he says. "It's very much ingrained in our philosophy that we look to make a positive contribution in everything we do." As part of this broader commitment, the company played a leading role in helping to develop the United Nation's Sustainable Development Goals (SDGs), with Polman serving on the UN High Level Panel and – subsequently – as one of the UN Secretary General Ban Ki Moon's "Global Advocates"

Polman recognises that Unilever's size puts it in a privileged position but only if it uses its power wisely. "We are in 190 countries and reach two billion people a day, and the question we always ask is how we use that to make an impact. How can we use this to make more transformative changes in the industry? How can we encourage the industry to move out of deforestation? How can we use the industry to address food waste and recycling?"

This does not come at the expense of performance. Unilever's share price has appreciated 168 per cent since early 2009, and the company is widely admired for its achievements. One of the world's most desired employers, it attracts talented employees who share its vision for a brighter future. To help with this, Polman made crucial changes early on.

"There was a risk of losing our way by having a short-term focus on the market," he says, "so we abolished quarterly profit reporting and earnings guidance. We had to create an environment that allowed people to take the right decisions for the long term. Also, it's always important to keep in mind that the consumer is the ultimate boss."

Polman believes there is yet more to be done, particularly when it comes to encouraging other companies to operate in a similar manner. But he believes that Unilever – and its army of beloved brands – is leading by example. "We are showing there is an alternative business model that is more inclusive, more equitable and more sustainable," he says. "We want to be locally relevant and globally efficient, and we are showing that you can have good financial results for the stakeholder and also a business model that doesn't take from society more than it gives."

Ship shape

Stena Line

When Dan Sten Olsson outlines the philosophy that shapes the approach of Stena, the company founded in Sweden by his father in 1939 and which he has run as CEO since 1983, he delivers the perfect line: "We are small enough to care but large enough to cope."

The Stena Sphere has interests in ferry operations, shipping, offshore drilling, property, waste management and metal recycling, making it one of Sweden's largest family-owned conglomerates, employing 19,000 people. Stena Line, the company's ferry business, operates 16 ships, 12 carrying the British flag, serving 10 routes around the British Isles. The asset value of drilling rigs, ferries, ports and property operated by Stena in the UK is approximately £2.8 billion, with Stena Line employing over 1,000 British seafarers and a further 1,350 on shore.

That makes it Britain's biggest ferry company. In recognition of this, Dan Sten Olsson was awarded a CBE in 2010, receiving the honour from The Earl of Wessex, aboard the British warship HMS *Kent*. "I would like to say how delighted I am to accept such a prestigious accolade," Sten Olsson said after the ceremony. "I would like to say how grateful we are for the support we have received in the United Kingdom – not only in a commercial sense but also from British society in general."

Stena Line operates in eight geographical business regions in Europe from its head office in Gothenburg, Sweden. It is owned by Stena AB, one of the three principal divisions of Stena Sphere. The company operates 22 routes in northern Europe, with 34 vessels, and also owns five ports, making it a crucial part of the European logistics system.

"Our vision is to connect Europe for a sustainable future," says Carl-Johan Hagman, the CEO of Stena Line.

It forms a part of a wider shipping interest that dates back to 1948, when the first Stena ship – a three-masted schooner called *Dan* – was purchased. Stena's vessels are now in constant motion through Europe and beyond. It's estimated that, in 2014, Stena's ships sailed the equivalent of 270 times around the world to deliver raw materials, freight and passengers.

Stena Line transports around 2.7 million passengers a year between Ireland and Britain, plus a further 780,000 to Holland. It also transported 520,000 freight units on the North Sea and 745,000 on the Irish Sea, firmly establishing its position as a market leader. In addition to investments in new ships and routes, Stena Line has invested £80 million in a state-of-the-art new port and terminal facility at Cairnryan, Scotland, which opened in November 2011. In creating the UK's third largest gateway, this project was assigned "National Project" status by the Scottish Parliament. The multi-million-pound port facility enhances the country's travel and freight productivity and helps to generate millions for the economy through quality employment opportunities and associated business and tourism expenditure from Stena Line customers.

The company has two priorities: to deliver good-value, tailor-made products and services to freight customers, and to provide value-for-money products and services to its passengers – all the time ensuring that everyone has an enjoyable time onboard. In January 2015 the new sulphur emissions regulations (SECA) came into force: like the unpredictable price of oil, it is

an example of the complexities of international business. Hagman believes that if Stena Line is the best at what it does, it will thrive regardless of external factors. "Irrespective of whether markets are up or down, our focus and ambition is to be best in class when it comes to operations and business execution," he says. "Operational excellence, through high-quality, high-service, reliability and being very close to our customers is our strategy through the 22 ferry routes in Stena Line."

A core message is sustainability. Shipping is already the most energy-efficient mode of transport in relation to cargo volume, but Stena Line is always looking at ways to improve this. "Stena Line is working consciously towards creating the eco-friendly shipping of the future and we are leading the way in this area," says Hagman. More than 200 projects have been completed under Stena Line's energy-saving programme since 2006, including installation of frequency-controlled equipment for pumps and fans, improvement of combustion in engines, and cargo handling. In Gothenburg, the ferry Stena Danica was connected to the district heating grid, powered by 100 per cent renewable energy, and in some ports – including Hook of Holland – Stena Lines ships are connected to shore power at the quayside to further reduce fuel consumption and emissions.

The fleet's new pride and joy is the Stena Germanica. It started life in 2015 as a pilot project to become the world's first ferry to be run on methanol, and trial tests have been promising. Initially, one of the four main engines was converted to methanol, to be followed by the other three. Running fully on methanol will significantly reduce emissions – by 90 per cent for sulphur oxides (Sox) and particles (PM) and by 60 per cent on nitrogen oxides – while running on bio-methanol will also eliminate CO_2 emissions.

Hand-in-hand with sustainability comes social responsibility, and the stated aim for Stena is to act ethically in everything it does. Hagman also discusses the importance of safety and community involvement, with Stena Line – like all Stena companies – taking an active role in supporting selected international projects.

Stena considers itself a company built on care. "We care, we innovate, we perform," says Olsson. "That's what unites us. Our success over the years has been achieved by continually caring about our customers, by providing innovative solutions and by perfect performance. We deliver quality by always keeping the promises we make and our goal is always to be the best at what we do. To run a profitable organisation enables us to continue our operation and invest in our own future as well as in the future of our customers and society. Hopefully our approach is visible in everything we do and benefits not just ourselves but also future generations."

This is a message that's picked up by Hagman. "Stena Line is positioned in the forefront of the shipping industry when it comes to sustainability," he says. "Fuel efficiency, sustainability and safety are issues that traditionally have been hallmarks of Stena and they will, to an even great degree, be part of our future. Our business can only be sustainable if we, every day, through effective performance, contribute to our client's success. My goal is to build a sustainable company for the long term."

East meets West

Reignwood Investments UK Ltd

The classical facade and vast tower of Ten Trinity Square may not belong to one of London's most recognised buildings, but it is surely one of the most attractive, and is certainly among the most historically important, even in this gilded city of landmarks new and old. Built in the 1920s, the elegant City of London office block was for decades the home of the Port of London Authority (PLA), the body that controls trade and shipping on the Thames, as well as looking after the surrounding London ports, which were then at the centre of world trade. The vital importance of this role meant that the PLA has always had close ties with the Royal Family, something that continues to the present day when it helped organise the Diamond Jubilee flotilla in 2012.

Today, however, Ten Trinity Square is preparing for a new life, having been meticulously restored by its new owners, the Chinese investment company Reignwood Investments. When the project is completed towards the end of 2016, Ten Trinity Square will consist of several state-of-the-art apartments and penthouses, a five-star hotel, a private members club and a host of luxury amenities and services. More impressive still, it will be a physical manifestation of ever-improving international relations.

"East meets west describes the defining dynamic of this century," says Songhua Ni, the Executive President of Reignwood Group and President of Reignwood Investments UK Ltd, and this synthesis is embodied by Ten Trinity Square.

Reignwood Group was founded in 1984 by Dr Chanchai Ruayrungruang, a Thai-Chinese entrepreneur with strong roots in China. His aim was always to enhance relationships between east and west through bringing the best of western business values to China, while using the firm's expertise and experience to transform iconic brands in Europe and the US. The company's investments now span a range of sectors including consumer products, hotels and residential property, golf courses, wellness centres, aviation, offshore engineering and finance. In the UK, Reignwood's interests include the landmark development at Ten Trinity Square, as well as Wentworth Club.

These grand, ambitious projects are at the core of Reignwood's strategy. "Reignwood believes that cultural differences risk getting in the way of business relationships," says Ni, "and it is seeking a better level of understanding among all sides to everybody's benefit. Many of our investments in China target both Western and Chinese business people and provide a forum for them to come together. This is an ambitious, growing company with a clear vision for its future. Reignwood's businesses and investments are focused on meeting the needs of consumers and businesses in China, Asia and the west, through a shared understanding of each other's culture and heritage."

As Ten Trinity Square was once the embodiment of the PLA's values, it will now be emblematic of Reignwood's. The Grade II* listed building, close to the Tower of London in the City of London, has been diligently restored since Reignwood purchased the property in 2010. The building was

originally the work of Sir Edwin Cooper, who sought to create something that illustrated the wealth and importance of the Port of London Authority. It has a huge square tower, raised on pillars, that dominates the skyline west of Tower Hill, and the vast building takes over an entire block in an exhibition of columns, domes, towers and statues, centred round a circular rotunda.

The PLA sold the building in the 1970s after which it was used as offices. When they took on the project, Reignwood Investments were determined to do more than merely reproduce interiors. They set about restoring and preserving surviving features, with stone-restoration experts working on exterior stonework and carvings, while others set about improving plasterwork, wood carvings and marble floors. The extensive work resulted in the discovery of several significant architectural finds as well as an antique clock in the United Nations room – the location of the reception for the historic inaugural assembly of the United Nations in 1946.

When the work is completed, Ten Trinity Square will be an exclusive and harmonious arrangement. It will feature residences, the Four Seasons hotel and a private club, all of which reflect the vibrancy of modern London while honouring Cooper's original design, with the restoration led by French designer Bruno Moinard. But it will be even more than this.

"London's great clubs once played a vital role in shaping debate and facilitating exchange," says Ni. "Ten Trinity Square Private Club will revive this proud tradition for a new, globalised era. The club is being created at a time when London is establishing itself as the fulcrum between these two worlds of East and West."

He promises that Ten Trinity Square Private Club will be unlike anything else in London. It is being created from the sumptuous boardrooms and executive offices of the original building, carefully retaining the finest features of carved walnut panelling and high ceilings. The club will include a library, cigar lounge, bar and the Château Latour wine room and restaurant. "The club is for global leaders," says Ni, "whose careers and interests mean that they travel frequently between East and West."

A similar mindset is behind the work at Wentworth. "A round of golf is one of the most productive times when people can discuss and resolve issues in a non-confrontational and confidential environment," says Ni. "At Wentworth we are bringing some of the key lessons we have had from managing golf and country clubs in China. Our Jack Nicklaus-designed courses are among the best venues of their kind."

This philosophy will drive future investments. "Reignwood believes that the United Kingdom and China can be complementary partners," says Ni. "Chinese companies value the strength of the UK business environment, its business-friendly policies and robust rule of law. They admire its well-educated and supportive workforce. The UK is in need of capital investment to retain its place as a premier European and global economy. China has an abundance of capital that it is looking to invest in world-class assets. So Reignwood Investments is an ideal partner for the UK. Our future investments in the UK will continue to focus on areas where we think we can bring unique value to restore iconic brands to their former glory."

A meeting of minds

The European Azerbaijan Society

The European Azerbaijan Society (TEAS) exists to bring together Azerbaijan and Europe in political, cultural and business terms. It also highlights the increasing ties between westward-facing Azerbaijan and Europe, particularly regarding energy links, but also in terms of shared perspectives and visions, emphasising the country's unique geopolitical role as a paragon of stability, despite being located between two giant neighbouring nations – Russia to the north and Iran to the south.

TEAS is headquartered in London with offices in Paris, Strasbourg, Berlin, Brussels, Istanbul and Baku. It organises a rich and varied programme of events, including the TEAS Business Forum series, aimed at increasing collaboration between European and Azerbaijani companies; cultural events that demonstrate the rich blend of musical and artistic talent in the country; and political meetings, primarily aimed at emphasising Azerbaijan's religious and cultural diversity. It also helps raise awareness of the unresolved Armenian–Azerbaijani conflict over Nagorno-Karabakh, which has led to the displacement of an estimated 875,000 Azerbaijanis.

Despite the enormous economic burden posed by this, Azerbaijan continues to account for 70 per cent of the economy of the South Caucasus. According to the World Economic Forum, the economy grew by over 300 per cent in the last decade, although the recent decline in oil revenues calls for a rapid expansion of the country's non-oil sector. Here, however, Azerbaijan has no shortage of opportunities – it is blessed with an excellent climate and already has an extensive agricultural sector. Its abundant wave, wind and hydroelectric power provide opportunities for the generation of renewable energy, and its historic towns and dramatic landscapes are set to be the backdrop to exotic holidays for years to come. Furthermore, from 2020, gas from the Caspian and Central Asia will be delivered direct to Italy through the Southern Energy Corridor, an Azerbaijani initiative that will help the EU in its drive towards achieving energy supply diversity and security.

Azerbaijan's connections with the UK are long-standing, with the UK providing more that 50 per cent of foreign direct investment and more than 500 UK companies being active in the county's capital Baku. Its relationship with Her Majesty The Queen dates back exactly 60 years when a Karabakh horse – bred in the eponymous region – was given to the Royal Stable by the Soviet government. In 2012, TEAS was a sponsor of the Royal Windsor Horse Show, held to commemorate The Queen's Diamond Jubilee. As with this year's event, Karabakh horses and traditional dancers participated in the event, complemented by an Azerbaijani pavilion, dispensing hospitality and information on the country.

The most recent connection has been the role played by TEAS in supporting The Prince of Wales's Mosaic International Leaders' Forum, which is aimed at developing the talents of young people in 18 Muslim-majority countries.

In short, Azerbaijan is a secular, westward-facing republic on the fringes of Europe. Its energy links and business opportunities make it evermore relevant to Europe, and its hosting of such international events as the European Games in 2015 and Formula One this year have proven its mettle.

Long range vision

Schroders

Schroders' reputation for astuteness and probity in managing assets attracts a broad spectrum of clients: institutional and retail investors as well as financial institutions rely on its plentiful range of investment services, which include equities, fixed income, multi-asset, alternatives and real estate. For over 200 years the company has put its clients' interests first through prioritising long-term growth over short-term profit.

"In our decision-making we aim to ensure that we prosper for another 200 years," says Michael Dobson, Chairman. "The key to that has always been adaptability and stability – it's essential to be able to change and stay relevant, while holding true to what you are."

Over its history, Schroders has taken commercial decisions and made investments considered contrarian by some competitors. But time has proved the ultimate arbiter of the firm's strategic good sense, and significant long-term investment decisions have subsequently born fruit.

Under the reign of King George III in 1804, two brothers from Hamburg, Johann Heinrich and Johann Friedrich Schröder, went into partnership in London with the intention of acting as commodities merchants in the city's thriving commercial environment. Clients and trading partners quickly came to entrust them with requests to access the city's commercial and financial services, and the brothers responded by developing the firm as a merchant bank.

As early as 1924 Schroders began to provide asset management services and since 2000 it has operated solely in this area, playing an important role in actively channelling capital to companies to support them in investing for growth. This dedication to business investment continues to benefit the growth of Britain's economy, as well as the firm's clients.

Although headquartered in the vibrant financial hub of London, Schroders today is very much an international operation. It supports offices in 28 countries, and from assets under management of £313.5 billion, some 60 per cent of its revenue comes from outside the UK. Little wonder it has twice received the Queen's Award for Enterprise in the field of Export Achievement since its decision in the 1960s to reach out overseas: in 1993 for Schroder Capital Management International and in 1998 for its International Energy and Project Division.

In 2013 Schroders expanded its wealth management business through its acquisition of Cazenove Capital. With a history as long as Schroders' own, this was a natural partnership, and it now also specialises in taking care of the interests of private clients, charities and financial advisers.

Looking ahead, Schroders is keeping abreast of developments in the marketplace and the evolving needs of its clients. "Schroders plays an important role in helping a broad range of investors meet their financial goals as they provide for retirement, seek to offset future liabilities or build pools of capital to fund their investment needs of the future," says Dobson. "Helping our clients achieve their investment aims has always been at the core of our business and is key to our past and future success."

A solid understanding of the past, and a prudent eye on the near and distant future, suggests that Schroders will continue to prosper and grow for many generations to come.

Hot properties

Concept Business Group

Beaufort Gardens is easily one of London's most desirable addresses. A hundred years ago, this was a bustling hub of high society. Today, with its stately Georgian facades set in leafy backstreets in a peaceful corner of Knightsbridge, it's easy to see why the address has retained its appeal for well-heeled buyers across the decades. These days, however, luxury homeowners are looking for more than just elegant period architecture and a prestigious postcode.

"Increasingly, developers targeting luxury-sector buyers have to look beyond the property itself to the kind of lifestyle it can offer," says Nicholas Trimmatis, CEO of exclusive property development and investment company Concept Business Group. This means creating an environment that caters to the requirements of wealthy buyers, not just in the look and feel of a place but in the amenities and features it offers.

Arriving at CBG's Beaufort Gardens residences, owners use a private lift to reach their apartments and unlock the door through thumbprint keypads fitted with sensors that will send a text-message alert if a problem is detected. In addition to the peace of mind afforded by state-of-the-art security systems, apartments come complete with concierges, valets and porters, who are on hand to unpack luggage, fill the fridge, download music, book theatre tickets, arrange a nanny or charter a jet as required.

"In central London, you're dealing almost exclusively with high-net-worth buyers and they have specific expectations," says Trimmatis, explaining that developments producing multimillion pound units must be prepared to accommodate increasingly sophisticated demands. These include built-in features, such as private swimming pools, high-tech gyms and cigar rooms; top-notch management services; and, of course, a prime setting that offers proximity to key destinations.

While most of CBG's developments are concentrated in central London, the company is quick to identify promising opportunities around the city. An ambitious new project currently underway in Woolwich will see CBG transform a historic area of London around King Henry's Dock into a desirable destination for 21st-century living. "The plan is not only to build a property," says Trimmatis, "but to create a neighbourhood in an area of south-east London that is undergoing a lot of regeneration. There's no development like this anywhere in London."

A Greek national, Trimmatis studied for his degree in London 24 years ago, before adopting it as his home. Hailing from a family of property developers, he was quick to spot the investment potential when a small apartment in Knightsbridge came on the market. Today, that first residence is part of an extensive portfolio of

properties he has purchased and developed over the years in some of London's most exclusive neighbourhoods.

Trimmatis is an established figure in London society, not least because of the many charitable endeavours he undertakes through CBG. The company supports more than 12 charities, including several of those overseen by the Royal Family. "We never miss an opportunity to extend our support and are honoured to work with the Royal Family to benefit a number of their organisations," he says, "including the Duke of Edinburgh Awards and the Outward Bound Trust."

For Trimmatis, it's the international environment offered by London that makes it such a rewarding place to live and work. "For myself and my family, London is the greatest place in the world," he says. "For anyone who loves their job enough to call it a hobby, this is the best city in the world to be in." He describes London's multicultural appeal as the perfect backdrop for property developers.

"London is not only a big market in itself but it acts as a base for the region," he says. "Around 60 per cent of all European real estate transactions take place in the UK." With demand exceeding supply, London also presents an extremely appealing prospect for investors looking to capitalise on the city's bulging real estate sector. This has the added advantage of high liquidity and, crucially in the current environment, reliability.

"Every ten years, regardless of any crises, the London property market doubles," says Trimmatis. "That is because people are coming here from all over the world to invest, fuelling further demand so that it outstrips supply." This is particularly true of central London, where luxury developments are highly sought-after from a growing pool of international buyers.

CBG has global client base, with clients from the Middle East, Russia, Europe, the USA and the Far East. Many are repeat buyers, assured from past experience that the company will provide a sound placement for their investment. "Loyalty is extremely important to us," he says. "We have built up a strong relationship with many of our clients, who know they can rely on us to deliver the quality and service they are looking for, while finding them something unique in the market."

This also applies to the company's commercial developments, which subscribe to the same high-end profile as CBG's residential properties. Recent projects include the former Volvo headquarters in Marlow, currently being redeveloped into a prominent address for a multinational company, complete with dining spaces and entertainment areas. CBG is collaborating with architect Sir Terry Farrell, best known for his work on the MI6 building. "This new property really sums up what we do," says Trimmatis, adding that commercial ventures now account for 50 per cent of CBG's portfolio. "We've taken an old building and breathed new life into it, recreating not just the environment but also the lifestyle that it will make possible."

When CBG started trading back in 2000, its founding principle was to present a property with a concept which offered the buyer something special. Over the coming years, the company will continue to refine this proposition, exploring new ways to anticipate the demands of today's high-end buyer and create bespoke environments tailored to suit a particular lifestyle.

"People come here for many reasons – business, culture, education, leisure – and it's our job to make their dream life in London a reality," says Trimmatis. With his expert understanding of the needs of his clients and personal love of the city, no one could be better suited to showcasing London at its most luxurious.

Teatime classics

Thomas Tunnock Ltd

From its origins in a single bakery shop 126 years ago, Tunnock's has grown to become a giant in the world of British confectionery, selling its iconic fare to 35 countries and earning its owner several visits to Buckingham Palace. Every minute, the company produces an astonishing 2,100 caramel wafers and 1,050 teacakes from its 200,000 sq ft factory in Uddingston, south-east of Glasgow.

The factory is just 100 yards from the bakery which was bought for £80 in 1890 by an apprentice baker called Thomas Tunnock. By 1906, he was employing six boys, including his son Archie, to deliver rolls from the oven to customers in the village. Thomas soon branched out into purveying for weddings and special occasions.

The economic downturn of the First World War led to the bakery's closure in 1919. After the untimely death of Thomas Tunnock in 1920, Archie left the army and used his £100 demob money to reopen the bakery, this time featuring an upstairs tea shop. As the business developed Archie realised he needed to make something with a longer shelf life than bread and cake, so he bought a dozen dry wafers and learned how to make caramel and chocolate. The result, in 1952, was Tunnock's now famous caramel wafer biscuit, which still carries the original red and gold foil wrapping.

Four years later, his son Boyd Tunnock, who had finished his National Service as a Cook Sergeant, was given the task of developing a new product. After a great deal of market research he hand piped an Italian meringue-style mallow onto a biscuit base before covering it in milk chocolate. The Tunnock's teacake was born in 1959.

Nearly sixty years on and Boyd Tunnock, now aged 83, says the company is going from strength to strength. In its most recent full financial year the company enjoyed a turnover of around £50 million and a profit of some £7 million. It started exporting in 1957 to a buyer in Newfoundland, Canada with whom it still does business. It ships its confectionery products to some of the coldest countries (Iceland) as well as the hottest (Kuwait and Saudi Arabia) in the world.

The teacakes received a huge fillip in 2014 when they were featured in a dance routine at the launch ceremony of the Commonwealth Games in Glasgow, which were officially opened by Her Majesty The Queen. Tunnock said the company had been asked by the organisers if they would be happy with them using the brand, but had no idea what they were planning. "It was a howling success," Tunnock recalls. Sales soared since images of the teacakes went round the world, increasing by 66 per cent and pushing Tunnock's to a record turnover.

Boyd Tunnock, who assumed the post of Managing Director of Tunnock's in 1981 after his father died, was made an MBE in 1987 for services to exporting and received his award from The Queen at a ceremony at Buckingham Palace. Three years ago Boyd Tunnock was able to present The Duke of Edinburgh with a packet of Tunnock's caramel wafer biscuits when he found himself seated next to him at a dinner to mark the Duke's awards scheme. In 2004, he was made a CBE in The Queen's Birthday Honours list for his services to charity and was awarded the honour by The Prince of Wales.

Tunnock has been heavily involved with charities. He has been chairman of Malin Court Housing Association, which runs a home for the elderly in Turnberry, Ayrshire, for the past three decades. He is also chairman of the Salvation Army Advisory Board for the West of Scotland and has held the same position on the Lifeboats of the Clyde Appeal committee. Last November Tunnock gave £250,000 to an appeal to bring an independent lifeboat station into operation at St Abbs in Berwickshire after the RNLI closed its site. "I'm reasonably good to charity," he says, "but I don't do it looking to get thanks. I do it because it is the right thing to do."

Despite a history going back to the Victorian era, Tunnock's has always managed to attract fans among celebrities. Pop group Supergrass visited the factory before performing at the first T In The Park concert at Strathclyde Park in 1994. Hollywood actress Andie MacDowell has been a huge fan of the caramel wafers, while Coldplay's frontman Chris Martin revealed his secret passion for teacakes and caramel wafers in 2008, calling them "the Lennon and McCartney of chocolate biscuits".

While the firm has focused on a select range of products – which also includes the caramel log, the wafer cream and the snowball – it has constantly invested in the best technology to increase production and keep pace with the ever rising demand. In 1999 Boyd Tunnock placed an order for a robotic system to pack caramel logs and, as a result of its success, bought its first teacake robot in 2006. The investment has significantly increased productivity and enabled the company to run 24-hour shifts.

But Tunnock's is ultimately a people business. It employs 550 people, almost all of who are based in Scotland at its fully unionised factory. "We are not over-burdened with management," says Boyd. "We tend to be light at the top and heavy at the bottom." Boyd's daughter Karen and son-in-law Fergus are part of the senior management team and, since 2013, five generations of the Tunnock family have worked for the firm when Tunnock's third grandchild Stuart joined the business after spending seven years building jet engines at Rolls-Royce.

Boyd Tunnock puts the company's 126 years of success down to "persistence". "If you try something and it doesn't work, then try again," he says. "And keep quality high – make sure you read complaints because you are reading the future. They are your customers so treat them with respect."

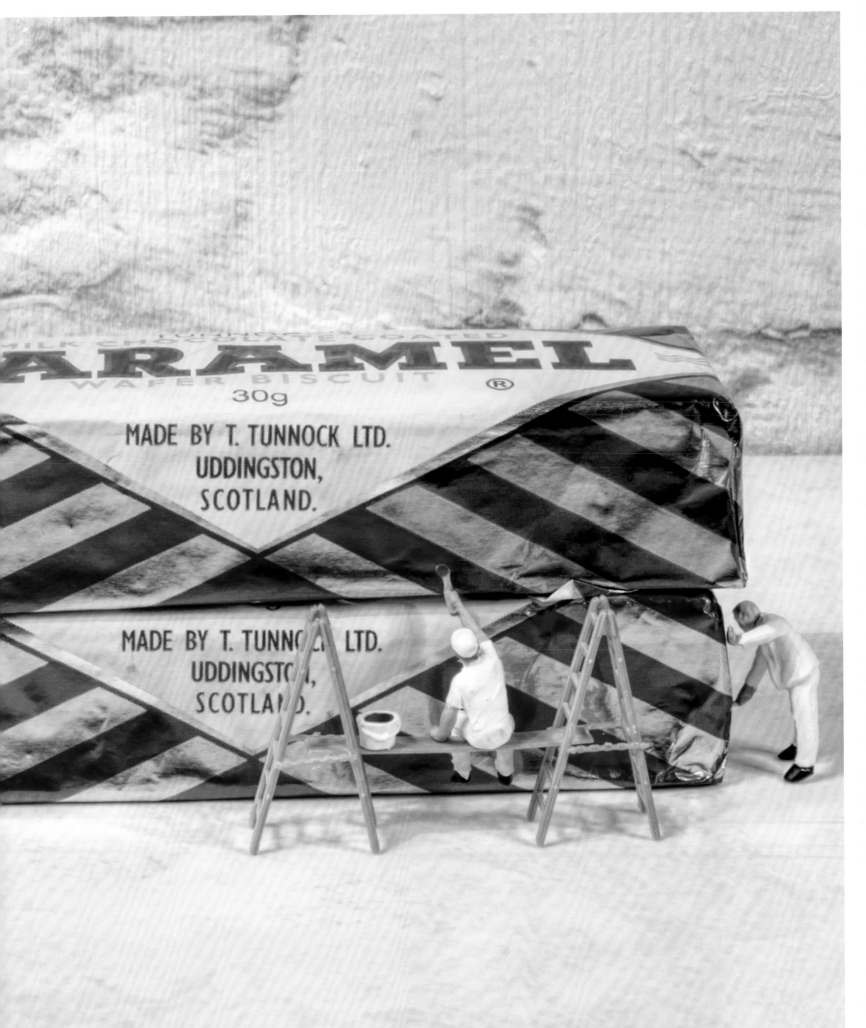

A healthy attitude

Boots UK

When Jesse Boot left school in 1863, aged 13, to help his widowed mother in the family herbal store, it is unlikely that this ambitious and principled young man could have foreseen what was to come. More than 150 years later, the Boot family's humble Nottingham shop has grown to be a trusted national retailer with an outlet on nearly every UK high street.

"The Boot family was always driven by a firm belief in improving society and helping ordinary people have access to medicine," says Boots archivist Sophie Clapp. "That legacy continues to this day, with Boots UK offering a specialist care and support role in the 2,500 communities in which it is based."

With a pharmacy still at the heart of every store, Boots has always adapted to meet the changing needs of the UK, introducing new products and services and new ways to help customers feel good. "As one of the nation's longest serving health and beauty retailers, we care about raising the health and happiness of the communities we serve," says Simon Roberts, President of Boots. "We always have, and we always will."

The sense of social purpose has also remained. Through long-standing partnerships with BBC Children in Need and Macmillan Cancer Support, Boots UK helps to support local projects across the UK, and also introduced the new role of Boots Macmillan Information Pharmacist to help offer information and support to those affected by cancer. In a new partnership with the National Literacy Trust, Boots Opticians is helping to raise awareness of the link between eye health and literacy. "These kinds of key partnerships

are absolutely part of our social mission," says Roberts. "It's our ambition to champion everyone's right to feel good, whether in the fields of pharmacy, healthcare or beauty advice."

Boots UK has an illustrious history of royal patronage. Jesse Boot himself was knighted in 1909; the then King and Queen visited the Boots factory during the Second World War; and the company was awarded a Royal Warrant for Boots Opticians in 1956 and Boots UK in 1971. In addition, the company is one of the hosts of the Patron's Lunch – the enormous street party held in June to celebrate Her Majesty The Queen's patronage of more than 600 charities.

This continues more than a century of social commitment. The company's work with the National Literacy Trust, for instance, follows on from the Boots Booklovers Libraries – a scheme created in the early 20th century that encouraged improved literacy by enabling people to borrow books for a reasonable price. Additionally, as early as 1911, Boots had appointed a welfare professional to look after the interests of its female staff members, and the company revolutionised cosmetics for ordinary women with the creation of its affordable Boots No7 range.

"Our business is based on the values of trust, care, partnership, innovation and dedication," says Roberts – old-fashioned, traditional values, placed at the heart of a thoroughly modern company that is continually evolving to serve Britain better. Jesse Boot would surely be proud.

The golden rule

Goldcorp Inc

Back in 1994, a couple of like-minded businessmen, Ian Telfer and Frank Giustra, bonded over a common belief in the glittering future of gold. They turned their belief into assets and their assets into a top-tier gold-mining company; 22 years on, Goldcorp goes from strength to strength, firmly maintaining the independent and innovative thinking that made the company successful in the first place. The firm now has mines and projects in six countries and employs more than 16,000 people.

"In a lot of operations in our industry, processes haven't changed significantly in 50 years," says Brent Bergeron, Executive Vice President, Corporate Affairs and Sustainability. "At Goldcorp, we are trying to attract the top talent with the highest potential to do things differently. We bring in exceptional people from various sectors and continuously push the envelope to make our operations even better."

This is not just about mining more gold, more efficiently – far from it. Goldcorp's core values and the strategy that guides the company include growing sustainability, fostering partnerships in the community as well as the corporate world, and improving safety. "The industry is always trying to become safer," says Bergeron. "We don't compete on that, ever. We all share information so that everyone learns from any incidents, and any new discoveries that can help reduce harm are shared, too."

The company's safety vision originated from a discussion with executives about whether they would feel safe enough to work in the company's mines. The response was usually positive but, when asked whether they would let their children, partners or parents do the same, the answer was somewhat different. And so Safe Enough For Our Families was born. "We know this is a high-risk industry but we want to improve safety as much as we possibly can," says Bergeron. "Our number-one priority is zero fatalities."

The company's approach to excellence in employee safety extends to its approach to local communities as well. "The entire industry has had

to make shift in how we deal with communities and governments," says Bergeron. "Goldcorp is emerging as one of the leaders in those areas."

Mines are usually in remote areas, with strong community ties. Goldcorp is finding ways to create value and improve the lives of people in these communities – and to do so in ways that will outlast the mine itself. The company has a strong commitment to local hiring practices and the sourcing of local goods and services. It also has a robust community investment programme that supports initiatives in education, health, infrastructure and the preservation of local arts and culture. "We work closely with First Nations communities in Canada," says Bergeron. "We want to become partners and make sure we don't disrupt their traditional way of life or cause any problems."

Goldcorp sets things up so that everyone has a stake: if the mine is successful, so is the local community. "We keep communities informed, build collaboration and encourage people to participate in the design and development of our operation," says Bergeron. This ties in with local people's own priorities. "For instance, the Cree Nation in northern Quebec is investing for future generations of its own people," says Bergeron. "We've adapted our corporate responsibility approach to suit specific aspirations of that commitment. We know we have the ability to positively affect lives in a positive, sustainable manner, and create value for all of our stakeholders – not just investors but communities, our employees and their families."

The company's approach to environmental stewardship is also breaking new ground. "How companies use water is of growing importance to our

stakeholders," says Bergeron, "and in this industry we are always going to be working in areas either with an abundance or scarcity of water. It's extremely important to lower our footprint when it comes to water use." The company has achieved water recycling rates of 97 per cent at some mines. Its approach to energy conservation is equally ambitious: for instance, Goldcorp's Musselwhite Mine in northern Ontario has completely eliminated the use of diesel-fuelled generators.

The sustainability principle aims to create collateral benefits that will continue once the mine is depleted of gold. "We have a product that people use for jewellery, for financial measures, in technology applications and for cancer treatments. We are constantly consuming our reserves, so it's vital for the company to maintain its growth profile but we aren't pursuing growth for the sake of it. We want to produce better, more profitable ounces."

That means higher-grade gold, via low-cost extraction. Destroying the planet in the service of short-term profit helps nobody. "We have a philosophy we call Operating For Excellence, which involves looking at ways to become more effective and efficient, by sending teams of people into our mine sites to look at ways of improving productivity and lowering costs in ways that can also benefit the environment."

Goldcorp wants, says Bergeron, to be the best and most sustainable company it can be. The company understands that gold's value, however great, is not enough: a conscientious, sustainable company that is an asset to its employees, its investors, its stakeholders and the planet is more precious than any metal could ever be.

Driving progress

Arnold Clark Automobiles

In 1954, a teenage Scottish mechanic called Arnold Clark left the RAF and decided to use his demob money to buy and restore a Morris Ten Four motor car, which he went on to sell. The profit made on that single vehicle helped to set up a car dealership, one that still bears its founder's name.

Clark – now Sir Arnold – is today the head of Europe's largest independent car dealer group, with an annual turnover of more than £3 billion. It sells more than 250,000 new, nearly new and used vehicles a year, and employs over 10,000 people.

"Value for money and customer satisfaction are absolutely paramount for us," says Sir Arnold. It's why his company has been named Automotive Management Retailer of the Year for 2016. It's also why the company's seventh decade is proving to be its most successful yet.

These days, it offers a lot more than cars, including finance, insurance, servicing, MOTs and extended warranty plans. "At all times, our focus is on offering the best deal in the marketplace," says Sir Arnold, "whichever product or package is being sold."

To ensure this, in 2003 the business acquired its own training facility, which was honoured by a visit from The Prince of Wales last year. Over the past decade, Arnold Clark has become a leader in online customer support, from its ratings system to Your Car Preview, which enables customers to watch a film of service personnel working on their vehicle. There's a comprehensive safety check before purchase and a vehicle health check afterwards, so the buyer of an Arnold Clark car can have perfect confidence in their purchase at all times.

The company's emphasis on quality of service extends further still. Arnold Clark was heavily involved in the 2014 Commonwealth Games, instructing over 700 volunteers at its Glasgow training facility in everything from driver etiquette to the city's best routes. The company also donates or loans dozens of vehicles to charities each year and, in 2015, gave more than £900,000 to charities – including the Prince's Trust, Ardgowan Hospice, Medics Against Violence and Tayside Children with Cancer, as well as a single gift of £350,000 to Glasgow's new Royal Hospital for Children. The company also lets various charities auction sailing trips on Drum, the award-winning yacht built for Duran Duran's Simon Le Bon, and now owned by Sir Arnold.

For a car company, another way of trying to create a better world is to promote electric vehicle technology, and Sir Arnold is excited about the possibilities of hybrid and fully electric cars. The business now boasts 32 electric vehicle charging points across the UK, and keeps customers informed about the latest developments in sustainability via its online newsroom.

"We recently bought the Volkswagen XL1, a pioneering, plug-in hybrid, which is being billed as the world's most fuel-efficient car," says Sir Arnold. "It's one of only 200 that the German manufacturer has so far produced." Arnold Clark is determined to ensure that customers can be as quietly confident in their future purchases as they are in their present ones. Six decades of experience is taking the company and its loyal customers full-speed into an exciting future.

Oat cuisine

Mornflake

Mornflake is Britain's longest established oat miller and has been at the heart of British food for more than 340 years. As one of the UK's few remaining major, independent food producers, Mornflake harnesses a unique combination of family dedication and time-honoured expertise to raise the bar for the cereal industry in quality and innovation.

"This is a 15th-generation family business," says Managing Director, John Lea. "Our longevity and independence not only brings the benefit of experience and the utmost care and attention to milling the best oats, but it also enables us to be faster, more entrepreneurial and innovative." These credentials are evident through Mornflake's acclaimed, extensive range from classic rolled oats to oatmeal and oatbran, as well as ready-to-eat muesli and granola.

Centuries of know-how have earned the Cheshire-based miller the International Monde Selection Gold Award for outstanding quality every year since 1964. Mornflake is proud to mill oats from Her Majesty The Queen's Estate at Sandringham, and also mills organic oats from the Duchy Farms of The Prince of Wales's Highgrove Estate. Mornflake remains at the forefront of organic oat milling both in Britain and abroad.

Mornflake's unrivalled longevity and focus on innovation have made it an integral part of British food history. During the Second World War, John Lea's father, Philip, was requested by the Ministry of Food to put aside his ambitions to join the Royal Air Force to instead "feed the nation". Rationing resulted in home-grown oats becoming a staple part of the British diet – something that Mornflake is proud to be instrumental in.

Mornflake also invented the stabilisation of oats, enabling them to be conveniently stored in our cupboards as we do today – it was the first company in the world to do this. As one of the original millers of oatbran, Mornflake is one of the few with the expertise to mill this rich source of beta glucan soluble fibre, which is proven to lower cholesterol. Together with the rest of the Mornflake oats range, it is accredited by Heart UK.

Based in Crewe, Mornflake exports its oats to more than 60 countries, earning the company the Queen's Award for outstanding achievement in International Trade, as well as being granted Champion Export Status by UK Trade & Investment. While future plans include further innovation and reaching a wider audience, a key goal is to conserve the British oat crop. Mornflake encourages the growing of British oats by "contract growing" on farms throughout the UK. "Our commitment to contract growing for over 40 years has helped to stabilise the UK oat crop, conserving it as an essential part of our agricultural economy," says John Lea. "This also means our oats have full provenance and traceability from 'seed to spoon'."

As a celebration of its commitment to British land Mornflake is co-exhibiting with Cheshire neighbours the Cholmondeley Estate in the Great Pavilion at RHS Chelsea Flower Show 2016. "We represent the agricultural underpinning of the estate within the exhibit," says John Lea. "Oats were known as the oil of the Middle Ages and at one time our oats would have fed the horses that worked the land to serve these estates. We are proud of our heritage and we utilise our experience and time-honoured skills. But ultimately, we look forward as a business and this is key to our success."

Play your cards right

Hallmark Cards

On a January day in 1910, a teenager called JC Hall stepped off a train in Kansas City carrying two shoeboxes. Inside were picture postcards and they were all the 18-year-old had to his name. But those postcards were the start of what is today the world's largest supplier of greeting cards – Hallmark. More than a century later, the values and vision of JC Hall (pictured, above) of providing customers with a world-class product are very much alive, according to Hallmark's international CEO Steve Wright.

"It's about a reflection of the individual – the process of selecting a greetings card is very important both for the sender and the recipient," says Wright, who is based at Hallmark's UK head office in Bradford, West Yorkshire. "All our research shows that people take a lot of care in selecting the right card, particularly women. It's a reflection of the depth of a relationship for the person who opens it and the personal touch, the thought that has gone in to choosing it and the message. Those values will always be important despite the growth of technology."

To ensure that the messages and the designs are just right, Hallmark employs a highly skilled, talented and creative team of around 150 in the UK. Responsible for almost 20,000 designs available in any one year, they range from long-standing employees to recent college graduates who have a variety of skills, from illustration to surface pattern design.

What everyone on the Hallmark design team has in common is flair – and team spirit. The creative process is collaborative, with designers and writers working closely together.

"Sometimes the editorial comes first, sometimes the design – the skill lies in matching the image and message together," says Creative Director Jo Bennett. "We subscribe to trend agencies and we blend this with our understanding of emotional relationships. A lot is down to understanding these relationships. The card that customers send their mum is very different from one they send to a friend. Often the person buying the card isn't the person sending it – a dad will buy a card for his daughter to give her mum. It's about the importance of the message."

In a bid to nurture and invest in new talent, Hallmark sponsors two New Designers awards every July which it has done for the past 20 years. "The prize includes a placement at Hallmark," says Bennett, "where they bring new blood and ideas into the business." Many become regular freelances and there are success stories of those who are still working with the company 15 years later.

The benefit of working for a global company is that staff will find their designs in demand around the globe. Registered in 1958, Hallmark UK is an important creative hub for the family-run company. The firm's UK design

content is shared by other Hallmark companies such as Australia, Japan and Belgium. "British content fits very well with the market in Australia, for example, where people relate to UK tastes," says Wright. "Even in Japan, which is very different, they like to translate our designs for their customers."

Hallmark's relationship with the UK is long-established. Founder Joyce (JC) Hall was a personal friend of Sir Winston Churchill, who gave several of his paintings to the Hall family. This investment in creativity and artistic talent is still one of the founding principles of the Hall family which owns one of the biggest art collections in the world and supports galleries.

"Here in the UK we're constantly looking at the latest innovation, consumer insights and emerging trends to create new, eye-catching designs for cards, stationery and gifts," says Wright. "This commitment goes beyond our products – we're passionate about working with and developing people who have the potential to achieve great things with the focus on recruiting raw creative talent. The pillars of the business and what Hallmark stands for are quality, integrity, innovation and trust. Innovation really comes through the creative recruitment and direction."

As one of the world's biggest senders of greetings cards, the UK is among Hallmark's most important markets. Marks & Spencer is a major customer along with Waitrose, Morrisons and Tesco. A great deal of effort is put into getting the appropriate range of cards for each retailer, and the company is constantly analysing data from many sources to stay aligned with retail and social trends. "In today's world," says Bennett, "the spectrum of what we celebrate and how we want to express ourselves is evolving and therefore influencing our creative development."

"We're also reflecting the move towards communicating by technology such as text and SMS messaging," she says. "We follow all the global design trends, we aim to keep abreast of those trends and link them to our work. It's an evolutionary product that we are dealing with." To demonstrate this, one message inside a Hallmark card reads: "Sister – another birthday, another selfie."

However, the company is still very much a family-owned business. Today, two of JC Hall's grandchildren – Don Hall, President and CEO and Dave Hall, President –are at the helm of the business. Hallmark Cards is motivated by the values of the Hall family who have always believed in doing the best for their customers. Designers may now use computers instead of creating everything by hand but the company is dedicated to ensuring the product is of the best quality.

There is also an emphasis on social responsibility – for example through altruistic work with schools as well as with charities. Hallmark has a long-standing relationship with Barnardo's. When Her Majesty The Queen opened the children's charity's new offices, Wright was among those who attended a special lunch to celebrate the event. Then there is "Million Makers", a scheme that supports the Prince's Trust – teams of Hallmark employees compete against those from other companies to raise money over six months to help transform lives. Hallmark teams have won the "Million Makers" challenge in the Yorkshire/Humberside region on two occasions.

Keeping in touch with the needs of customers while remaining true to its creative values are the "hallmarks" of this business. JC Hall would, no doubt, have been very proud.

A moveable feast

Samworth Brothers

You may have seen a Samworth Brothers lorry on a British motorway. "They're the big cream ones," says Chief Executive Alex Knight. "On the side you'll see our motto: 'Quality is a way of life'. This describes everything we do to ensure the high quality of our products, our facilities, our relationships with customers, the commitment of our people. Quality is paramount to how we operate."

Samworth Brothers is a family business still owned wholly by the Samworth family after four generations. It produces a variety of chilled foods for retailers while also being responsible for well-loved and iconic British food brands such as Ginsters, the UK's best-selling Cornish pasties, and Soreen, the popular malt loaf brand. The business is a champion of traditional Melton Mowbray pork pies through its Dickinson & Morris and Walker & Son brands, and is also looking forward to new food trends with the recent acquisition of the sports nutrition brand, SCI-MX. It has businesses in Leicestershire, Cornwall, Manchester and Gloucester.

"When you look at our core product range, it is clear to see that our heartland is high-quality food," says Knight. "We make a wide range – pies, pasties, sandwiches, desserts, ready meals and salads for top UK retailers." Supporting quality British food has always been integral to the ethos of the company.

"We are a British company in so many ways," says Knight. "We are proud of being in Britain, proud to produce high-quality food that is

delicious and appealing to our consumers, and from ingredients that most often come from local producers and farmers." Some of that food was found in hampers produced by the company for Her Majesty The Queen's Diamond Jubilee in 2012 and the company is equally delighted to be celebrating The Queen's 90th birthday.

The company has also maintained a close relationship with two of The Prince of Wales's charities. Samworth Brothers businesses across the country are involved with Prince's Trust programmes to help young people get into jobs, education and training. The company also shares many of the aspirations of the Prince's Countryside Fund. "A lot of our raw materials come out the ground and we have a very close relationship with many farming communities", says Group Executive Board Director Mary-Ann Kilby. "We are working with the Prince's Countryside Fund and Business in the Community, and have been a lead sponsor of the Rural Action Award. It reflects our own approach. We like to ensure that, right through our supply chain, we are looking after homegrown produce and people."

Social responsibility has always been a cornerstone of how Samworth Brothers operates, with charitable undertakings rooted in local communities. It runs a highly successful Sports Opportunity Fund that helps young people develop confidence, self-esteem and better life skills through sport. The company also organises the Samworth Brothers Charity Challenge, a major triathlon-style fundraising event that takes place every

two years and has raised more than £1.7 million for good causes to date. Ginsters has a successful partnership with the Help For Heroes charity, while Soreen is involved in a partnership with the Youth Sport Trust, helping young people get involved in sport.

In Leicestershire, where the company has 11 businesses, there is a very close and positive relationship with the Leicestershire Cares charity, with many local employees actively involved. This is important to Samworth Brothers as it is a company that believes in investing in people and has many long-serving staff. "We're a very people-focused business," says Knight, "and we've always felt a strong responsibility for the communities in which we operate."

George Samworth, who founded the original Samworth business in 1896, was a well-known figure in the farming communities of the West Midlands as he developed his pig-dealing business. Subsequent Samworth generations have helped the business flourish by responding and adapting to the UK's ever-changing food tastes.

Throughout the company's history, it has maintained an adherence to three core principles: people, quality and profit. It prefers growth to be organic, but it occasionally acquires other businesses. One recent acquisition was the sports nutrition firm SCI-MX, which represents a degree of diversification for a company that is aware of changing trends in diet and food. "Sports nutrition is a massively growing market but a lot of it doesn't taste as nice as it could and with our food-production capacity we can help with that," says Kilby. This means staying abreast of nutritional and dietary trends and developments and finding ways to innovate and improve the healthiness of the product without harming the quality or taste of what the company produces.

"In this industry there's sometimes a fight for the bottom," says Knight. "People want to cut the quality of the product to lower the price. We feel our responsibility is to improve the quality of the food we are all eating and to ensure that we can continue the sustainable delivery of food. There are important issues to confront like protein, fats and sugars. People still want treats so we have to find ways to make those treats healthier. One of the ways we do this is by working with university students to find solutions. We want to get young people involved in the research, get them interested in the food industry and attract the best of them to work with us."

Which brings us back to Samworth Brothers' interest in people and quality, embodying the best of British values. "It's about the food, the engagement with the community and the way we do business," says Knight, who says that The Queen's birthday will be commemorated by an internal cooking competition. "Samworth Brothers is a very special family business and we want to join with the Royal Family with its own celebration of the last 90 years."

Food for thought

Dunbia

Dunbia is a textbook example of how to grow a successful business. Starting out with one village butcher's shop in 1976, brothers Jim and Jack Dobson have since built a multinational food company operating across 11 sites in the UK and Ireland. Within seven years of buying their first shop in Moygashel in County Tyrone, Northern Ireland, the Dobsons had built a slaughterhouse in nearby Dungannon and embarked on a series of acquisitions. Dunbia now has 11 sites, with operations in Scotland, Wales, Nottinghamshire and Lancashire, as well as the Republic of Ireland. It operates offices in Paris and The Hague in Holland and employs 4,300 people.

"We believe our staff are among the best and most loyal in the business and have contributed to our success," says co-founder and Group Chief Executive Jim Dobson. "Ultimately, we're just small farmers but we found our niche. In four decades we've gone from a two-man operation to having a professional board." The chairman of Dunbia is former cabinet minister Lord Mawhinney, and the company is enjoying strong growth. In 2015, pre-tax profits rose by 40 per cent to £6.6 million while turnover rose from £764 million to £827 million. Dobson puts this success down to recent investments in processing plants coming to fruition.

Dunbia is now the second largest processor of red meat in the UK, processing beef, lamb and pigs. It serves retail, commercial and manufacturing sectors and supplies some of Europe's leading retailers and food-service providers. It exports to 36 countries worldwide, selling a wide portfolio of meat products, and has picked up 30 industry awards in the last four years. In 2011, Jim was awarded an OBE by The Princess Royal at Buckingham Palace; last year he was named UK Director of the Year by the Institute of Directors. In the same year Jack Dobson, Dunbia's Group Executive Director, won EY Industry Entrepreneur of the Year.

The company also works with charities in which the Royal Family is involved. The North Highland Initiative addresses the challenges facing rural communities in Scotland, while the Cambrian Mountain Lamb Initiative promotes rural enterprise in mid-Wales. Both are supported by The Prince of Wales. Dunbia also provides extensive support to Caring for Life in Leeds, a charity – whose patron is The Countess of Wessex – that helps vulnerable people gain a sense of achievement through farming and catering.

Celebrating Dunbia's 40th anniversary, Jim Dobson puts the company's success down to its long-term relationships with customers and suppliers. "The structure of the rural areas in which we work is very much family-owned farms and we relate to them," he says. "Farmers are our supply base – we work closely with them to support the rural structure of the UK and Ireland."

With over 100 new products a year and 30 industry-led agri-research projects, the company is constantly innovating to stay ahead of its rivals. "Our industry is constantly presenting new challenges," says Jim, "Our strategy is to remain focused on our suppliers, customers and staff and work in partnership with them to drive our business and our industry forward."

Staying power

King Power

As the name suggests, King Power is a company with a proud tradition of supporting royalty. In 2004, the Thai travel retailer, which has shops in major international airports throughout Thailand as well as several downtown complexes, set up the King Power Foundation to support charities and celebrate auspicious occasions like the Thai King's birthday or the 60th anniversary of his accession to the throne. In 2009, King Power received its greatest honour when King Bhumibol Adulyadej bestowed his emblem of the state, the Royal Garuda, upon the company. Much like the UK's Royal Warrant, the Royal Garuda is generally only granted to an entrepreneur who conducts business with honesty and integrity. The royal seal of approval is now prominently featured on the facade at every King Power shop.

King Power's relationship with royalty even extends to the UK. In 2015, a King Power team took part in a competition at the Guards Polo Club in Windsor, winning the Cartier Queen's Cup. Her Majesty The Queen presented the trophy to Vichai Srivaddhanaprabha, Chairman of King Power Group.

Srivaddhanaprabha founded King Power in 1989 in Bangkok with a single-minded vision. "We aim to be the leading travel retailer providing the best travel-related businesses and services worldwide," says Srivaddhanaprabha. He saw an opportunity to use duty free commerce as a way to elevate Thailand in the eyes of the world through the country's distinctive culture and history.

The first step was to launch Thailand's first downtown duty free shop at Mahatun Plaza, Bangkok. In 1999, it began to manage the inflight duty free operation for Thai Airways. The big leap came in 2006, with the opening of a vast store: the King Power Duty Free Downtown Complex on Rangnam

Road in the centre of Bangkok. The complex not only contains an immense duty free mall but also a five-star hotel, state-of-the-art theatre, hotel and restaurants. The development demonstrates how King Power responded to the evolving needs of local and international customers.

Aside from offering visitors a large-scale shopping opportunity, King Power Downtown had restaurants and theatres and stimulated cultural appetites. The VR Museum opened to the public in July 2011 with the aim of promoting the culture and history of Buddhist art and culture, while giving visitors the chance to learn about the beauty and finesse of this unique style of religious art. Visitors can see rare pieces, such as the world's first Buddha image sculpted in the Gandhara artisan style, which was influenced by the ancient sculptures of Greco-Roman origin. Very rare acquisitions of amulets are also on show: the prominent Benjapakee, an acclaimed collection of five major Buddhist icons, is one of the museum's most prestigious collections.

The success of King Power Downtown was followed by similar enterprises. King Power Pattaya was launched as the first duty-free shopping venue in the eastern seaboard, with easy access to U-Tapao International Airport. With its close proximity to Suvarnabhumi Airport, King Power Srivaree Complex is built for ease of access and convenience in preparation for travellers' upcoming trips, as is King Power Phuket, the fourth of King Power's downtown complexes.

Over the years, King Power has received numerous national, global and industry awards in recognition of its performance. Its duty free

outlets have won Frontier Awards, for instance, while the independent international organisation Superbrands has given it seven awards.

The company employs more than 9,000 people and is driven by a strong sense of best practice. "Our reputation, our integrity and our professionalism are fundamental core values of the King Power group," says Srivaddhanaprabha. "We will always endeavour to provide the highest standards to the benefit of our customers, commercial partners and suppliers; and at the same time remain a company sincerely committed to our responsibilities to society as a whole."

King Power is heavily involved in social responsibility projects via the King Power Foundation, supporting breast cancer charities, children's hospitals, veterans groups and environmental projects. Srivaddhanaprabha established the foundation under the guiding ethos of boosting initiatives that support the underprivileged within Thai society. Its primary aim is to help disadvantaged children and youth on a path towards a better life, through education and health services, often via charities supported by the Thai royal family.

The sport of polo has also been a major passion for the company. Fuelled by his own personal passion, King Power Group's founding Chairman Vichai Srivaddhanaprabha established the Thailand Polo Association (TPA) under the official governance of Sports Authority Thailand (SAT). Through the TPA, Srivaddhanaprabha has brought Thai polo onto the world arena and raised it to international standards. In a proud milestone in the TPA's history, the sport of polo was included for the first time at 2007 SEA Games on Thai soil.

The King Power Group also supports the King Power polo team. Vichai's sons Apichet and Aiyawatt Srivaddhanaprabha have led the teams as active patrons. Recently, King Power had a proud moment in their first Gold Cup entry, almost making history by progressing into the final of the Gold Cup for the British Open championship. The association has also hosted major polo competitions, including Thailand Polo King's Cup, All Asia Cup and the Ambassador's Cup. The Thailand Polo Association is proud to have the King Power polo team as emerging ambassadors for the sport internationally, at the Chakravarty Cup, the Queen's Cup and the British Open in the UK and at the Cartier Cup in Dubai.

In a further expansion into sport, King Power purchased Leicester City Football Club in 2010. "Football is a personal passion and reflects my deep interest in sport and the possibilities it offers for developing youth talent, particularly in Thailand," says Srivaddhanaprabha. Leicester City's incredible success in the 2015/16 Premier League season is, King Power hopes, a great omen for the parent company's own exciting future.

Fast track to success

Rail Delivery Group

For all the challenges faced by the UK's rail network, today's railway is an amazing success story. Decades of decline have been reversed: passenger numbers have doubled in the past 20 years, with the annual number of train journeys growing from 801 million in 1996/97 to 1.6 billion in 2014/15. Today the railway transports 2.5 million people into the UK's largest towns and cities every day.

Passenger rail travel is now growing faster in Britain than in Germany, France or the Netherlands, and with the freight sector enjoying 70 per cent volume growth since the mid-1990s, the UK has one of the most successful railways in Europe. "That success reflects the fact that people want to use the railway," says Paul Plummer, Chief Executive of the Rail Delivery Group (RDG).

Rail plays an ever crucial role in Britain, with long-term growth in passengers and freight. The purpose of the RDG is to enable Network Rail and train- and freight-operating companies to succeed by delivering better services for their customers. Alongside it sits the Rail Supply Group which aims to make the UK a global leader in the supply of innovative railway technology.

The railway network has been transformed since the mid-1990s, thanks to the introduction of market forces and competition, and an industry structure that brings together private-sector innovation and government policy focused on long-term investment. Between 1979 and 1997, passenger numbers grew by an annual average of just 0.42 per cent. Since then, journeys have increased by around 4 per cent a year. "As people get better services," says Plummer, "it becomes a virtuous circle of further improvements and greater demand. But this also provides challenges, and nobody in the railway is in any doubt about the need for further modernisation and improvement."

The railway industry is also an important contributor to economic wealth and job creation. The railway and its supply chain employs around 216,000 people and contributes as much as £10.1 billion to the economy per year. On top of that are the indirect benefits, such as an £11.3 billion gain from improved productivity, a reduction of 7.7 million tonnes of harmful CO_2 gases thanks to lower road use and £12.9 billion of travel time savings per year. As the British economy has grown, rail has been the fastest growth of any mode of transport in two decades.

The immediate challenge that the railway industry faces is to cope with the impact of this phenomenal success. Passenger numbers could double again over the next 30 years as the UK urban population grows. "That is quite mind-blowing in terms of the consequences and the need for further investment," says Plummer.

There are almost 30 per cent more daily train services than there were 20 years ago on a network that has hardly increased over that period. As a result, there is more overcrowding, delays and disruptions – something that regular commuters will be familiar with. Britain's network is the second most congested railway in Europe. While the industry has succeeded in reducing the causes of disruption, the impact of each individual disruption is increasing because of the sheer number of people using the railway. In order to ease the bottlenecks and put the railway on track for further expansion amid growing demand, the members of the RDG have embarked on a major investment and modernisation programme.

Independent analysis might show that Britain's railway performs more efficiently than many of its counterparts on a number of measures, but Plummer says the industry is not complacent. "The railway is very focused on modernising and improving the whole customer experience," says Plummer. "That is about improving reliability, providing better passenger information, and modernising the way in which we communicate with passengers so they can use the railways in the easiest possible way."

Network Rail is investing £40 billion in its Railway Upgrade Plan, one of the biggest in rail's history, to improve reliability and increase capacity. This has already seen improvements to King's Cross, Reading and Birmingham New Street stations and the opening of the Borders Railway between Edinburgh, Galashiels and Tweedbank – the longest stretch of domestic railway to be built in the UK for 100 years.

The next phases will include the electrification and new trains for the Great Western routes and the High Speed Two (HS2) project linking London, Birmingham, the East Midlands, Manchester, Leeds

and Sheffield. The train operating companies will bring 3,700 more carriages into service over the next two to three years as part of an investment worth almost £10 billion, and providing greater capacity and more comfort for passengers.

The railway has experienced highs and lows over the 90 years of Her Majesty The Queen's life and The Queen has played a significant role at key moments in its history, both before and after her Coronation. Two years before ascending to the throne, the then Princess Elizabeth carried out one of her first official railway duties when she named a new steam engine after herself on a visit to the train works at Swindon, Wiltshire.

More recently, in February 2016, The Queen attended the ceremony held to unveil the renaming of Crossrail as the Elizabeth Line effective from December 2018. She has officially appeared at many significant developments of the network including the Borders Railway, the unveiling of the rebuilt Reading station in July 2014, and the re-opening of St Pancras International and the High Speed 1 service in November 2007. The Queen and other members of the Royal Family have also made frequent use of the Royal Train, which is maintained by a member of the RDG.

As the industry looks ahead to the 200th anniversary of the first regular passenger service in the world in 1830, the outlook is for further improvements, investment and modernisation led by the HS2 project. Plummer says that while HS2 is a critical project in terms of expanding and improving the railway, the focus is on the network as a whole. "The outlook is for continued growth and improvements in customer service," he says, "so we can provide better connections between cities across the country."

Winning dinners

Harrison Catering Services

In January 2004, Her Majesty The Queen and The Duke of Edinburgh sat down to lunch at the opening of the £64 million University of Oxford Chemistry Research Laboratory and were served with the same food as that enjoyed by hundreds of thousands of British schoolchildren all over the country every weekday. This meal was supplied by Harrison Catering Services, an independent family firm that provides daily meals to hundreds of schools and businesses, providing a strong emphasis on creative, home-cooked foods and nutrition for children.

"When we started in 1994 our sector was increasingly looking at reducing labour costs and moving towards convenience foods and snacks," says Chairman Geoffrey Harrison, who had a background in contract catering. "The economics of the business was people trying to save space and it was all centred around doing something quick and easy. I believed there were still many people who wanted a nice lunch with a knife and fork, eating great food with good ingredients. It was going against the flow, but we built a business on just that. The tenet on which we formed the company is still true now."

From the beginning, Harrison recruited a nutritionist and was guided by the simple notion that children aren't much different from adults. "There is nothing wrong with a burger as long as you don't eat it every day," he says. "It's about having that varied diet. We believe that the way to stop children eating burger and chips every day is to make the alternatives better. They want the same as grown-ups – good service, decent food, and they want to be served with a smile without queueing for long. It's incredibly rewarding when you see so many children enjoying the food."

Harrison founded the company 22 years ago. Two years ago, he handed over the day-to-day running to his children, Claire Aylward and Gareth Harrison. "Gareth is responsible for operational, craft and purchasing," explains Aylward, "while I'm responsible for sales and marketing, HR and nutrition." Here, Harrison intervenes. "They are in charge … most of the time," he says, with a smile. "However, serious decisions are collective. We spent a long time on succession planning. One of our advantages was that Claire and Gareth had worked here from the start and gone up the ladder. It wasn't about parachuting people in from outside. They knew everybody and had earned respect as they worked their way up. That's the great thing about a family business. We knew they were right for the job."

Aylward believes the company derives considerable benefits from being a family firm. "People feel like they are part of the Harrison family," she says, "not just a payroll number in a large organisation. We take an interest in what they are doing. We train extensively to get the best out of them and we make sure they are happy in their work. Our staff turnover is half the industry average. That's good for them, for our clients and customers and for us. It's part of what makes us stronger and different."

It certainly seems as if staff relish the opportunity they get from working with Harrison Catering Services. The management team makes regular site visits, "not to catch people out," explains Harrison, "but because we are interested in what they are doing".

One recent visit took them to a school in Ealing, West London where a chef, Naseema Rasheed, won School Chef of the Year. "Her authentic dishes are being circulated to primary schools throughout the country," says Harrison. "One chef can reach so many people. Her name and school will be on the bottom of the featured menu. She came to us six years ago and was told she could work in a supermarket or be a dinner lady – she now has a degree in hospitality and controls more than 20 staff while producing 890 meals a day. She's running a £386,000 turnover business." Rasheed's food is drawn from her Indian heritage, including recipes that have been in the family for years. Again, this is something that the company encourages. "It's really important that we reflect the demographics of the school," says Aylward, "and produce something that is authentic."

In a similar vein, the company wishes to stimulate and encourage young people's enjoyment of food and nutrition. "Feeding children in a school environment gives us the chance to educate them," says Aylward. "We can introduce them to flavours they might not otherwise try." The company works with the Royal Academy of Culinary Arts in the Chefs Adopt a School programme, which sees professional chefs spend time with children, talking to them about flavours and nutrition.

Harrison's biggest commitment in this area is the charity founded by Geoffrey himself, the Geoffrey Harrison Foundation. "I firmly believe that if you give everybody a fair start, what they do subsequently is down to them," says Harrison. "We fund the Junior Chef Programme at two London universities, a Saturday-morning course for 15-year olds-running for ten weeks that culminates in them cooking a meal for their parents and guardians." When Harrison attended a meal produced at the end of the course for the first time he was astonished to be served a three-course French meal. "I wasn't sure what they could achieve in such a short time. It was excellent and 75 per cent of them will go on to a full-time course in the industry. It's a great life skill and very heartening. Head teachers call the college asking how they get these kids to come along every Saturday for two months when they can't get them to be engaged at school."

Like so much to do with the company, this experience is hugely rewarding. "The business of feeding young people is so stimulating," says Harrison. "Children want the same overall eating experience as adults. They want to go into an environment where the staff are looking after them and it's much easier to get the catering staff to smile if they are serving something they want to be associated with. If you are serving great food, the staff want to be part of that and the kids respond to it."

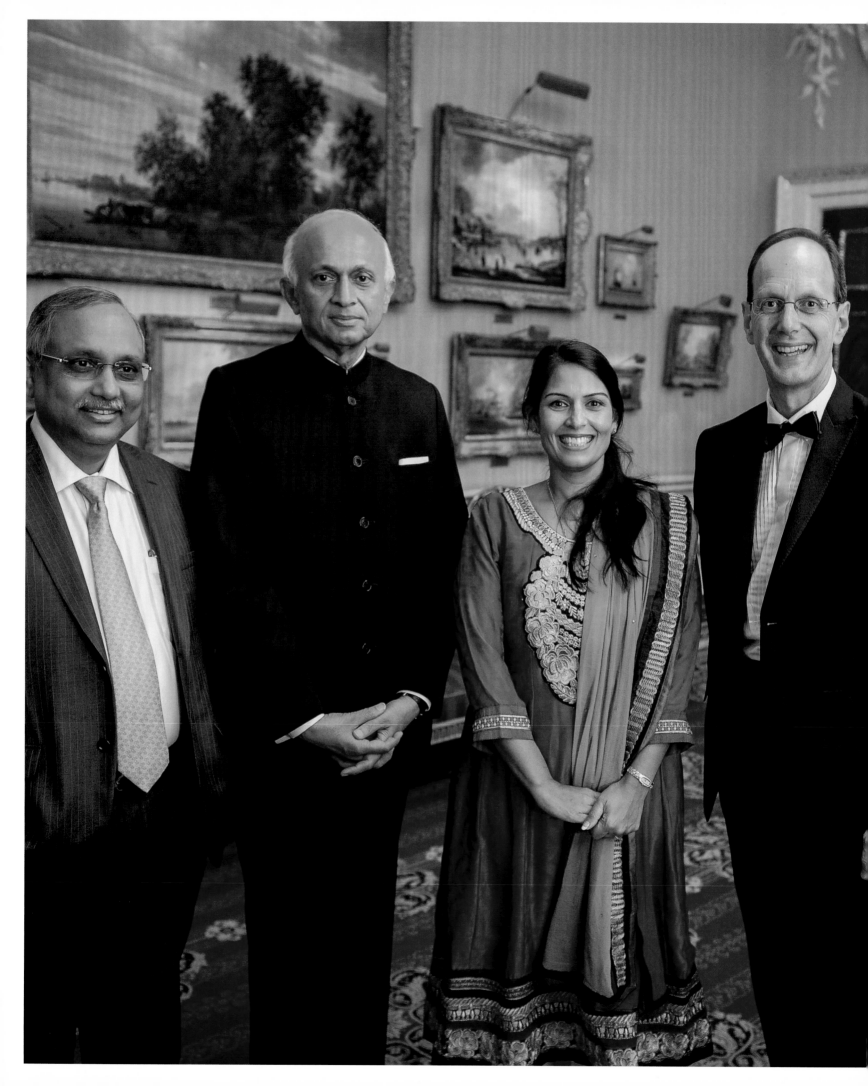

Ties that bind

Confederation of Indian Industry

The history of the Confederation of Indian Industry (CII) is the story of the transformation of a small association, representing a segment of industry, to the premier business association of modern India. The journey began in 1895 when five engineering firms banded together to seek business opportunities. More than 120 years on, the association has nearly 8,000 members and more than 200,000 indirect members, and a rather comprehensive focus for India's development and global engagement.

For the CII's UK chapter, the key task is to promote ties between Indian industry and the UK. As the UK's third largest investor, India plays a vital role in the economy. More than 800 Indian companies operate in the UK, with Britain's fastest-growing Indian companies generating around £22 billion of turnover.

"Our goal can be defined as strengthening India–UK business relations, bilaterally," says Chandrajit Banerjee, Director General of the CII. "It's about representing Indian industry and encouraging them to consider expansion opportunities in the UK, as well as helping UK companies explore emerging opportunities in India." The organisation also works with large as well as small and medium-scale businesses, with a diverse sector-spread across technology, engineering, manufacturing, pharmaceuticals, financial services, tourism and hospitality.

Rolta UK Limited – small business, big plans
One of these firms, Rolta, has its headquarters in Mumbai but its UK base in Reading – the British equivalent of Silicon Valley. It has ranked among

Forbes Global's Best 200 Under a Billion four times in six years, with a focus on innovation leading to its impressive growth. Providing IT solutions for a variety of sectors – private and public – including security, utilities, oil and gas, manufacturing, retail, healthcare and financial services, the company helps others achieve operational excellence with customisable software products. Those investing in the latest advances are reaping the rewards of knowledge, says Ravi Pandey, President of Rolta in Europe, the Middle East and Africa, as well as Asia and the Pacific. The company is at the forefront of moves to capture smart data across an entire operational chain.

"In the past," says Pandey, "machines were dumb and so could not produce smart data. This changed but the technology industry was slow to catch up. Operations Technology (OT) lagged behind Information Technology (IT); but at Rolta we set out to champion the OT data vital for any increase in operational efficiency. Adopters now have not only 360-degree data, but also the data analytics capability to use it to make insightful, operational improvements that save money and increase efficiency – with the certainty that the underlying data is 100 per cent automated and so 100 per cent accurate."

Cadila Pharmaceuticals – a commitment to innovation
Innovation is also at the heart of another CII member, Cadila Pharmaceuticals. Established in 1951, it's one of the largest privately held pharmaceutical companies in India, which develops, manufactures, sells and distributes pharmaceutical products across more than 45 therapeutic areas.

Dr Rajiv Modi is Chairman and Managing Director of Cadila Pharmaceuticals, and also serves as the Chairman of the CII's National Committee on Pharma. "We strive towards fulfilling our vision of providing high-quality medicines at affordable prices to people around the world through innovation and research," he says. Cadila Pharmaceuticals' association with CII has been enriching, helping the company with awareness and access to global industry best practices and many national and international programmes.

Based in Ahmedabad, the company has a presence in over 90 countries. In the UK, it partners with Helperby, a spin-off of St George's University Hospital in London, on a programme to help against antimicrobial resistance. It also works with the Wellcome Trust to conduct global trials on treatments for cardiovascular diseases and an affordable surfactant to help reduce the number of deaths of pre-term babies. Cadila Pharmaceuticals is also a pioneer of Corporate Social Responsibility in India. Its various projects include the Kaka-Ba Hospital in the remote village of Hansot in Gujarat, which is an exemplary rural healthcare delivery model.

Air India – bringing India and the UK closer
Perhaps one of the most well-known companies with a footprint in both countries is Air India, whose own origins stretch back to 1932 when it started as Tata Sons, with just two aircraft carrying mail across India. Renamed Air India in 1946, the Star Alliance member's fleet now numbers over 100, with its own engineering facilities and ground-handling departments.

"Our link with the UK goes back 68 years," says Tara Naidu, Air India Regional Manager for the UK and Europe. "We started flying to Heathrow in June 1948 – one of the first airlines to do so, and we have been members of the CII for some time. Who better than the national carrier of India to help foster business links between India and the UK by carrying the passengers?"

With six new Dreamliner planes on order and a thriving business-class service, expansion is on the cards for Air India. Among its new European routes, a direct flight from Heathrow to Ahmedabad is in the pipeline, and the company has longer-term plans to fly to more destinations in the Americas. And with a 1.5 million-strong Indian diaspora in Britain ready to take advantage of increased flights, the long-lasting bond between the countries is as strong as ever.

These ties are further bolstered by the numerous royal trips to India down the years. The Duke and Duchess of Cambridge are the latest royal visitors to India, following in the footsteps of The Prince of Wales, most recently in 2013, and Her Majesty The Queen's own three visits between 1961 and 1997.

Such royal connections have even helped inspire India's future entrepreneurs. The not-for-profit Bharatiya Yuva Shakti Trust, launched by The Prince of Wales in 1992, is based on the principles of the Prince's Trust. With support from the CII, the organisation now operates in six regions across India and aims to transform job seekers into the job creators of the future. With ever-stronger links between India and the UK, perhaps these success stories of tomorrow will one day make their own mark on both countries.

Defence of the realm

Analox Military Systems

"Making safety affordable." In three words, Vicky Pigg, the Sales and Marketing Director, explains the guiding principles behind Analox Group. "We're the modern version of the canary in the coal mine," she explains.

Analox Military Systems (AMS), a branch of Analox Group, specialises in the design and manufacture of atmosphere-monitoring equipment such as submarines that sustain or support life in hostile environments. This dual interest in the military and international trade has brought them into direct contact with the Royal Family, including The Duchess of Cornwall at the commissioning ceremony of the submarine HMS *Astute*, and The Duke of York, when he was UK trade envoy.

AMS was set up as a dedicated division five years ago. "The needs of our military customers were different to our commercial customers in terms of product life cycles and the timescales involved," explains Pigg. "The expected life of a submarine is from 25–35 years, then add the submarine design timeframe to it – you could be looking to specify and provide equipment now which won't enter into service until 2020 and then needs to be supported for 25 years – that equipment will outlive many of our careers so it has to be designed to be supported throughout its life."

AMS's achievements include designing the only submarine escape analyser to meet NATO requirements, now in use with more than 20 nations. It focuses on core technology and innovates to either break into the market or develop it.

Because of the importance of what it does – products that mean life or death for users – AMS works closely with clients. "We talk to them about the problems that need to be overcome and then supply the product they require," says Pigg. "You need to understand the customer's application and then find the technology that will fit, so you need to build a partnership. We also try to use local and UK companies within our supply chain where possible." Recent client feedback reflects the success of this approach, with one customer describing AMS as "an illustration of high-end, quality British engineering".

Pigg emphasises the engagement of AMS's own staff in this process. "People take real pride in what they do and will work very hard to make sure the clients get what they need," she says. "When you are making this sort of equipment, you absolutely want to get it right and everybody who works here feels that way." Employees are encouraged to play a positive role in wider society, with staff given one day each year to raise money for a charity of their choice. Additionally, AMS supports two charities – Help For Heroes and the Great North Air Ambulance Service.

All this has ensured that AMS continues to grow, adding 20 per cent more staff in the last year. "We're incredibly proud to be designing and manufacturing life support equipment from our base in Yorkshire and exporting around the world," says Pigg. "We want to be the first choice for submarine atmosphere monitoring equipment. Ultimately we're hoping to do our bit to keep UK manufacturing alive and well."

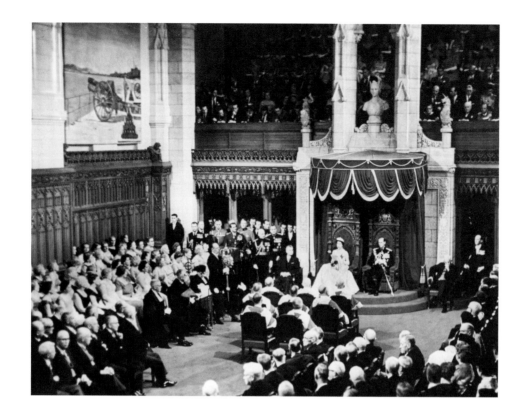

A common bond

The Commonwealth, past and present

It just so happens that the central philosophy of the Commonwealth as we know it dates back to the year of Her Majesty The Queen's birth. It was in London on the 22 November 1926 that King George V hosted the seventh Imperial Conference, where government heads of the UK and seven dominions of the British Empire – Australia, New Zealand, the Irish Free State, India, South Africa, Canada and Newfoundland (then a separate dominion) – signed up to the Balfour Declaration. Chaired by Prime Minister Stanley Baldwin and officiated by Lord Balfour, the declaration established that all of the assembled dominions were "autonomous communities within the British Empire", equal in status and not subordinate to the UK.

It was the first step in the transition from Empire to Commonwealth. The next key landmark came with the London Declaration on 28 April 1949, which was called to address how a newly independent India could remain within the Commonwealth while adopting a republican constitution. The declaration stated that King George VI remained, not as

imperial emperor, but as "the symbol of the free association of the independent member nations and, as such, Head of the Commonwealth".

This was a role that The Queen was to make her own when she ascended to the throne three years later. She leads a voluntary association of 54 independent countries that can have very different constitutions while retaining Her Majesty as Head of the Commonwealth. For instance, 15 Commonwealth realms – including the UK, Canada, Australia, New Zealand and many Caribbean countries – recognise The Queen as Head of State, while others, including India, Pakistan and most African Commonwealth countries, are republics. Other Commonwealth realms have an indigenous monarchy (including Lesotho, Malaysia, Swaziland or Tonga), a sultanate (Brunei) or – in the case of Samoa – an elected Paramount Chieftaincy.

In a speech given during the 1977 Silver Jubilee celebrations, The Queen spoke of how – for nearly a third of the world's population – the role of the monarch has changed throughout her lifetime. "I have seen, from a unique position

of advantage, the last great phase of the transformation of the Empire into Commonwealth and the transformation of the Crown from an emblem of dominion into a symbol of free and voluntary association," she said. "In all history this has no precedent."

Before ascending to the throne, The Queen had already taken part in several tours to Commonwealth countries, including Canada and South Africa. Since 1952, she has visited almost every country in the Commonwealth and made many repeat trips. On her first tour of Commonwealth countries in 1953–54, The Queen covered 43,618 miles, and was received by immense crowds. In Australia, for example, nearly three quarters of the population came out to see her. In 1957, The Queen opened the 23rd Canadian Parliament, becoming the first monarch of Canada to open a parliamentary session. Four years later, she toured Cyprus, India, Pakistan, Nepal and Iran; on a visit to Ghana that year, she dismissed fears for her safety, even though her host, President Kwame Nkrumah, who had replaced her as head of state, was a target for assassins.

'The Queen has been absolutely determined all through," wrote Prime Minister Harold Macmillan at the time. "She is impatient of the attitude towards her to treat her as a film star. She has indeed 'the heart and stomach of a king'. She loves her duty and means to be a Queen."

The Commonwealth includes some of the world's wealthiest nations (such as the UK, Australia, Canada, and New Zealand), some of the world's poorest (Malawi, Rwanda, Sierra Leone) and many of the emerging powerhouse economies that are transforming the 21st century's global landscape, including India, South Africa and Nigeria. There are different cultural mores, and countries where the predominant religions might be Christianity, Islam, Hinduism or Buddhism. All, however, try to fulfil

OPPOSITE: COMMONWEALTH COUNTRIES ARE REPRESENTED AT THE THAMES DIAMOND JUBILEE PAGEANT IN 2012. RIGHT: THE QUEEN ON TOUR IN SOUTH AFRICA IN 1995 – THE YEAR AFTER THE COUNTRY REJOINED THE COMMONWEALTH

certain codes regarding public service, transparency, human rights, democratic process, an independent judiciary, freedom of expression, equality of opportunity and good governance.

As a result, membership of the Commonwealth has become seen as a force for good in the promotion of democracy and development, and in the pursuit of equality and opposition to racism. One of the first priorities of a post-apartheid South Africa, for instance, was to rejoin the Commonwealth, a membership that was revoked in 1961 as it solidified its racist segregation policies. Even countries that were not part of the British Empire have recently been admitted: Mozambique, a former Portuguese possession, joined in 1995, while Rwanda, a colony of Germany and then Belgium, joined in 2009, rightly believing that membership would assist it in its desire to re-establish democracy after a devastating civil war. The Palestinian Authority has even expressed an interest in joining the Commonwealth.

The Queen keeps in touch with Commonwealth developments through regular contact with the Commonwealth Secretary General and his secretariat, and has regular meetings with heads of government from Commonwealth countries. Each year, she attends the Commonwealth Day celebrations

in London and an interdenominational service held in Westminster Abbey, followed by a reception hosted by the Commonwealth Secretary General. She also hosts the Commonwealth Heads of Government Meeting every two years.

The Commonwealth Games, which takes place every four years, is seen as the perfect platform for promoting relations between the Commonwealth countries and celebrating their shared sporting and cultural heritage. The Queen was there to open the last games in Glasgow in 2014.

On her Commonwealth visits, The Queen has always made sure she sees and experiences a wide range of communities, cultures and regions, and also supports the work of charities and public organisations in each country.

"I believe we can be pleased with how far the Commonwealth has come in its 60 years and yet how true it has remained to its origins," said The Queen at the 2009 Commonwealth Heads of Government Meeting. "But this does not mean we should become complacent and rest on past successes. The Commonwealth must show that it is relevant to, and supportive of, our young people who need to be convinced that the Commonwealth can help them to realise their ambitions."

In mint condition

The Royal Canadian Mint

At the turn of the last century, new coins destined for a bank on Canada's West Coast would have had to travel nearly 5,000 miles from the UK before finally reaching businesses and consumers in the rapidly growing Dominion of Canada. That epic voyage was dramatically shortened when Britain's Royal Mint opened a branch facility in Ottawa on 2 January, 1908. Since then, every new coin jingling in a Canadian pocket or purse has been the work of the Royal Canadian Mint.

Canadian-owned and operated since 1931, today's Royal Canadian Mint strikes more than 20 million circulation coins a day from its high-speed Winnipeg facility, while the original Ottawa operation continues to stand out for industry-leading collector coins, medals and precious metal investment products.

The Royal Canadian Mint is a supplier of choice to foreign central banks and other mints, which value the development and application of cutting-edge technology underpinning its expertise. It also produces the world's most popular and secure one-ounce gold bullion coin, the 99.99 per cent pure Gold Maple Leaf. Several factors have made the mint successful in the international bullion market, including beautiful, secure and high quality products, as well as strong relationships with its global customer base.

"While the art of minting calls for preserving time-honoured techniques and traditions, we have also become progressive, innovative leaders of our industry by exploring the potential of science and technology," says Royal Canadian Mint President and CEO Sandra Hanington. "The beauty of our coins is key to our ongoing success, which we achieve through innovation and quality, to create design and technical features that no one else has."

In a year that celebrates a milestone birthday for Her Majesty The Queen, the mint is a proud partner in the celebrations, through collector, circulation and bullion coinage all bearing The Queen's effigy. Since 1953, the mint has struck more than 50 billion circulation coins featuring four evolutions of her effigy.

The mint has countless ways to express Canadian pride through the hundreds of exceptional, handcrafted collector coins it produces every year, to the delight of Canadians and collectors world-wide. Many of these coins celebrate the strong connection between Canadians and their Royal Family. Events such as The Queen's Diamond Jubilee, the wedding of The Duke and Duchess of Cambridge and even the birth of Prince George have all found a place on Canadian coins, thus forming a unique and precious record of Canada's royal history. A new chapter begins in 2016 as the mint releases gold and silver commemorative coins for The Queen's 90th birthday that will feature some of its renowned technology and innovation.

"The mint has the ability to tell the many stories of Canada through our coins and we are very aware that the element linking each story is the

CANADA

50 DOLLARS

300 DOLLARS 1952 - 2012

CANADA

LM

presence of the monarch's effigy on our coins," says Hanington. "The fact that The Queen is on every circulation, collector and bullion coin that we produce brings each one special meaning."

The Royal Canadian Mint's ability to marry artistry with innovation continues to take the celebration of Canada's royal heritage to a higher level. Working with talented Canadian artists, from its own engraving staff to coin designers from all over the country, the mint makes full use of 3D computer-assisted design technology to create spectacular results. While modern engraving may have set aside a few artisanal processes, the hand of the engraver still controls the digital sculpting tools that render an artist's drawing with incredible realism.

Technology allows the mint to test new ways to turn artistic vision into reality. In 2012, a pure gold coin was embellished with an inset Canadian diamond, visible on both sides of the coin, to mark The Queen's Diamond Jubilee. Such innovations are highly prized, offering a new way to appreciate a shared history.

Many other Royal Canadian Mint advances have given rise to uniquely Canadian keepsakes. Enamelling and holograms have come into their own on the mint's collector coins, including a new "achromatic" hologram, which creates the powerful illusion of a three-dimensional engraving on a totally flat surface. Hand-painted enamels are also meticulously applied by mint specialists after coins have been struck individually.

Colouring innovations have even extended to Canadian circulation coins. The 2004 Remembrance-themed poppy 25-cent coin was the world's first coloured circulation coin. That first technological advance spawned many successors and, in 2015, paved the way for a new, high-resolution pad-printing colouring technology, which made its debut in Canada on a 25-cent coin celebrating the 50th anniversary of the modern Canadian flag.

The Royal Canadian Mint strives to connect emotionally with the people of its country by producing coins that make them proud to be Canadian. In 2015, it held a unique public design contest to redesign all of Canada's circulation coins to celebrate the 150th anniversary of Canadian Confederation in 2017. More than 10,000 designs were submitted from coast to coast to coast and the final designs were chosen by a public vote. The coins will be unveiled and released in early 2017 and, as always, the royal effigy will be engraved on the obverse.

The Royal Canadian Mint has carved out an important way to celebrate Canada's history, culture and values – all while cherishing its unique connection to The Queen and Canada's Royal Family.

Cultivating excellence

Lincoln University

When The Duke of Edinburgh arrived at Lincoln's campus in New Zealand in 1973 it was via unorthodox means – sitting on a hay bale on a trailer pulled by a tractor, having been "hijacked" by agricultural students eager to demonstrate that, at Lincoln, things are done differently.

The institution was founded in 1878 as a school of agriculture, with early studies including pioneering work in soil chemistry, superphosphate use and manures. Lincoln University remains a specialist centre of land-based learning but it has come a long way from the "dirt, odour and sweat" that characterised its early years.

Lincoln University – named after the Canterbury township of Lincoln in which the original campus is based – has 350 academic and research staff and some 3,500 students. Academic disciplines cover the core agricultural sciences as well as broader land-based subjects including agribusiness, agritechnology, bioprotection, conservation, tourism, environmental management, landscape architecture and property. The university is the third oldest in New Zealand and has unique importance given the country's two largest export earners, agriculture and tourism.

"When Lincoln was founded, the driver was to educate young men in the colonial way of farming," says Ian Collins, Lincoln University's heritage writer. "Today there is an equal mix of men and women, and the land-based disciplines are approached in a global context."

The university has two campuses in New Zealand's South Island, and operates several farms – from deer to dairy to high country sheep. These are used for research, student learning and as demonstration farms to pass knowledge on to the farming sector.

Students at Lincoln learn not just in their own study area, but also in the wider context of the global population and environment. The university's programmes fit within one or more of the institution's missions, to help: Feed the World, Protect the Future, and Live Well. Research themes also address these global challenges, providing answers to such issues as increasing food production, mitigating environmental impacts, getting food from producers to markets, climate change, and international rural development. The global significance of Lincoln's work has resulted in the institution being ranked 13th in the world in the small universities category, and in the top 3 per cent overall.

As befits a country that produces great sportsmen and women, Lincoln offers academic scholarships with corresponding sports programmes to students showing promise in both areas. All Blacks captain Richie McCaw attended Lincoln on a sports scholarship. Other prominent alumni include Sir Don McKinnon, a former New Zealand Deputy Prime Minister and Commonwealth Secretary-General. An alumnus with a royal link is Fred Wilkinson, a floral designer to Windsor Castle and Buckingham Palace.

Lincoln's influence is felt throughout the world, with alumni working as diversely as managing conservation land in Nepal, conducting academic research in China, wine-making in the USA, or cattle breeding in Tasmania. People who have learnt how to make a living in land-based sectors, while protecting that land for future generations.

"We are to New Zealand what New Zealand is to the world," says Collins. "Known for our excellence in agriculture, tourism and related areas, small but proud, informal and innovative, punching above our weight."

First among equals

Brisbane Girls Grammar School

There have been many milestone moments in the long history of Brisbane Girls Grammar School. Among them is the letter of thanks sent by Her Majesty The Queen in 1954 after receiving a declaration of the school's loyalty to the throne. In 1970, 30 school prefects met Her Majesty in Brisbane, and seven years later The Queen and The Duke of Edinburgh were greeted by the school's girls as part of their Silver Jubilee Commonwealth tour. More recently, head girls from the Girls Grammar met The Duchess of Cambridge on the 2014 royal visit to Australia.

Perhaps the most significant year in the records, not just for the school but for girls' education in Queensland as a whole, is 1875, when Sir Charles Lilley paved the way for a pioneering school that would offer girls the same educational opportunities as their brothers. "The courage and vision of its founders in establishing a school for girls, at a time when girls' education was not widely valued, thrives to this day," says Brisbane Girls Grammar School Principal, Jacinda Euler. "The school's students, staff and leadership continue to lead with passion, creativity and excellence."

Today, its recognition as one of Australia's leading girls' schools is built on the precedent set by its enlightened founder, whose belief in the importance of making education accessible to young women was quickly validated by the performance of its students. From 1878 until 1909, students from Brisbane Girls Grammar School won the Fairfax Prize for academic proficiency on 19 occasions, setting an early precedent for the strong academic performance that characterises the school today.

"Brisbane Girls Grammar consistently achieves outstanding academic results," says Euler. "The school equips girls with the ability to think and to question, and instils in them a deep love of learning. Our girls go on to some of the finest universities in the world and pursue an extraordinarily diverse range of career paths. As a reflection of our life-wide approach to learning, a small number of students are choosing to defer their studies and take part in organised exchanges, employment opportunities or volunteer work around the world."

Service, primarily in the form of contribution to community-based activities and awareness raising, is an essential element of the learning experience at Brisbane Girls Grammar School, where students are given the opportunity to develop and participate in projects designed to make a difference in the lives of others. This is part of a richly varied co-curricular programme that includes more than 120 activities, from traditional sport and music pursuits to more niche activities such as the Balance Programme, which develops mindfulness and self-management techniques to help girls navigate adolescence.

"Our teachers model intellectual passion, pedagogical expertise, curiosity and care and we maintain high expectations for our girls," says Euler. This stimulating and nurturing environment leaves students with a lasting affection for the school when they leave to forge successful futures. Its alumnae includes the first female director of the Australian National Gallery and the first woman to be appointed as president of an Australian appeal court. It continues the school's early status as a champion of gender equality – and the right of all women to receive an exceptional education.

Forging ahead

Ara Institute of Canterbury

When The Prince of Wales visited New Zealand's Canterbury region in November 2012, he found an area still coming to terms with the devastating earthquake that had struck it a year and nine months earlier. But he also encountered enterprising people eager to rebuild what they'd lost – a sense of purpose epitomised by the representatives of Ara Institute of Canterbury that he met during his visit.

Catering to around 25,000 students on campuses across Christchurch, Timaru, Ashburton and Oamaru, Ara Institute of Canterbury offers a broad range of innovative, industry-relevant bachelor degrees and vocational courses.

"Starting with foundation studies, our programmes include anything from business studies, ICT, engineering and architecture to midwifery, radiography, social work, sports sciences and highly regarded degrees in Japanese and Māori," says Kay Giles, Chief Executive of Ara Institute of Canterbury.

Although the institution only started offering degrees in 1995, it has been around for over a century, as its oldest forerunners – technical colleges based in Timaru and Christchurch – were founded in the early 1900s. They operated as separate institutes until 2016 when they merged to become Ara, a Canterbury-wide organisation.

As well as offering programmes and qualifications that meet both regional and international demands, the new institution includes nationally recognised centres of excellence in several different fields. They include the School of Food and Hospitality; the New Zealand Broadcasting School, with many graduates involved in New Zealand's radio and TV stations; and the School of Nursing, whose facility was opened by The Princess Royal in 1990.

"We also run a very successful trade school, which has the highest proportion of female students of any trade programme across New Zealand," says Giles. "Offering a vast range of courses, including a dedicated programme for the Māori community that is tailored to their needs, the school has played a vital role in rebuilding Christchurch after the earthquake. This shows that Ara Institute of Canterbury really focuses on servicing the needs of the local community, and as a result, we have a very high standing across the region."

The institution's efforts to integrate the Māori community are also very highly regarded, epitomised by the fact that, as well as learning about Ara's contribution to the rebuilding efforts, The Prince of Wales met students from the Māori trade programme, He Toki ki te Rika, during his 2012 visit to Christchurch.

"That was a fitting way of acknowledging that Ara Institute of Canterbury has, for over a century, played a vital role in bringing different communities together, as well as international students who have contributed to the local economy," says Giles. "Having recently rebranded and grown in size, we now want to take these efforts to the next level by building even stronger partnerships with different industries and providing even more training for rural communities. It's a very aspirational vision for the future, but we are building on 100 years of success."

Worldly wise

The University of Otago

In its 147-year history, the University of Otago, in Dunedin, New Zealand has been graced by visits from Her Majesty The Queen, The Duke of Edinburgh, The Prince of Wales, The Princess Royal and, most recently, by The Duchess of Cornwall. The institution's prominence is reflected in its international make-up. Around 70 per cent of its faculty members are either from overseas or have gained their higher degree abroad, and more than 80 per cent of its students come from outside the city, with many hailing from countries around the world. This leads to a vibrant and close-knit campus-style university where diversity can thrive.

Since its establishment in 1869, the University of Otago has remained loyal to the values of equity and academic freedom. It was the very first university to be established in this part of the British Empire, and was one of the first in the Empire to admit women to its classes. Today, the university is strategically committed to furthering the aspirations of Māori and its Pacific neighbours.

"The numbers of Māori and Pacific students at Otago continue to grow, and we have the highest completion rates in the country," says Professor Helen Nicholson, Otago's Deputy Vice-Chancellor (External Engagement). "For many years the university has put in place considerable resources to ensure their success and continues to do so."

Otago successfully balances the traditions of its history with modern scholarship. It is an academic leader in the humanities, sciences, health sciences and business, offering around 190 undergraduate and postgraduate programmes. More than 4,500 of the university's 20,000 students study at the postgraduate level, with a higher proportion of PhD students than any other university in the country. Students are taught by leaders in their fields, a fact recognised by New Zealand's prime minister, who has presented Otago with more Supreme Awards for teaching excellence than any other university.

Otago's research excellence is internationally recognised and underpins all academic activity. It has leadership roles in two new national Centres of Research Excellence, it has partnership roles in the country's National Science Challenges, and it hosts 14 multidisciplinary research centres, including two of the world's most highly regarded health and development longitudinal studies.

Otago's students make up 20,000 of Dunedin's 120,000 population and the university is a strong contributor to the city's economic, cultural and sporting life. The university's rugby club has produced more All Blacks than any other club in New Zealand, while its rowers win accolades at both national and international regattas. And Otago takes seriously its responsibilities to good citizenship. The newly established University Volunteer Centre already has relationships with more than 160 community organisations and has more than 1,000 student volunteers. It was the first New Zealand university to achieve Fair Trade status, it is part of the Green Star programme, and the principles of sustainability are embedded across all aspects of the university.

"We take a holistic approach to our students' educations," says Professor Nicholson. "While academic excellence is, of course, a priority, cultural, social and sporting experiences are all part of life at Otago. We know our students are going to work and communicate across the world, and we want to prepare them for that."

Fruits of the earth

Nature's Path

"Always leave the Earth better than you found it." This is the simple wisdom passed on from a father to son that has guided a life-long quest to bring delicious, healthy organic food to the world. Nature's Path began as a one-product operation based in the back room of a restaurant in Vancouver, Canada in 1985. It has since grown into an international organic food company, much-loved around the globe, selling more than 150 products including porridge, granola bars and the UK's number-one gluten-free and organic breakfast cereal.

Co-founder Arran Stephens was raised on a farm on pristine Vancouver Island, British Columbia, where his unorthodox father taught him pioneering farming methods. This was 1951 and his large berry farm featured a prominently posted sign saying: "No sprays or poisons used", instead preferring to employ radical composting methods using seaweed.

The family farm was using organic methods way ahead of its time. It instilled in Stephens a belief in the methods and philosophy of organic farming, and the value of acting like "good compost" – leaving a better, cleaner, environmentally sustainable world for the next generation.

In 1967, inspired by his extensive travels through India, a 23-year-old Stephens opened Canada's first vegetarian restaurant, the Golden Lotus, using his last $7 and a $1,500 loan. Stephens had no experience in business or cooking – his background was in art and poetry. At first it was an uphill struggle and he would often use quieter moments to practise meditation. But, after the restaurant received a glowing review in a local paper, the tables were packed practically every evening thereafter.

A year later Stephens returned to India where he met and married an educated young woman called Ratana (meaning "jewel" in Sanskrit). Together they returned to Vancouver, sold the restaurant to a co-operative formed by the employees, and opened Canada's first supermarket-sized organic food store. The focus was on fresh organic whole foods and was one of the first stores in the city to stock tofu, soy milk, whole grains, fresh organic produce and sprouted breads. Stephens began milling, baking and growing food to sell in the store that could not be obtained elsewhere. And so items such as granola, vegetarian pastries and energy bars started appearing on the shelves. Every year, for several years, sales doubled.

In 1981, they sold the supermarket and moved back into the hospitality industry when they opened another much larger vegetarian restaurant, this one called Woodlands. Here, Stephens started producing sprouted Manna Bread in the back room – and so began Nature's Path organic foods.

As Stephens branched out into developing a line of organic cereals, it wasn't long before Nature's Path had outgrown the back room at Woodlands, as well as several other larger venues. Stephens and his wife then gambled everything on a purpose-designed cereal factory that they built from scratch.

With passion, tenacity, good fortune and a talented team, Nature's Path grew from these humble beginnings to become the largest organic breakfast brand in North America, selling in 50 countries worldwide, and employing more than 600 people.

Of the 600 valued team members are included the Stephens's offspring, three of whom are involved in leadership roles in the family business. Nature's Path is highly respected as an employer, offering competitive pay, benefits, incentive compensation as well as leadership programmes. This has helped the company retain its edge as more and more companies move into the crowded organic and health food market.

As a family-run company, Nature's Path has the freedom to put its money where its heart is. Passionately committed to people and planet, as well as profit, it supports food banks, endangered species, community gardens and other social causes, demonstrating a spirit of generosity that has been ingrained in its culture from its very beginnings.

Investing in farmland and supporting scores of independent farmers on more than 100,000 organic acres, Nature's Path is also helping to keep millions of pounds of pesticides, chemical fertilisers and genetically modified organisms out of the environment and off our plates. In 2010, it helped establish the Sustainable Food Trade Association and became zero-waste certified, with a commitment to complete carbon neutrality by 2020. Nature's Path also owns more than 6,600 acres of farmland, which it farms organically, often in co-operation with family farmers. Stephens explains the philosophy underlining everything the company does. "We've always operated under the principle: Do the right thing and you'll be taken care of," he says. "Treat your people well and be customer-driven. Serve them well."

Today, Nature's Path remains proudly independent as a multi-generational family enterprise, championing causes that often marry both entrepreneurialism and activism. It posits that business must help lead the way towards environmental sustainability.

In the early 1990s, Nature's Path entered the UK market. Gurdeep Stephens, daughter of the company's founders, was living in London at the time and was invited to speak to some of the UK's largest food companies about Nature's Path mission. She expressed her hope that everyone would participate in the growing organic movement and invited them to compete with Nature's Path. She recalls receiving many puzzled looks at the time, but is now happy to see the world waking up to the goodness and profitability of organic production, which now has global sales in excess of $80 billion.

In keeping with the vision and ethos underlying Nature's Path, its founders make an impassioned plea. "Our every choice ultimately impacts upon Mother Earth," says Arran Stephens. "How we leave the Earth will be our collective legacy. When we make good choices, good things grow. So let us collaborate, and together let us leave the planet better than we found her."

The power to succeed

The Bishop Strachan School

When the Bishop Strachan School Chapel Choir set sail for England in May 1953 on a seven-week trip to be part of Her Majesty The Queen's Coronation celebrations, its members were simply confirming a tagline that the school lives by to this day. "Girls can do anything" is explored to its full at the Toronto school – Canada's oldest independent day and boarding school for girls – which celebrates its 150th anniversary in 2017.

Bishop Strachan's 900 pupils benefit from an innovative approach to education from the moment they arrive at junior kindergarten at the age of 4. The school is one of Canada's leaders in the Reggio-inspired teaching method, where children are encouraged to develop their interests and express themselves – an approach that is combined with the teaching of traditional core skills of literacy and maths to ensure the best start in life.

"The world needs more women with strong voices," says the Head, Deryn Lavell. "When I think of our vision and what we call 'The Signature of a BSS Girl', I see talented, strong, inspiring women. We teach our girls to be adaptable and curious, to understand and respect the world."

Through the school's state-of-the-art maths, science and arts facilities, pupils learn not only the skills necessary to empower them in the 21st century but also how to apply them. A recent initiative saw them work on a project to help redevelop Toronto's waterside in collaboration with architects and city planners. The students learnt about urban planning and architectural design, and created projects to offer up solutions to make Toronto a more sustainable city, presenting their findings to city councillors.

"We encourage our pupils to innovate, be creative and to develop their imaginations," says Lavell. "This sort of project-based learning, while ensuring academic rigour, also gives our pupils confidence and engages them with their environment. The results are often astounding."

The school, founded by the Rev. John Langtry, has Anglican roots but represents all beliefs. "The idea of our chapel is to provide the spiritual heart of the school," says Lavell. A third of the 80 boarders are from Canada, with the majority coming from Asia and from other parts of the world. "Toronto is an incredibly diverse city and we are an attractive school for that very same reason," says Lavell. "We also offer a generous bursary to encourage talented girls to apply."

Building a strong community is vital to the school's success, and parents get involved by fundraising and volunteering in the classrooms. It's important to Lavell that girls appreciate Bishop Strachan's heritage (the school is particularly proud to have been visited by The Duke and Duchess of York in 1901), but even more important that they are aware of today's strong female role models. "Her Majesty The Queen, for instance, is a trailblazer and an example of a strong leader," says Lavell. To support the girls as they grow, the school offers a mentoring programme in which alumnae provide guidance and advice that helps young pupils to reach their full potential.

Pupils graduate with the confidence to take on the world. "What makes us so special is our relevance to modern society," says Lavell. "The need for women who know the power of their own voice is greater than ever."

Great expectations

York House School

In 1932, in the grip of the Great Depression, seven visionary women put their own money into establishing a school for young women in Vancouver, Canada. Against the tide of popular thinking they firmly believed that, with a progressive education, women could be empowered to fulfil any ambition.

The school was named after the English city of York, birthplace of the school's founding principal, Lena Cotsworth Clarke. Taking as its motto "Not For Ourselves Alone", York House School aimed to instil a sense of social responsibility and citizenship in its charges.

"This motto still resonates today," says Chantal Gionet, Cotsworth Clarke's present-day successor. "And it continues to be a guiding principle." Indeed, it's no great surprise that every year a number of York House girls participate in the Duke of Edinburgh's Awards programme, the vision of which to "inspire and promote lifelong improvement for all young Canadians by encouraging personal development and achievement" chimes so harmoniously with the school's own ethos of fulfilling each student's potential. The school is actively engaged with the local community throughout Greater Vancouver and, in addition to promoting international exchange partnerships, York House works with community projects in Guatemala and Honduras.

While continuing to honour its traditions and values, the school works hard at helping its girls to keep up with the demands of the modern world. In a constantly changing environment, in which job security is no longer guaranteed, the school strives to empower each student to be bold, courageous and resilient, and embrace an entrepreneurial spirit. "We provide an exceptional academic education," says Gionet, "But we also recognise the importance of educating the whole child: socially, emotionally, physically and intellectually. We also know that we must prepare our students for the future by challenging them to think creatively and critically, and providing real-life learning opportunities that are an extension of the classroom."

In 2013, the newly reconstructed Senior School was opened. Its award-winning West Coast design marries polished concrete, wood, glass and stone throughout. Soaring glass panels and skylights allow natural light to drench the main entranceway. Names of thousands of alumnae, staff, students and famous women are screen-printed onto glass panels that guard the stairways. "It's truly awe-inspiring when you walk through the front doors," says Gionet. "The openness and the light make you feel as though anything is possible."

Many York House girls are third-generation, which engenders a special sense of engagement and pride. A growing number of alumnae chapters are being formed around the world, to provide an invaluable support network for former pupils. "We are proud to say 'once a Yorkie, always a Yorkie'," says Gionet. York House girls grow up with the firm belief that they have access to any career, and its alumnae are represented in almost every walk of life – from mothers to lawyers and doctors to business owners and aerospace engineers.

"Our girls, past and present are all individuals with their own distinct personalities and talents," says Gionet. "But, regardless of what they do, they want to make a difference in the world. One distinct characteristic of a Yorkie: they're bold, yet humble at the same time."

Northern exposure

University of Northern British Columbia

Her Majesty The Queen's 90th birthday celebrations have extra resonance for Canada's University of Northern British Columbia (UNBC), and for the thousands who came to witness her open the university in August 1994. Many more watched the broadcast of the ceremony on national television, and it is a day that is remembered fondly.

Since that time, UNBC has had a vital impact on the region, enabling its young citizens to study closer to home, rather than having to move farther afield. Sited on a plateau between the coast and the Rocky Mountains, with expansive panoramic views, the beauty of the university campus greatly enhances the quality of life for students and staff.

"What is exciting about the founding of this university," says the university's President Daniel Weeks, "is that it was precipitated by a grass-roots movement of people in the North who shared a transformational vision. Around 16,000 people put their signatures to a petition to urge the government to get it started.

"So many of our graduates are now leaders in the business world and in industry, and they tend to hire our students," he continues. "This creates an incentive for local people to stay in the area."

UNBC's largest campus is situated within the city of Prince George, which has a population of around 75,000 and is regularly referred to as British Columbia's Northern Capital. "Forestry, minerals, oil and gas were the driving forces behind opening up this part of the world," says Weeks. "But its long-term prosperity is dependent upon having an educated leadership to steward those resources."

UNBC's work is research-intensive, and its flagship programmes are in health sciences, business, environmental resource management and related sciences. With an enrolment of about 4,000 – including around 550 graduate students – its small scale favours interaction between researchers in a range of disciplines. In keeping with the aspirations of its founders, much of the university's work focuses on the social, economic, environmental and cultural issues that affect Northern British Columbia.

Among UNBC's long list of successes, the number one ranking in the 2016 Maclean's University Rankings for a university of its size stands out. "We are very proud," says Weeks. "The judging criteria are based on a range of indicators. These vary from the number of books in the library to student faculty ratios, student satisfaction and the nature of our programmes. The university was built to empower the people of the North, and we believe that we are living up to that."

In 2015, UNBC hosted the Canada Winter Games Closing Ceremony and, coinciding with the 25th anniversary of the university's foundation in 1990, the Governor General, David Johnston, attended the closing ceremony. "The Governor General is The Queen's representative in Canada, so it was a delightful bookend to Her Majesty's opening visit," says Weeks. "Her reign is being felt daily in Northern British Columbia."

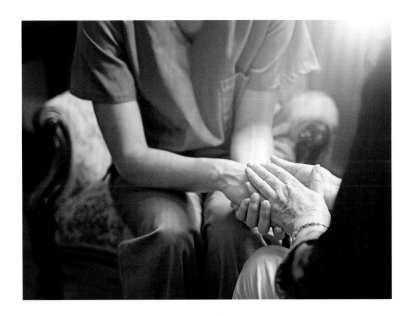

Nursing times

Canadian Nurses Association

When a group of 400 international nurses visited the UK in 1909, their trip coincided with the late Queen Victoria's birthday, so the delegates decided to pay their respects. Of all the countries represented, it was only the Canadian nurses that were given permission by the King to go inside Victoria's mausoleum, with the founder of the Canadian Nurses Association (CNA) placing a wreath on her tomb. Given such a long connection with royalty, it was no surprise that Her Majesty The Queen was made Royal Patron of the CNA in 1957.

The CNA was formed in 1908 to support nursing across Canada. "CNA is a powerful, unified voice for the nation's registered nurses," says Karima A Velji, the CNA President. "We represent registered nurses from coast to coast to coast. We advance the practice and profession of nursing to improve health outcomes and strengthen Canada's publicly funded, not-for-profit health system. The CNA is a key player in helping shape public policy on issues like primary health care, chronic diseases, quality end-of-life care and the effective use of health resources." It does this by focusing on healthcare solutions, optimising the use of evidence and expertise to encourage governments and others to improve healthcare policy, and to ensure that the nursing voice is heard on key issues.

Barb Shellian, the organisation's President-Elect, explains that an important element of this involves listening to nurses themselves. "Through surveys, workshops and focus groups, we regularly consult with our members, especially before governmental meetings, when we invite members to share their knowledge and expertise," she says. Over the decades, the CNA has provided valuable input into issues of mental health, health promotion, disease prevention, healthy ageing, patient safety and social determinants of health. It has done this by harnessing the vast knowledge of its governing board, its individual members and more than 45 nursing specialty groups across Canada. It also provides nurses with ongoing education opportunities such as certification in 20 specialties in Canada and shares Canada's nursing expertise with the world through the ICN, the International Council of Nurses, whose president, Judith Shamian, was previously president of the CNA.

The CNA has to accommodate numerous challenges that are particular to Canada – namely, the country's size. "Because of our unique geography, there are close to 7 million Canadians in remote and rural communities," says Velji. The CNA is currently working with the Canadian Indigenous Nurses Association to build capacity so that indigenous people are able to receive the training to serve as nurses in their own communities.

Canada also has a long history of providing nurses to its military, something of particular interest to the Royal Family, who have themselves given the Commonwealth's armed forces so much time and personal service – The Queen included. For this reason, the CNA's office in Ottawa has a memorial garden dedicated to the Canadian Nursing Sisters of the Second World War in recognition of the support provided by the CNA to Canada's military in these vital years.

Victoria values

Melbourne Girls Grammar

Catherine Misson is the Principal of Melbourne Girls Grammar (MGGS), one of the leading independent day and boarding schools in Victoria, Australia. Founded in 1893, the school has an enviable reputation for fostering academic high achievers with rich extracurricular interests. "Our girls are confident about having their own opinions and know how to express them with humility and grace," says Misson. "We are a school that is seen to produce women leaders."

The inner-city campus in South Yarra mixes open spaces and sports fields with light-filled, spacious learning studios that complement the school's forward-thinking, digitally engaged teaching. With around 1,000 girls from kindergarten to Year 12, the school specialises in providing personalised learning experiences. "We are willing to run a significant number of senior courses to ensure that girls have access to their preferred learning pathways," says Misson. She and her dedicated staff know well that girls who combine extracurricular activities across sports, music and drama also achieve the best academic results.

Small class sizes also help cement pupil–teacher relationships. "Our pastoral care is at the heart of achieving and maintaining a positive approach to learning," says Misson, "and it comes out of the very close culture we have of girls knowing and trusting teachers."

Trust and communication are also vital when teaching in a digital world. MGGS's teachers constantly adapt to new technology, using it to customise class management to the girls' needs. "We are a fully BYOD – 'bring your own device' – school and we have high-speed WiFi throughout the campus," says Misson.

Girls at MGGS are encouraged to push themselves, but within a supportive network of teachers and Personal Dimensions Mentors who help students balance the demands of school work, extracurricular activities and home life. MGGS is not, however, a hothouse narrowly focused on exam success. "We talk openly to parents to get them to understand how important it is to allow a girl to fail and to learn from that within a safe environment," says Misson. "It's not about grades, but the personal achievement of each pupil."

International students and those from further afield in Australia vie for places at MGGS's boarding house, drawn by the school's reputation, its safe environment and its record of getting girls into top universities such as the University of Melbourne. It was in the boarders' dining room in 1954 that portraits of Her Majesty The Queen and The Duke of Edinburgh were unveiled in honour of their first state visit, with students providing a Red Cross Guard of Honour outside Government House to welcome The Queen.

The school has a proud history and a current generation of inspiring alumni that includes human rights lawyers, high court judges and senior figures in public health. "Our girls will always step forward and express their opinions," says Misson. "They recognise that we are part of a sisterhood and that gives us all an aim for our endeavours."

Globally speaking

EC English Language Centres

When EC English Language Centres first began, in the early 1990s, its "classroom" was the basement of Andrew Mangion's family home in Malta. "There were just a few dozen students," says Mangion, EC's Executive Chairman, "but then some of the best companies have started in basements and garages."

Today, the company is still based in Malta, one of Her Majesty The Queen's favourite destinations, and one that she has visited many times since the early days of her marriage. However, as EC celebrates its 25th anniversary this year, it is now a global organisation, attracting to its courses annually more than 40,000 students from 140 countries. The UK was the first country chosen by EC for its expansion, followed by South Africa, the USA and Canada.

"The brand is recognised and trusted worldwide," says Mangion, "and it is built on rigorous standards." As well as offering exceptional English-language teaching, EC also helps students to succeed in a global community.

"Advances in technology mean there's a need for connectedness among people," says Mangion. "Connectedness needs a language and being able to speak English opens doors – it's a lifeline to joining a global economy. It's why our lessons are conducted entirely in English." Employing 1,000 people across its schools, EC prides itself on the fact that it has teachers who understand what it's like to live in a foreign country – because many have lived and taught overseas.

Innovation is also key to the success of EC. It has been a pioneer in setting up schools in London, Malta, New York and Toronto exclusively targeted at more mature students through its "30+" programme. "They are for those who want to share their experience with more mature, like-minded students," says Mangion. In addition, the focus is on "blended learning" – that means not only face-to-face but also online education. With such an international body of students, pupils learn from each other. "Israeli students learn alongside Saudi pupils," says Mangion. "It helps break down stereotypes and makes them better global citizens."

EC's constant striving to achieve excellence has not gone unnoticed. In 2011, it won the STM Star Chain School Award, and the Star Innovation Award in both 2009 and 2010. To ensure the highest performance, teachers are continually monitored through observation and student feedback. This is achieved via the Net Promoter Score (NPS) system, an evaluation tool used by companies such as Apple and Virgin to improve customer satisfaction.

Going forward, the school plans to increase its collaborations with universities. In 2014, it opened its first school on a US campus for international students needing to improve their English. The plan is to set up more of these campus schools.

From its humble beginnings, EC has become a global brand without compromising its values. As Andrew Mangion knows, that takes passion, determination, commitment – and an unquenchable desire from both teachers and students to learn.

The art of learning

The Corelli International Academic School of the Arts

Students at the Corelli International Academic School of the Arts could be said to be a microcosm of the Commonwealth. They hail from almost every country within it, as does the school's teaching cohort. It makes for a lively and vibrant school brimming with personality. But it also has a unique feature – Corelli is New Zealand's only Cambridge certified school of the arts.

David Selfe, himself a graduate of London's Royal Academy of Music, co-founded the school with his wife Kirsten in 2001. Both are passionate about the importance of the arts in education. Corelli does have a rigorous academic programme: its schooling, based on the Cambridge tradition, gives a students an excellent chance of getting into a top university. But alongside that rigour comes an artistic curriculum that offers everything from ballet to hip-hop, from filmmaking to fashion design and emerging contemporary art.

"Countless studies have shown the importance of the arts in helping children learn," says Kirsten. "But it's more than that. Students can be themselves here, which makes children happy, and if they're happy, they learn. It's a great confidence booster too: get them on stage and they become less afraid of trying new things academically, of asking questions."

The school is located in picturesque Browns Bay on the North Shore of Auckland City. The area conveniently offers numerous high-quality amenities, such as sports fields, a library, a swimming school, tennis courts and the beautiful Browns Bay beach.

By adding two hours to the normal school day, Corelli is able to devote around 35 per cent of its timetable to the arts. The school has a capacity for 200 students, aged between four and 20, and puts on a staggering 62 shows a year, which can range from a clarinet solo to a comedy sketch.

"It's a different show every week," says David. "The fact that we have the content to do that many illustrates how much the students want to do it. We have some students who want to be the next Lady Gaga; others who want to be engineers or psychologists. Having a creative curriculum will help them in any one of those fields. It generates faster thinking, boosts the cognitive process, and encourages them to reason more."

No wonder, then, that Corelli has received six Top School ratings with Cambridge International Exams, while Auckland University describes it as a school that punches above its weight. Currently Corelli is developing a strong relationship with the Wallace Arts Trust – a major arts centre, which has a vigorous school programme and promotes the arts in the same way as Corelli.

"Everybody does well because we don't try to fit the student in a box," says David. "We find the child's passion first. If you can find that light-bulb moment you can teach them anything, because after that it's just a matter of facts and experience. Our students are children of the Commonwealth being taught by teachers of the Commonwealth. Each child is allowed to be an individual, to be themselves. They can step from here to anywhere."

Meter masters

Secure Meters Ltd

When Secure Meters was established in 1987, the aim of its founder, Sanjaya Singhal, was to combat energy fraud in India, which was rife at that time through tampering of meters. He was looking to develop a revolutionary technology, and his search ended in Devon, England, where he found an inventor, John Fielden, offering a suitable solution.

Since those early days, Secure has expanded from a company with a workforce of only two in India into an international business with more than 3,000 employees in six different countries. In the UK, Secure has grown from having 70 employees in 1995 to around 600 today.

Secure is now at the forefront of smart meter technology, and has collected a number of awards along the way – including the Queen's Award for Enterprise in the Export category. A recent survey, carried out by the accounting firm Grant Thornton, ranked Secure among the UK's fastest-growing Asian-owned businesses.

"The government is encouraging the use of smart meters to assist Britain's transition to a low-carbon economy," says Singhal. "We have more than a million meters already deployed in the UK, and another million or so on contract." Secure's products enable householders to monitor their energy use, and control central heating and hot water. Singhal attributes the company's success to the business living its core values at all times and across all geographies. Its unwavering commitment to research and new product development, on which it invests about 7 per cent of its sales, gives Secure the ability to compete effectively with much bigger players.

A rare and special aspect of Secure's employment culture is its respect for the women in its workforce. The company is based in Udaipur, Rajasthan, where women are traditionally viewed as homemakers. Until Secure arrived, job opportunities for them were scarce. Now, on day shifts, approximately 500 out of 600 workers on the shop floor are women. All women staff enjoy parity of pay with their male colleagues, a rare phenomenon in the region – particularly at shop-floor level. The company has invested in a skills school and, at any given time, some 40 people are undergoing training in industrial skills. Large numbers of women engineers also have jobs in Secure's development and sales teams. "To be honest, I hadn't realised at first that we were doing anything special," says Singhal, with characteristic modesty. "We just thought it was a normal and right thing to do."

This year's celebrations for Her Majesty The Queen's birthday bring Singhal an especially pleasurable reminder of his visit to Buckingham Palace, when the company won the Queen's Award for Export. There were about 80 other winning companies there, and Her Majesty spent a minute or two with each. "When we met her, she knew exactly what we all did and why we had won the award!" says Singhal. "She had retained a brief for all 80 companies, all in her head. A monarch who works as hard as that to encourage trade and industry for her nation is doing a fantastic job."

Positive thinking

Loreto Mandeville Hall Toorak

When violinist and former Loreto Mandeville Hall Toorak pupil Brigid Coleridge performed at Buckingham Palace and was introduced to Her Majesty The Queen, she was but the latest example of the Australian school's 127-year-long tradition of excellence.

Based in a leafy suburb of Melbourne, this independent school for girls aged 3 to 18 was established in 1924 by the Sisters of Loreto, a Catholic order founded by Yorkshirewoman Mary Ward in the early 1600s. In educating girls, Ward was far ahead of her times. Today, there are about 200 Loreto schools around the world and, as one of Australia's leading schools, Loreto Toorak is a prime example of the Loreto quest to combine academic and extracurricular quality with a focus on social change.

"We've been named the top independent girls' school in the state of Victoria," says Dr Susan Stevens, the second lay Principal in the school's history. "Two years ago, our rowing team won the Australian schoolgirls' championship; one of our students is now a Rhodes Scholar and another was named Young Australian Writer of the Year 2014. But, above all, we teach our girls to act and think in ways that make the world a better place. The Loreto Sisters' guiding principles are freedom, justice, sincerity, verity and felicity, and we transmit those values via curricula that focus on traditional core subjects but also include innovative courses and new educational approaches that foster frequently neglected life skills."

Situated in beautiful grounds centred on the historic, National Trust-listed mansion Mandeville Hall, it now boasts state-of-the-art facilities that allow it to offer unusual and highly inspirational subjects such as archaeology, neurobiology, forensic science and aviation, with several qualified pilots among the older students.

"We want to educate society's future leaders," says Dr Stevens. "To achieve that, we've also established ourselves as one of the leading schools worldwide in the field of positive education, which focuses on teaching life skills such as resilience, optimism and determination. This subject area is generally part of university education, but it has become another defining feature of Loreto Toorak, as we try to enable our girls to handle whatever life throws at them and make a positive contribution to society."

In fact, the school's students do that from a very young age by getting involved in social projects such as local environmental initiatives. The older girls also tutor at schools that cater for less privileged students and stay with indigenous communities in remote areas to understand their culture.

"In Year 11, students take part in one of the Loreto Sisters' many social justice programmes in the developing world," says Dr Stevens. "They spend two weeks working in orphanages or schools for children with disabilities in rural Vietnam, which gives them a totally different perspective on life."

Throw in the fact that the school orchestra regularly tours the world, and produces the likes of Brigid Coleridge, and Mary Ward would probably consider Loreto Toorak a worthy modern torchbearer for her ambition to help young girls achieve.

Faith in education

Baradene College of the Sacred Heart

The day begins early at Baradene College, a girls' school in central Auckland, New Zealand. By 6.30 am, the campus is already buzzing with activity as girls gather for cycle squad, pile into the school van to head out to rowing training or meet in the auditorium for choir and orchestra rehearsal. At 3.10 pm, the bell tolls to mark the end of lessons – but students will eagerly head back out to the sports fields or make their way to the performing arts centre to engage in another round of extracurricular activities.

"We strongly encourage academic success," says the school's Principal, Sandy Pasley. "But we also stress the importance of extracurricular activities. We want the girls to develop a sense of social justice and an understanding of local and global issues, both social and environmental." It's an approach epitomised by the likes of internationally respected landscape designer and Baradene alumna Xanthe White. An advocate of sustainable design, White's highlights to date include a silver and silver-gilt award at the Chelsea Flower Show, as well as two introductions to Her Majesty The Queen.

Indeed, diversity of experience is a key feature of life at Baradene, a Catholic secondary school which welcomes 1,180 girls between the ages of 11 and 18 from many backgrounds and encourages them to engage in a broad range of activities. "We educate the whole person," says Pasley. "As a Sacred Heart school we uphold the beliefs of our founder Saint Madeleine Sophie Barat, whose educational philosophy prioritised a deep respect for intellectual values, a personal and active faith in God, social awareness, community support and personal growth. It's why charitable activities are part of the fabric of the school."

Founded in 1909, Baradene has always had a culture of encouragement and support. Its aim has always been to foster a sense of belonging in students, helping girls reach their potential and develop lifelong friendships.

"The faith-based education they receive gives our girls the ability to withstand the highs and lows of life with hope for the future," says Pasley. "That pastoral care is mirrored in its approach to everything. We have a wonderful reputation as a vibrant and caring community that encompasses the values of faith, learning, social justice and personal growth.

"We offer a supportive learning environment where we educate to each girl's needs and talents," continues Pasley. "Staff members work with one another and with students to create a learning environment in which each person is valued and respected for who she is. Natural abilities are brought to light and shared, differences and limitations are recognised and accepted, leadership is fostered at many levels and young people are encouraged to find hope, purpose and meaning in their lives."

Baradene is one of the top-ten schools in New Zealand. At the end of each year it sees some 93 per cent of Year 13 students gain acceptance into top universities, both local and international. However, it's not just the stellar academic record that sets Baradene College students apart and makes them desirable candidates for university and high performers in their future careers.

"Baradene girls leave school as independent, resilient young women," says Pasley, "who are prepared to make a difference through self-knowledge, energy and purpose."

My brother's keeper

CBC St Kilda

"We want our boys to be successful, but not just for themselves. If your only goal is personal success, it has been a hollow education." Gerald Bain-King, the Principal of the CBC (Christian Brothers' College) St Kilda in inner Melbourne, is referring to the ideals of social justice and community that are as relevant to life in the Roman Catholic boys' secondary school today as they were when it was founded in 1878. CBC St Kilda turns out what Bain-King proudly calls "terrific young gentlemen" in an environment of unambiguous values and skilled, structured teaching.

CBC St Kilda is part of Edmund Rice Education Australia, founded on the teachings of Rice's Congregation of Christian Brothers. Rice, an 18th century Irish visionary, believed that education could raise boys out of poverty, knowing they also needed to be well dressed and properly fed to avoid the suffering and stigma of poverty.

"He was an early proponent of the whole person approach," says Bain-King. "Throughout our history, boys from low social backgrounds were taught they could become people of significance. Today, we are committed to maintaining a mixed school population."

The approach of CBC staff is one of collaboration and communication. "If there is an issue or problem, the teachers help the boys understand what has happened," he says. "It's not about blame, but resolution. Similarly, where schooling in the past was often rote learnt, we know that education is actually about how you learn, not purely what you learn. It is important that the boys become thinkers and authors of their own understanding."

The school fully embraces digital learning platforms. "However," says Bain-King, "while we engage completely with the digital domain, we keep hold of our sacred values through community between people, through sports and the arts and the invitation to join in."

In keeping with the founders' ideal of a desegregated society, educational programmes at CBC can be both academic and practical. Students can either choose academic subjects such as English literature, history, physics and languages, or undertake studies in areas such as construction, work-place skills and hospitality. "Teaching students about values and emotional intelligence is as important as academic subjects," says Bain-King.

For this reason teachers at CBC are attuned to the boys' developmental needs and work with families to help them deal with peer pressure and finding their place in the wider world. "Our church says families are the primary educators of their sons, responsible for morals and good manners," says Bain-King, "so our role is to engage parents throughout their son's education, so learning from home and school is united. We learn from each other through our community."

Boys at CBC, who include around 25 per cent non-Catholics, learn in an uplifting environment based on integrity and a strong social conscience, a school ethos that informs every aspect of a pupil's learning experience. "Everything we do is about learning," says Bain-King. "There is no such thing as a non-educative moment in the school."

Teaching quality

The Mico University College

Late in 2015, The Princess Royal made a three-day visit to Jamaica and among those fortunate enough to have played host to her was the Mico University College in Kingston. Part of the reason that this venerable college featured on the royal itinerary was because it holds the enviable record of being the oldest teacher training institution in the western hemisphere.

In August 1836, the Mico opened its doors to 10 newly freed, poor black student teachers – three men and seven women. Its aim was to train native school teachers at elementary level who could then go on to transform the educational landscape in Jamaica.

Today, as it celebrates its 180th anniversary, the Mico University College continues to give a sterling service in the education of teachers. It is an internationally recognised brand supported by four pillars – leadership, service to others, integrity and excellence in performance.

"Our core business is teacher education," says Pro Chancellor Professor Neville Ying. "However our holistic and multidisciplinary approach has resulted in our graduates making outstanding contributions globally in diverse fields such as teaching, law, business, politics and religion."

The Mico offers undergraduate degree programmes through its three faculties: Education & Leadership; Humanities & Liberal Arts; and Science & Technology. It also offers four master's programmes through its Graduate School of Education in collaboration with its R&D arm, the Institute of Technological and Educational Research (ITER). The vision of the Mico is to be the university of choice in the Caribbean for teacher education and the centre of excellence for pedagogy in science, mathematics, specialised diagnostic and therapeutic services for children, and research to inform the development of policies in education. The institution has an academic staff of more than 150, and a combined population of day and evening students numbering over 2,000.

The Mico is known for taking students from humble beginnings and equipping them to attain the highest levels of achievement. Once described as "the poor man's university", its alumni includes two Governors General of Jamaica – Sir Clifford Campbell and Sir Howard Cooke. Recently, the institution's Pre-University Men's Programme (PUMP) was introduced to target young men at risk and encourage them to pursue university degrees.

"The Mico's alumni speak highly of the institution's credibility and student-centred focus," says Professor Ying. "Our growth from being a teacher training college to a university college was as a result of the high-quality programmes during our exciting journey of institutional development, and support from the strong and continuing partnership with the Jamaican government, our founders, and the Lady Mico Trust."

With the Mico on the path to achieve full university status within the next five years, it's clear that it continues to blaze a trail of excellence, equipping its students with the knowledge, skills, attitudes and values to be innovative and enquiring, to face the challenges of a complex yet exciting global village. "We are now giving focused attention to the effective integration of information and communications technology in our teacher education programmes, to equip our students for the digital environment of the 21st century," says Professor Ying. "The Mico remains committed to using teacher education as a key driver for sustainable national development."

Fresh ideas

Calvary Christian College

Queensland was named after Victoria, but it's an area of Australia that Her Majesty The Queen has visited several times since 1954, when she became the first reigning monarch to tour the country. And this most regal of states is currently home to a revolution in education, according to Steven Coote, Principal of Calvary Christian College in Brisbane.

"We are focused on creating a school that is committed to challenging the status quo of what schooling looks like so that we can equip our students with an understanding for their future," says Coote. "We want to produce creative and divergent thinkers, learners who will be inventive and innovative. We want to grow young people who can make the world a better place."

Calvary Christian College was founded in 1984 and now occupies two campuses with around 1,100 students. The school was established as a ministry of Logan Uniting Church, but is non-selective. Its Christian worldview is central, but is part of a thoroughly modern model of education.

"The exponential change across the globe requires that our young people must be able to create and be responsive to the world and what it demands," says Coote. This requires changes in the classroom, something Calvary embraces to the extent it has replaced the word "teacher" with "learning designer" to reflect the way educators design the "conditions for success for every student".

Coote believes that it's necessary to create an environment where children are comfortable with a degree of ambiguity while they process solutions. "We will still contribute to the conversation and help them interrogate questions, and we will teach them explicitly where needed, but we want to allow them to construct their learning so they are confident with the answers they come up with," he says. Pupils are encouraged to ask big questions, assess information, and formulate and then test a hypothesis in ways that are creative and innovative.

The school has identified four stages in this process – learn, explore, create and belong – which takes the student from basic numeracy and literacy through to the pastoral side of the curriculum, where children can share their learning and think about using it to improve the world.

"We even have a Centre for Innovative Learning Design on campus," says Coote, "an embedded space for us to evaluate and design models of learning that are available not only to our own staff, but to other educators across the world."

Calvary is committed to embedding the critical and essential skills of numeracy and literacy and also runs a rich co-curricular programme. The assessment process that the school uses allows teaching staff to gather data to ensure that each child will achieve the best outcome. It also recruits innovative staff who are ready to create the best possible learning environment for students, among whom are Coote's own children.

"I have two children at the school," he says. "We want to be the school of choice for parents and staff. We think our work is very important. We are speaking at conferences, producing publications – our reputation is growing and we want people to know about us."

Personal growth

Catholic Agricultural College

The traditions still alive today at Catholic Agricultural College were first inspired more than 200 years ago by Edmund Rice. A missionary and educationalist, Rice realised learning had the power to liberate lives, especially those of children in poverty. "The college strives to offer a liberating education, based on gospel spirituality, within an inclusive community committed to justice and solidarity," says Marie Barton, Principal. "Gospel values where Jesus Christ is the cornerstone of a full Christian life are the core beliefs of our community underpinned by quality relationships."

When Her Majesty The Queen spoke at the Commonwealth Heads of Government Meeting in Perth, Western Australia in October 2011, she observed that, "This city is known for its optimism; this state is known for its opportunity and potential." These qualities are exemplified by the state's Catholic Agricultural College, located in the beautiful Chittering Valley, which has been at the forefront of agricultural and vocational education for many years. It ranks consistently high in state-wide graduation tables and has been in the top five vocational education and training (VET) schools in the state.

The learning environment is based on integrating theory, practice and technology. Here, the 159 male and female pupils who range in age from 12 to 18 all study agricultural science and also have the opportunity to learn subjects ranging from wool handling to horse breeding, from hospitality to retail services. This equips both day and residential pupils with the necessary skills for securing a job in Western Australia where the majority of opportunities are in agriculture and trade.

"One family recently moved interstate so their child could join our equine programme for example," says Barton. "We are a registered training organisation, offer strong programmes and our rural location a little removed from Perth is very attractive to many of our families."

The majority of students are mainstream. However, the college has built a reputation working with those who have become disengaged from education, have significant gaps in their learning or have special educational needs. "We've had great success with students who have struggled in mainstream schools and they've been among our leaders in recent years," says Barton. "We endeavour to celebrate diversity and liberate those at the margins through nurture and a sense of belonging to our small community. We promote self-growth and healthy relationships through honest feedback and restorative practice."

Looking to the future, Barton says the college is committed to ensuring its graduate students are well-prepared for the workforce and make "a significant and positive contribution to their communities." This is all the while honouring the college's core gospel values of excellence, respect, tolerance and honesty, as well as celebrating diversity. Its students are also encouraged to show initiative, responsibility, leadership and involvement in their community.

They are values that are still as relevant today as they were all those years ago when Edmund Rice was helping to transform lives. Today, with the Catholic Agricultural College being a key member of the Edmund Rice Education Australia network, there is no doubt that the venerable missionary and educationalist would have been proud.

Smart prospects

Onehunga High School

Onehunga High School mixes tradition and innovation in a thriving community of 1,200 students in one of Auckland's oldest suburbs, overlooking the spectacular Manukau Harbour. The school was opened in 1959 – just a few years after Her Majesty The Queen and The Duke of Edinburgh visited Auckland – and has since developed into a vibrant, multicultural environment.

"We aim for innovation within the curriculum," says Principal Deidre Shea. "Being able to offer strong academic classroom teaching alongside practical courses in catering, construction or technology is an innovative way to give each student the chance to achieve excellence."

In an atmosphere that stresses integrity and respect, the school prepares students for the National Certificate of Educational Achievement, which readies them for further education. Academic mentoring helps students structure their studies and subject selection. The Royal Society of New Zealand has recognised the outstanding results of some students and lists them on its Young Achievers Database. In addition, several staff have been awarded Royal Society fellowships.

Within the Pathways programme, students can focus on a wide curriculum that includes automotive technology, catering and hospitality, building and construction or

business studies. The Business School at Onehunga High was the first of its kind in New Zealand and has strong links with universities. Senior students have the opportunity to travel to China and Taiwan to study overseas business practices.

Since 2013, construction students have worked with the NGO Habitat for Humanity, which helps build good-quality, affordable housing to give people a hand up. Each year, Onehunga students build a four-bedroom family home. "Practical involvement gives students huge confidence," says Shea. "For those who haven't decided what to do after school, it's the chance to try something in a safe learning environment."

The school also places great importance on sport and the arts. "In 2015, some of our students choreographed a piece with the support of the Royal New Zealand ballet," says Shea, "with music co-written by students and the Auckland Philharmonia Orchestra. Our students put on an incredibly professional performance. There wasn't a dry eye in the house."

The school's long history in Onehunga means that it is home to many second- and third-generation students. "It's a warm, welcoming community," says Shea, "with strong ties to families and local businesses." Its innovative teaching in traditional and non-traditional subjects and workplace skills allows students to thrive in whatever field they choose for their futures.

High fliers

Caribbean Aviation Training Center

In 2008, Prince William became the fourth successive generation of the Royal Family to become an RAF pilot. As is the case for anyone choosing to learn to fly, either as a leisure pursuit or as the first step in a career in aviation, his choice of flying school was paramount. Prince William, as an army officer, received his training at RAF Cranwell after having completed his officer training at Sandhurst.

Having a military background is something that sets the Caribbean Aviation Training Center (CATC) in Kingston, Jamaica, apart from others of its kind. Its founder and CEO, Captain Errol Stewart, also trained at the Royal Military Academy at Sandhurst.

For more than 15 years CATC has been providing multiple levels of flight training and education, from the Private Pilot Licence to the Airline Transport Pilot Licence, all to international standards. Around 60 pilots pass through its doors every year. "It's fair to say that all of our students have exhibited certain character in their way of flying," explains Brianne Stewart, Director of Marketing. "It's about how they handle themselves as individuals, and that's made possible thanks to our military background."

CATC pilots can be found all over the world, in particular the Middle East and the USA, where they pursue promising careers in the commercial or corporate airline industry. It's no wonder, then, that students from as far away as the UK and India have heard of this aviation school and want to train there. "The Cessna Pilot Center, a division of the Cessna company, voted us number one Cessna pilot center twice," says Stewart. "People come here because of our beautiful landscape, which makes the flying experience that little bit more special."

Among CATC's major achievements is setting up a mentorship programme for those aged nine to 15 years old, from which two full scholarships are awarded to participants who show a genuine passion for aviation. Sharing his love for flying is something that Captain Stewart is wholly committed to, whether that's through visits to local schools or setting up Jamaica's first airshow, Boscobel Jamaica, a display of flying prowess for the general public to feast on.

"We have a saying in Jamaica, 'Wi likkle, but wi tallawah', which means small but strong," says Stewart. "We may be a small institution within the Caribbean, but the strength of the students that we offer to general aviation far exceeds the smallness of the facility."

All The Queen's horses

A lifelong passion

Her Majesty The Queen's far-reaching influence on the horse world is the continuance of a royal tradition that follows the founding of the Royal Stud at Hampton Court in the 16th century, King Charles II moving his court to Newmarket every year and Queen Anne spotting the potential for a racecourse at Ascot.

Whatever the occasion – whether inspecting the showing lines at Royal Windsor, arriving to cheers at Royal Ascot, watching her family play polo or carriage driving, visiting her Highland and Fell pony stud at Balmoral, hacking out in Windsor Great Park on one of her ponies or presenting the medals at a rain-soaked European Eventing Championship at Blair Castle in 2015 – The Queen has lent a gravitas and expertise to the British equestrian scene that is the envy of the rest of the world.

Early photographs show a young Princess Elizabeth sitting confidently on a black Shetland pony, Peggy, a fourth birthday present, and she and Princess Margaret were sent to learn to ride and drive with riding instructor Horace Smith and his daughter Sybil in Maidenhead.

In 1945, the princesses won the private turnout (driving) class at Royal Windsor Horse Show with their pony Hans. The show remains an annual diary date and is the scene of The Queen's 90th birthday celebrations with horses flown in from all over the world for a spectacular pageant against a backdrop of a floodlit Windsor Castle.

The Queen's father, grandfather and great-grandfather owned racehorses – King Edward VII was the last monarch to have a Derby winner (his home-bred Persimmon in 1896)

PREVIOUS PAGES: PRINCESS
ELIZABETH RIDES HER PONY IN
WINDSOR GREAT PARK (LEFT);
THE QUEEN AT THE ROYAL
WINDSOR HORSE SHOW IN
1968 (RIGHT). OPPOSITE: A
FASHIONABLY ATTIRED QUEEN
ATTENDS THE SHOW IN 1952.
LEFT: THE QUEEN TAKES TO
THE SADDLE FOR AN OUTING
WITH THE ROYAL PARTY AT
ROYAL ASCOT, 1961

and his horses were trained at Kingsclere in Hampshire, where Her Majesty currently has some of her 25 or so racehorses in training with Andrew Balding.

The Queen inherited King George VI's flat racehorses (her mother had the jumpers). Her ownership got off to a thrilling and, no doubt, pleasantly distracting start when Aureole finished second in the Derby just days after the Coronation.

The distinctive royal racing colours – purple, gold and red with a black velvet hat with gold fringe – have been carried to victory on her behalf more than 800 times, and she was leading owner in the 1950s before the might of Middle Eastern-owned horsepower began to dominate. The Derby is the only Classic The Queen has yet to win – her last runner, Carlton House, a gift from Sheikh Mohammed al Maktoum, was sent off favourite in 2011 and finished third.

In 2013, The Queen was named Racehorse Owner of the Year for her contribution to the sport and in recognition of her first Ascot Gold Cup winner, Estimate, trained by Sir Michael Stoute. It was her first Grade One winner since Dunfermline, winner of the Epsom Oaks in 1977, and pictures of a delighted monarch were beamed around the world.

The Queen sets aside diary time every year to visit her horses in training and is hugely knowledgeable about bloodlines. She stands two stallions at the Royal Stud at Sandringham, Royal Applause and the Derby winner Motivator, which was bought by The Queen's racing manager, John Warren.

The Queen is an elegant, competent horsewoman, as was demonstrated in a terrifying moment during Trooping the Colour in 1981 when blank shots were fired from the crowd.

The result could have been disastrous, but The Queen quietly reassured her mount, Burmese, and all was well. Burmese was a much-loved sight; a gift in 1969 from the Royal Canadian Mounted Police, the horse carried The Queen a remarkable 18 times at Trooping the Colour.

The Queen has followed eventing ever since Badminton Horse Trials was started by the 10th Duke of Beaufort in 1949; her annual visit would include hacking out with the Duke and Princess Margaret and watching the cross-country from a rug beside the lake with the rest of the crowd.

In 1974, she presented the trophy to her then son-in-law, Captain Mark Phillips, after his victory on her horse Columbus IV, a mount deemed to be too strong for Princess Anne. Another happy day was the 1971 European Championships at Burghley when she was able to present the gold medal to her daughter, winner of the individual title on Doublet, bred by The Queen out of a polo pony.

The Queen also owned Countryman III, second at Badminton with the present Duke of Beaufort, David Somerset, and ridden by Bertie Hill at the 1956 Olympic Games in Stockholm. The cross-country course there was fearsome and became slippery after overnight rain; Countryman became straddled over a fence that collapsed, but still completed the course and helped Britain win a first Olympic team gold medal in eventing.

It was The Duke of Edinburgh who said that "horses are great levellers" and The Queen has always taken the vicissitudes of ownership with equanimity, delighted by her own success, but equally pleased for others. Her tangible pleasure has, in turn, given great pleasure to everyone else.

LEFT: THE QUEEN IS AN ENTHUSIASTIC SPECTATOR AT THE EPSOM DERBY, 1978. OPPOSITE: AT TROOPING THE COLOUR IN 2007

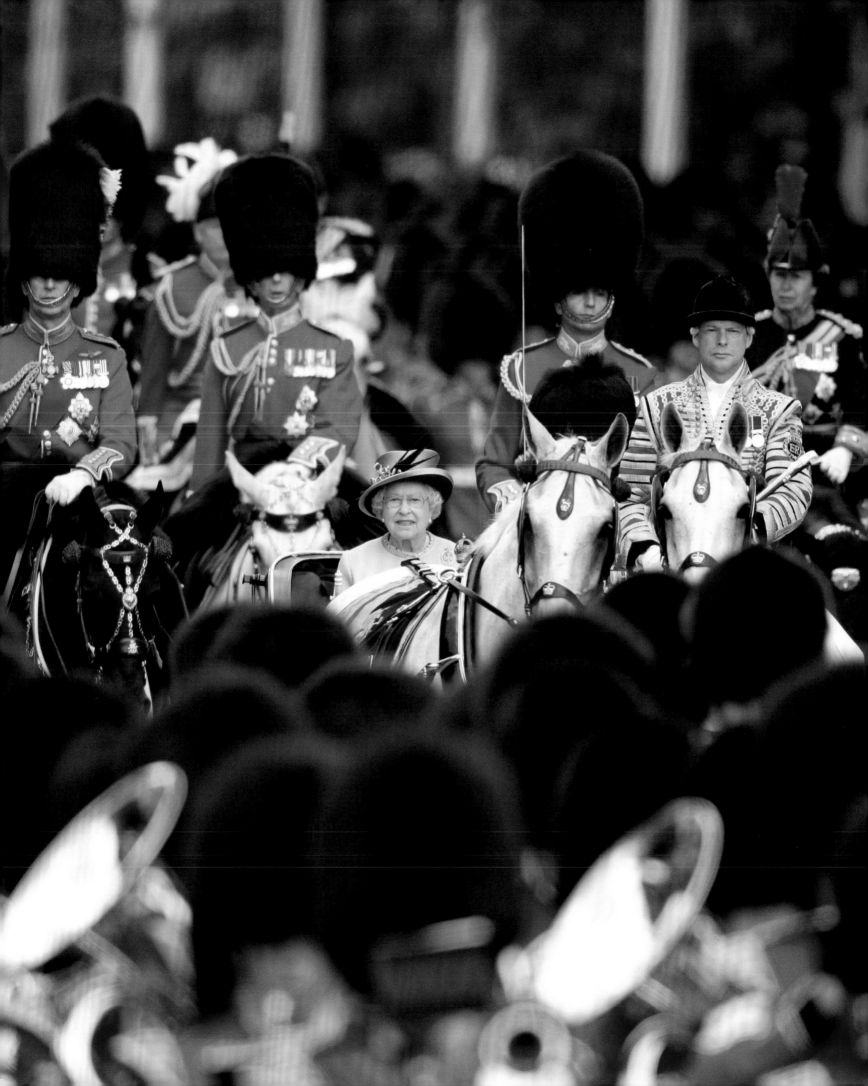

Winning ways

1966 and all that

It's no exaggeration to say that Her Majesty The Queen's Diamond Jubilee in 2012 ushered in a new golden age for UK sport, with that year's London Olympics leading the charge in what has been a remarkable era of sporting success. The likes of heptathlete Jessica Ennis, sailor Ben Ainslie, cyclist Victoria Pendleton and long jumper Greg Rutherford were all part of a Team GB that won more medals (65) at the games than any British team in more than a century. Since then, their compatriots have also dominated the Tour de France (Bradley Wiggins and Chris Froome), become heavyweight boxing champions of the world (Tyson Fury) and won Wimbledon (Andy Murray). Britain's tennis team came home with the Davis Cup, while the England cricket team has twice claimed the Ashes.

Although The Queen rarely attends Wimbledon, her childhood, Silver Jubilee and Diamond Jubilee all coincided with major victories achieved by her tennis-playing subjects (in the 1930s, British men clinched the Wimbledon singles and Davis Cup titles; in 1977, Virginia Wade won the women's singles trophy at SW19, the last Briton to do so; and in 2012, Murray won Olympic gold and the US Open, thereby becoming the first British man to win a Grand Slam singles title in 76 years). Yet arguably the UK's greatest sporting highlight of recent years was Murray's Wimbledon triumph in 2013. Prior to his hard-earned victory over Novak Djokovic in the final, the last man from these shores to win the world's most prestigious tennis tournament had been Fred Perry before the Second World War.

Unlike our current monarch, The Queen's father, King George VI, was a tennis enthusiast and is, to date, the only member of the Royal Family to have competed at Wimbledon. In 1926 – aged 30, and just two months after the birth of the future Queen – the then Duke of York entered the men's doubles tournament with 45-year-old Sir Louis Greig, whom he'd met during officer training at Royal Naval College. The pair lost their only match in straight sets, but some of The Queen's other relatives have enjoyed considerably more success, especially in one of her favourite disciplines, equestrianism.

In 1971, The Queen's second child, Princess Anne, won the European Eventing Championships and was voted BBC Sports Personality of the Year. Five years later, at Montreal, she also became the first member of the Royal Family to take part in the Olympics. Her daughter, Zara Phillips, went one better, winning the Eventing World Championship and the same BBC award as her mother (both in 2006) before picking up an Olympic silver medal as part of the Great Britain Eventing Team at London 2012.

Her husband, Mike Tindall, also contributed to one of the finest achievements ever by any team from the British Isles: England's victory in the 2003 Rugby World Cup. In a thrilling final, the pre-tournament favourites beat hosts Australia, with Jonny Wilkinson scoring the winning drop goal with only a few seconds of extra time remaining, thereby ensuring that England became the only country from the northern hemisphere to date to lift the Webb Ellis Cup.

Motor sport has seen a different kind of horse power propel British competitors onto the global stage. In Formula One alone, the country boasts 10 different world champions (the next best nations have three each) and a total of 37 constructors' championships (more than the combined total of all other countries) since the series was launched in 1950.

Our national game is another sport with strong ties the Royal Family, the current FA President being The Duke of Cambridge, who succeeded his uncle, The Duke of York. As part of this honorary role, he regularly presents the FA Cup trophy to the winners of the final – an occasion that The Queen first attended on 2 May 1953, exactly a month before her Coronation. That match, also known as the Matthews Final because of 38-year-old Stanley Matthews' match-winning contribution, turned out to be an all-time classic, with Blackpool beating Bolton Wanderers 4–3.

The Queen and The Duke of Edinburgh were also present to witness England's finest sporting hour (or two, as it were): the 4–2 defeat of Germany in the 1966 World Cup Final at Wembley Stadium. Even those who don't particularly like football or who support one of the other home nations grudgingly admit that no other performance in any sport has had such a profound impact on our national psyche as this match, which was decided by Geoff Hurst's hat-trick, including two goals in extra time.

Nine months later, in April 1967, the till then unbeaten world champions lost 3–2 against the Auld Enemy at Wembley. This defeat signalled the beginning of almost 50 years of hurt for the home team, but Scotland's "Wembley Wizards" were so accomplished at the time that there was little shame in the result. In fact, a month after the game, Rangers reached the final of the European Cup Winners'

Cup and Celtic became the first British football club to lift the European Cup (now the Champions League), achieving this feat with players who were all born within a 30-mile radius of the club's stadium.

Since then, British football has only ever really succeeded internationally in club competitions, with English teams dominating Europe in the late 1970s and early 1980s, and again, to a lesser extent, in the second half of the past decade. Yet, in 2015, the England women's team became the first British senior national side since Gazza and co. at Italia 90 to reach the semi-finals of a World Cup. And, with three home nations (England, Wales and Northern Ireland) having qualified for Euro 2016 this summer, the hope is that another landmark year for The Queen will also herald yet another sporting annus mirabilis for the nation.

OPPOSITE: THE PRINCESS ROYAL PRESENTS GREAT BRITAIN'S EVENTING TEAM, INCLUDING HER DAUGHTER ZARA PHILLIPS, WITH SILVER MEDALS AT THE 2012 OLYMPICS. RIGHT: OLYMPIC PENTATHLON CHAMPION JESSICA ENNIS

A leading role

Britain on the world stage

There's little debate that the highlight of the opening ceremony of the London 2012 Olympic Games, directed with such wit and imagination by British Oscar winner Danny Boyle, was the scene in which Her Majesty The Queen appeared alongside Daniel Craig's James Bond. This was a stunning coup but also a moment – amid the implausible sense of fun – of genuine importance. As the world watched, Boyle called forth a meeting between two uniquely British icons who, in very different ways, have drawn so much attention and so many visitors to our soil. It was the perfect example – and one The Queen explicitly understood – of what historian Dominic Sandbrook considers Britain's major contribution to the world in the past 90 years as the country emerged from Empire to reinvent itself as "a cultural superpower", the home of world-straddling superstars from Agatha Christie and J R R Tolkien, to Adele and Harry Potter.

You could argue that this all began in 1926, the year of The Queen's birth and also of John Logie Baird's demonstration of television in London. Television is one of the principal ways in which British creativity has been developed, amplified and exported, largely thanks to the BBC, which for generations has provided musicians, actors, artists, writers and directors

with their cultural education as children, and their professional training and exposure as adults. The BBC exemplifies that powerfully British combination of cultural knowledge, skill and ambition, and has a global reach that only Hollywood can match. A list of talent nurtured by the BBC would fill a book on its own. What was Danny Boyle's first important job? Working as a producer for the BBC in Northern Ireland. How did Daniel Craig get his breakthrough? Playing the role of Geordie in the BBC's *Our Friends In The North*.

It is fascinating to peruse a list of other figures born in the UK in 1926 who would go on to become significant leaders in the arts. Names such as David Attenborough, arguably the world's most popular broadcaster. There are film directors (John Schlesinger), actors (Kenneth Williams, Warren Mitchell), playwrights (Peter Shaffer), authors (John Fowles), comedians (Eric Morecombe), critics (John Berger) and musicians (George Melly). These cover the ground between popular and pioneering, but are often both at the same time. Britain's unique position as a bridge between Europe and America, so crucial in finance, industry and tourism, is also important, with Britain traditionally condensing the intellectual European

avant-garde in a manner deemed acceptable to mass audiences in America – something demonstrated by the likes of John Schlesinger and John Fowles.

Two other personalities born in 1926 are also illustrative of the way British creativity can cover so much as it conquers the world. In 1956, 30-year-old BBC cameraman and writer Michael Bond bought his wife a teddy bear from a shop near Paddington station in London. He decided to use the bear in a story, which was published in 1958 as *A Bear Called Paddington*. The Paddington Bear series of books, depicting the impact of a small, clumsy, polite bear from Peru on the home of a typical British family of the 1950s, were massive. They have been translated into 30 languages and sold more than 30 million copies worldwide. Paddington Bear has been made into TV series and became a hugely successful digitally animated film in 2014. Much like that other Bond, this is a glorious example of a British cultural success story – eccentric and ingenuous, rooted in British traditions that resonate internationally, and which is still developing today, as characters and plots adapt to the demands of another generation, using new talent and technology.

Also born in 1926 was George Martin, who would produce The Beatles, arguably the single most important cultural act of the past 90 years alongside Picasso and Dylan. Martin got his first job at the BBC before he joined EMI, recording classical music and albums for comedians, such as the *Beyond The Fringe* cast album featuring Peter Cook, Dudley Moore, Alan Bennett and Jonathan Miller. In 1962, he began working with The Beatles, producing almost every note the band released from debut single "From Me To You" on. Martin, with a background in classical music and comedy, was able to appreciate the wit of the Liverpool band and also support their increasing ambition, as John, Paul, George and Ringo transformed what was considered possible in popular music. The Beatles began to incorporate elements from music hall and the avant-garde alongside traditional rock, blues and country to create music breathtaking in scope and aspiration, but still extraordinarily popular.

This was more than just culturally important. It's estimated that during the 1960s, the international appeal of The Beatles was worth billions to the

UK – that's how they earned their MBEs, meeting The Queen at Buckingham Palace in 1965 – and they still bring around £82 million a year to Liverpool alone through tourism. Indeed, the value to the British economy of musical heritage tourism is estimated to be as much as £4 billion, something increasingly recognised by museums and galleries, as they hasten to introduce musical acts into their galleries, epitomised by the groundbreaking David Bowie exhibition at the V&A in 2013. Bowie's death in January 2016 led to an international outpouring of love and grief – hundreds of the messages scrawled next to his impromptu shrine in Brixton were from non-Britons who saw Bowie as a shining example of an unmistakably British talent, defined by the post-war culture in which he grew up.

Bowie, like the Beatles, understood that all cultural disciplines were intertwined, embracing film, fashion, TV and visual art. In London, tourists flock to the Tate Modern gallery, the most visited contemporary art gallery in the world, which draws 4.7 million annual visitors, often to see work produced by modern British artists such as Francis Bacon, Lucian Freud,

Bridget Riley, David Hockney and Damian Hirst – Hirst's value to the British economy could even rival The Beatles.

Further swelling the cultural coffers of the nation is it's long-established wealth of acting talent – an aristocracy of the stage whose knights and dames (Kenneth Branagh, Ian McKellen, Judi Dench, Helen Mirren, Maggie Smith, to name but a few) help draw over 14.7 million visitors a year to the West End alone. Another 2 million visit the Harry Potter Studio in Hertfordshire, infatuated by stories that are rooted in a British tradition of hierarchical boarding schools and mythology, combining Enid Blyton with C S Lewis updated to the modern day. Written by J K Rowling, the novels have been adapted for box office-dominating films showcasing a plethora of British acting talent and in 2016 a new Harry Potter story has been created for theatre, showing the series still has plenty of life and invention in it. Here too, as with James Bond and The Beatles, there's a royal connection – in 2006, Rowling produced a story called *The Queen's Handbag*, which was filmed with the Harry Potter cast, to celebrate The Queen's 80th birthday: a royal example of cultural magic from British creative talent.

Wired for sound

Sony Music UK

Perhaps the confession that somebody doesn't own a CD player isn't the most surprising thing to hear in 2016, but it still seems rather shocking coming from the boss of one of the world's biggest music companies.

"I don't have a CD player," admits Jason Iley, Chairman and CEO of Sony Music UK. "I stream music and have a turntable for vinyl." This balance between old and new is actually a neat reflection of Sony itself, which nurtures stars such as Mark Ronson while revering veterans such as Bruce Springsteen. "We have a lot of heritage artists and a lot of new artists, and the beauty is the way the two work together, so George Ezra signed to Columbia because that was Bob Dylan's label," says Iley, who notes that Sony looks after some of the most successful recording artists in the world but is constantly looking for the next international superstar: the next Michael Jackson, Barbra Streisand or Beyoncé.

The dramatic public response following the death of Sony artist David Bowie in January 2016 demonstrates the unique place that pop stars still inhabit in the world. The music industry in Britain is worth over £1 billion per year and Sony is a major part of that success. "Sony's established labels include Columbia, RCA, Simon Cowell's label Syco and Epic," explains Iley from the company's stylish office in Kensington, London. Recent label deals in addition to the above also include Black Butter, Insanity and Nothing Else Matters.

The acquisition of these smaller labels reflects Iley's determination to grow Sony by discovering exciting new artists. "When I look at iTunes' top 10 today, four are new acts we signed in the last year – that's the dream," he says. "This year we also have new music from Paloma Faith, Calvin Harris, The Script and Olly Murs, so this will be a big year for us."

Iley grew up listening to Pink Floyd and Bob Dylan, and soon developed his own tastes. His first gig was The Cure at Wembley – "we crimped our hair to look like Robert Smith" – and his first job was selling ads for *Deadline*, a UK comic founded in 1988 that featured as its main character Tank Girl (illustrated by Gorillaz co-creator Jamie Hewlett) and based in a recording studio. "I soon realised that comic shops had no money so there was no advertising there, but every act that

used the studio would read the magazine," says Iley. "I suggested we should illustrate musicians and put them on the cover. We did that with artists such as Blur, Senseless Things and Ride, and that meant I could contact record companies and get them to place advertising. That was my intro into music."

After continuing to work in marketing, Iley was offered a job at Sony – "one of the first albums I looked after was *HIStory* by Michael Jackson. I helped float his statue down the Thames!" – and then worked at Universal for 15 years, before being poached by Jay Z to run his Roc Nation label in New York. In 2014, he was coaxed back to London by Sony.

Iley brought with him one over-riding belief. "In music, the artist is king and always will be king," he says. "The quality of the record is the most important thing. If the artist delivers a great record, the public will buy it."

It's this belief in the pure primacy of talent that has helped musicians stick with Sony, knowing the company is with them for the long haul. "We cultivate talent," says Iley. "Mark Ronson is on his fourth album and selling more records than ever, Olly Murs is working on his fifth album, and Paloma Faith's third album has been her most successful to date. We stick with our artists and they sell more as their career develops. Over the last few years we have also re-focused our catalogue output, with AC/DC, Jeff Lynne, Dolly Parton and Barbra Streisand all enjoying huge success, and we recently had another number one album with Elvis Presley."

But Iley knows Sony cannot afford to stand still. "The catalogue is important and the artist is key, so we invest in A&R [artist and repertoire, the division responsible for new talent] to create the catalogue of the future," he explains. "The only way to do that is to sign new artists. You hope every artist will be the next Adele or Dylan, but you don't know, that's the beauty of the business. Look at Sam Smith, George Ezra or Ed Sheeran – two years ago, nobody had heard of them but now they are domestic-signed, global-selling artists. It doesn't matter if it's fashion, tech or music, we are always obsessed with that sense of discovery. There's always that hunger, and that's why we will always invest in new music."

For Iley, the greatest thrill comes when those breakthrough acts are British. "Throughout my career I've been fortunate enough to help develop some of the greatest acts in the world and the ones I'm most proud of are British – Amy Winehouse, Mark Ronson, Finley Quaye, George Ezra – those domestic acts that nobody heard of until you got involved with the process of taking them to the general public."

Sony can retain artists, Iley believes, because of the personal trust between artist and label, something that comes from Iley's own boss, Doug Morris, CEO of Sony Music. "Great leadership is so important," says Iley. "Doug is an understanding, passionate, brilliant boss and his ethos runs through the whole company. Every label has its own culture but when you have a boss that will back you, it gives everybody confidence."

That's vital in an industry where nobody can be entirely sure what will happen next and there are still important issues to resolve. "Streaming is undoubtedly the model for the future in terms of consuming music," says Iley. "That's a challenge that the industry needs to tackle. But the reason I love my job is I come in every day and anything could happen. Will we have four artists in the top 10 of iTunes? Will we win five Brit Awards? Will there be a new app that transforms how we listen to music? I have no idea. It's exciting! It can change in a minute."

The sport of kings

La Martina

The Royal Family and polo are inextricably linked. It's the sport most enjoyed by three generations of the household – The Duke of Edinburgh, The Prince of Wales and now The Duke of Cambridge and Prince Harry. The Royals' favoured polo club is Guards at Windsor, which was founded in 1955 with The Duke of Edinburgh as President and is considered the best in Europe by many. There the club shop is run by La Martina, the world's most prestigious manufacturer of polo equipment. "We became the official supplier of the club and have a shop that was opened by Her Majesty The Queen," says Lando Simonetti, La Martina's founder. "We are honoured to have this connection."

La Martina was founded 30 years ago in Argentina, where Simonetti played polo as a young man on his country estate. "In Argentina, we use horses to move our cows," he says. "Many riders started playing polo, two against two, for fun, We call it country polo. In the last 50 years, polo has been an Argentine game – it's where all the big tournaments happen."

The company began producing equipment for horse and rider – mallets, helmets, saddles – using the best materials and methods, and focusing on the safety of the player and horse. La Martina has since expanded into textiles and retail, manufacturing team kits and opening shops. "Polo is a little sport but it's played in almost every country," says Simonetti. "We became a small company that was shipping products all round the world. From that point on we became recognised as the best company for polo."

After 30 years of success, Simonetti is now looking ahead to the next three decades and beyond. The company sponsors tournaments and supplies the shirts for every international team that takes part in the Polo World Cup. It has 150 shops worldwide, including at Harrods as well as a flagship London store on Jermyn Street. Here it sells everything a polo player needs to look the part both on and off the pitch, from helmets and balls to team shirts and polo trousers, to handbags, scarves and sunglasses. La Martina sells the aspirational lifestyle of polo to the world with partners who reflect this attitude, including the likes of Maserati and Bentley.

The company's success has been the subject of a case study at Harvard University, and Simonetti has given speeches at a London business school on the same topic. He puts it down to the founding principles, simple concepts of fair play and honesty that are shared by everybody who plays polo.

"When you start a company for the family, you want to teach them to do business in the right way – don't cheat or take short cuts, be honest and get to the point," says Simonetti. "Polo is also a sport where you can't take short cuts or do sneaky things, because people and horses can get hurt. So our products are not for glamour, they are for protection and performance. That is the key for polo equipment. Our attitude from day one was: don't take any short cuts, always use the best material. We applied that same concept when we went into textile and when we went into shops. That was appreciated by our clients, suppliers and licensees."

La Martina now leads the polo world in safety and innovation while remaining a family business. "Polo is based on a few clear rules," says Simonetti. "It's driven by fair play, integrity and passion, and this attitude is one that everyone in the polo world shares. That's why networking is easy. A player is a gentlemen when playing a match and when doing business, because polo rules are life rules. La Martina shares this attitude: our most important value – transferred from the family to the company – is integrity."

La Martina is particularly proud of its London and Windsor enterprises because, as Simonetti explains, Britain is the home of polo. "Polo was created and invented by the British Army who needed a sport for the long

summers in India, not to get bored," he says. "They created a sport based on a game that had been played in Central Asia for centuries and they had a lot of fun. The best players at first were the Indians, not the English, and then it was the Argentinians. It's a sport created by England and is now dominated by Argentina, so we are right in the middle."

Simonetti's deep love of polo means he wants to use La Martina to bring the sport to the world. Polo, for him, is a passion, a lifestyle, and a historic sport with a unique culture that needs to be protected and preserved. One way La Martina does this is by supporting clubs and associations around the world. "We contribute to other universities and schools that have polo teams, like Harvard, Yale, Stanford, Eton and Oxford," he says. "We try to help them in any way we can by donating equipment for places that do not have the budget." The company also supports polo tournaments where The Duke of Cambridge and Prince Harry play for charity, and sponsors teams and tournaments around the world.

The princes' love of the sport was inspired by their grandfather, The Duke of Edinburgh, who has done a great deal for the image of polo in England through his patronage and support. "The Royal Family has always been committed to polo, even more than to cricket or tennis, because The Duke of Edinburgh passed on his passion to the rest of the family," says Simonetti. "At Guards in Windsor, they began with one field and now they have the best club in the world, not because of money but because it is run by a professional polo player. It is a real polo club and that's why it is fantastic. We are so honoured to be part of it."

Arabian nights

Royal Cavalry of Oman

Clad in costumes of brilliantly coloured silk and sitting astride Arabian horses whose bridles glint with silver, the men and women of the Royal Cavalry of Oman perform displays that combine speed, acrobatics and consummate horsemanship. They dazzled crowds at Her Majesty The Queen's Diamond Jubilee Celebrations in 2012; and were naturally invited to play a key part in the four-day Queen's Birthday celebrations at Home Park, Windsor Castle. "It is a great privilege to be part of the event and to be able to show off the skills of the cavalry," says Brigadier General Abdulrazak al Shahwarzi, Commander of the Royal Cavalry of Oman.

The Royal Cavalry of Oman was founded in 1974 by Sultan Qaboos bin Said al Said in order to preserve and promote pure-bred Arabian horses and the noble tradition of horsemanship in Omani society. "Initially, we had 20 horses," says Brigadier al Shahwarzi. "Now we have around 1,200 horses in four centres across Oman and we have nearly 850 employees, including cavalrymen and women, trainers, musicians, grooms and so on."

The Madinat Al Adiyat racetrack, near Muscat, is the heart of the cavalry's operations in Oman; and it is here that The Queen, on her second state visit to Oman in 2010, attended an equestrian show hosted by Sultan Qaboos. Among the cavalry's signature showpieces is the *rakd al arda*, in which two horses gallop side by side, with one rider standing upright, balancing on a traditional Omani saddle. Such feats are now often performed by the cavalry women, who train and ride alongside the men. "We have had female riders for 20 years," says Brigadier al Shahwarzi, "but, since 2009, they have been employed as actual members of the cavalry." Female riders are also included in the *firqah* (group), which is made up of riders who have particular talents for showriding and performances.

Away from the display arena, the Royal Cavalry of Oman is responsible for maintaining and monitoring the pure pedigree of its Arabian horses, which are bred for strength, endurance and grace. Thoroughbred horses are also bred for racing, appearing at fixtures across Europe and the Middle East; and for polo, with teams competing in Argentina, Spain and Portugal. The cavalry is a member of all the major international Arabian horse organisations, with whom it shares expertise and experience.

The Royal Cavalry of Oman uses the most up-to-date facilities at its stud in Salalah. Every horse's ancestry and medical history is recorded and updated on the cavalry database. "We have a foot in the past with our equestrian traditions, of course," says Brigadier al Shahwarzi, "but we also have a foot in the future with the latest breeding and rearing methods."

The Queen and Sultan Qaboos share decades of friendship, the longevity of their reigns (he has ruled Oman for 45 years) and a love of horses. The birthday equestrian spectacular, choreographed by al Shahwarzi, is therefore a very fitting birthday present for Her Majesty.

This storied land

Tourism Northern Ireland

Following the reception that Her Majesty The Queen received on her last visit to Northern Ireland in 2014, people in the country of all backgrounds and faiths are joining together to celebrate her 90th birthday. During that visit, The Queen also took in a tour of Titanic Studios, home of the hit television series *Game of Thrones*.

"The *Game of Thrones* phenomenon is a good metaphor for modern Northern Ireland," says John McGrillen, CEO of Tourism NI. "It is filmed in a former paint hall of the shipyard, which was weeks away from being demolished. A former BBC producer spotted it from the window of an aeroplane and, seeing its potential, encouraged HBO to make use of it."

Game of Thrones brings in tens of millions to the local economy each series, and at any point in time employs in excess of 500 people. The spirit of regeneration that has grown up around the studios is turning the once-great Harland & Wolff shipyard into a vibrant hub for the creative media and digital technology industries. It has also provided a healthy boost to tourism as fans explore the 20 or so film locations within an hour of Belfast.

Golf tourism is another growth area, not surprising given the success of Northern Ireland players, the quality of links golf and the return of the Open to Royal Portrush in 2019. Devotees of the Belfast-born author CS Lewis can also experience the Mourne Mountains, which inspired his vision of the kingdom of Narnia. Lewis once wrote of the landscape that he expected at

any moment to see a giant raise its head. He may even have been referring to the legendary Finn MacCool, who was said to have scattered the vast hexagonal rocks of the Giant's Causeway – sited within an hour of Belfast – as a walkway to Scotland.

During her last visit, The Queen planted a tree at her official residence, Hillsborough Castle, which has opened to the public and is now a popular function venue. In contrast to the castle's historic elegance is the ultra-modern Belfast Waterfront convention centre, located in the city centre. Its attractive riverside setting, wide choice of halls large and small and its versatile 2,000-seat auditorium are fast making it one of Europe's leading convention and entertainment venues.

Today's visitors seek out the history and culture of Northern Ireland as well as the beautiful scenery and dramatic coastlines. The vital mood is encapsulated in a new slogan for the capital city, Energy Unleashed, and in how the country is securing a reputation as the home of great events.

"When it comes to international sporting events such as the Giro d'Italia, the Irish Open and our all-Ireland bid to stage the Rugby World Cup in 2023, and now the excitement of staging the Open in 2019, everyone in Northern Ireland gets behind the effort," says McGrillen. "Coupled with all the recent investment, from Titanic Belfast to Derry's walls, there's never been a better time to come here."

The hit list

Celebrity Fight Night

Twenty-two years ago, a businessman and philanthropist from Arizona decided to organise a celebrity fundraiser for local charities. He persuaded boxing champion Michael Carbajal and basketball stars Charles Barkley and Dan Majerle to stage a comedy fight in oversized boxing gloves; and the audience absolutely loved it.

That man was Jimmy Walker, the event was Celebrity Fight Night, and the rest is showbiz history. The next year, Kenny Rogers performed a magical, 40-minute concert that changed the emphasis of Celebrity Fight Night from a local sports event to a celebrity-studded charity gala featuring stadium-filling entertainers.

In its third year, Celebrity Fight Night stepped into the full glare of the national spotlight when the world's greatest himself, living legend and former boxing champion Muhammad Ali, accepted an invitation to become the featured guest. At the time, Ali was being treated for Parkinson's disease at the Barrow Neurological Institute in Phoenix. "He decided to join us as the face of the event and he has been our guest of honour ever since," says Sean Currie, Executive Director of Celebrity Fight Night.

Although the celebrity boxing aspect of the event had initially been a way of differentiating Celebrity Fight Night from other charity events, that element was eventually dropped to make way for the music. "The quality of the entertainers who were coming in to sing was so impressive that we chose to elevate the musical entertainment," says Currie.

No longer featuring celebrity boxing, Celebrity Fight Night is a black tie affair including cocktails, dinner, live and silent auctions and performances from some of the world's leading music stars. The list of performers over the years reads like a Who's Who of the US film, music, sports and entertainment industries. Audiences have been treated to incredible performances by global stars such as Jennifer Lopez, Celine Dion, Robin Williams, Lionel Richie and Barry Manilow. British rock star Rod Stewart sang at the 2003 gala.

The fundraisers have amassed a huge amount of money for numerous charities, especially for the Muhammad Ali Parkinson Center at the Barrow Neurological Institute. The first event, held back in 1994, raised $100,000. Today, the event typically raises between $5 million and $9 million and is one of the largest-grossing charity events in the USA.

Guests pay up to $100,000 to host a table of 10 people, attend a VIP reception where they can rub shoulders with celebrities, and enjoy a banquet before the evening's entertainment even starts. Plenty more funds are raised during the auctions, where generous guests compete with each other in the bidding for an amazing array of prizes.

The Phoenix gala is a fantastic opportunity for guests to mix with some of America's biggest celebrities. "People enjoy it because they mingle with stars from Hollywood, professional sports and music in a way that they would never be able to anywhere else," says Currie. "We don't have a VIP area where the celebrities are behind a red velvet rope and the guests can only watch from a distance. They literally sit among them, have dinner with them and take pictures with them and feel like they are in Hollywood for the night."

Another feature of the gala is the Muhammad Ali Celebrity Fight Night Awards, which were established as a way to acknowledge leaders in the sports, entertainment and business communities who best represent the qualities associated with The Champ's fight to find a cure for Parkinson's disease. Previous award recipients over the years have included Halle Berry, Jim Carrey, Arnold Schwarzenegger, Larry King, Michael J Fox, Chevy Chase, Sharon Stone and Magic Johnson.

Celebrity Fight Night has celebrated its 22nd anniversary this year with celebrities and professional athletes from across the USA uniting to do their part to help win the fight against Parkinson's disease and support a range of other charities.

The event was held at the JW Marriott Desert Ridge Resort & Spa in Phoenix, Arizona and hosted by Grammy award-winning country music singer Reba McEntire for her 11th consecutive year. Performances were led by fellow country star and seven-time Grammy winner Carrie Underwood, musical duo Brooks and Dunn, vocal quartet The Tenors and stand-up comedian Sinbad, all directed by 16-time Grammy winner David Foster.

One of the prizes at the auction was a trip for a couple to fly to London and stay in the Grosvenor House Hotel on Park Lane for Her Majesty The Queen's Birthday Celebrations at Windsor Castle in May 2016. Another amazing charity experience organised by the foundation is a trip to Italy where donors enjoy five full days with the singer Andrea Bocelli, who accompanies the guests to the most magical sights in Florence and Venice. The culmination of this enviable experience includes a night at Bocelli's own home on the Italian coast where more star-studded entertainment is presented.

As the gala approaches its own silver jubilee in 2019, Currie says that the organisers are determined to continue to raise awareness of the Parkinson's disease research carried out at the Muhammad Ali Parkinson Center. "We plan to carry on Muhammad's legacy as long as we can, as long as people continue to come out and support what he stands for and what we are doing."

A vision for Europe

European Broadcasting Union

In the summer of 1953, Her Majesty The Queen was officially crowned at Westminster Abbey, in front of more than 8,000 guests, including prime ministers and heads of state from around the Commonwealth. To enable millions around the world to watch this event, the BBC had set up its biggest ever outside broadcast, with radio and television transmissions in 44 languages.

But the BBC could not have done this without the help of its partner, the European Broadcasting Union (EBU). The EBU provided the transmission links that carried coverage of the event, the guests and the crowds outside Westminster Abbey to millions of viewers across Europe and beyond. The Coronation was the first ever live satellite transmission across the channel.

The EBU was created three years earlier, in 1950, and held its first meeting in Torquay. Executives from the BBC and more than 20 other countries met with the aim of developing common solutions to technical issues and exchanging programme content to help fill their schedules. Today, the EBU has more than 73 broadcast members in 56 countries from Russia to Iceland, from North Africa and the Middle East to Scandinavia. Its members operate more than 1,800 TV and radio channels, broadcasting in more than 120 different languages to a potential audience of 1.03 billion people.

The organisation's mission is to make public service media indispensable. "Public service media is the cornerstone of society," says Ingrid Deltenre, Director General. "It strengthens democracy and democratic governance. It ensures that the whole of society, including those without political or economic influence, have access to information. It provides a voice for the voiceless." For the EBU, the role of the media is to provide the greatest possible part of society with a broad spectrum of views on issues of public concern. "This way public service media can promote tolerance and understanding amongst diverse groups," says Deltenre. "It also facilitates discussion around issues of national concern, like education, poverty and healthcare."

Public service media has many distinctive features, including universality, independence, excellence, diversity, accountability and innovation. "Without public service media," says Deltenre, "there are no checks or balances to ensure that

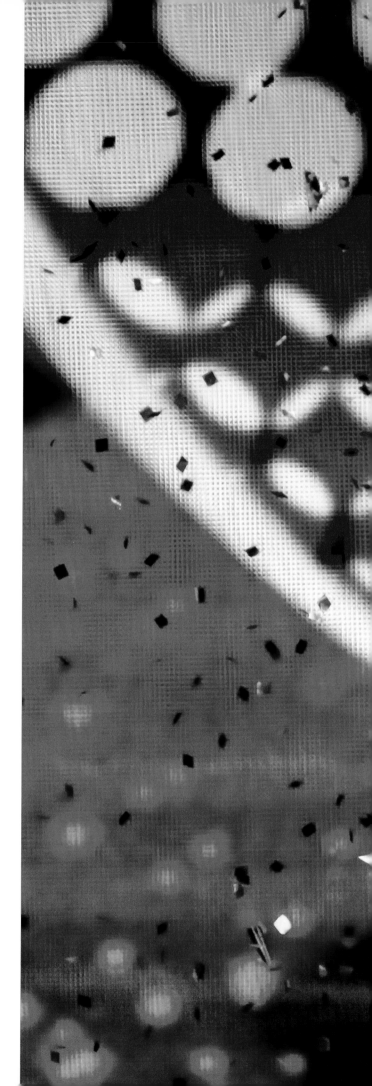

broadcasters treat all sectors of society in a neutral, non-preferential way. There is no counterpoint to those seeking to influence opinion or promote one belief set above others, whether political, social, religious, linguistic or racial. There is also no counterpoint to those motivated by profit above reaching a diverse, universal audience."

To this end, public service media is the beating heart of the creative industry. At its best, it provides innovative, attractive and trustworthy programming that meets the Reithian ideal that guides the BBC and many other broadcasters around the world who follow its lead: to inform, educate and entertain audiences across the whole of society – not just those that can afford to pay, nor those who belong to a particular sector of society or follow a particular creed.

Public service media brings huge economic benefit to society, as well as cultural value. The public service media share of the European audiovisual market is worth €33 billion (£25 billion) per year. It creates hundreds of thousands of jobs, including the flourishing independent production industry. Around Europe, public service media give excellent value for money to their audiences – on average, households in Europe pay €135 (£105) each year for their public service radio and TV channels.

One of the jewels in the crown of the EBU's creative activity is the Eurovision Song Contest. Launched in 1956, just three years after the Coronation, it is now the most watched live entertainment show on earth, with a worldwide audience of 200 million people. The contest even holds the Guinness World Record for the longest-running TV music competition. The country with the most victories is Ireland with seven, followed by

France, Luxemburg and Sweden with six each. Perhaps the most famous winner is Sweden's ABBA who triumphed in 1974.

The EBU is proud to play a leading role in the public service media community. It provides a range of services to its members, from lobbying hard to protect its members' interests, to helping them resist excessive government interference in their activities.

"We stay faithful to our roots in the field of technology," says Deltenre, "helping broadcasters establish common technical standards like high-definition (HD), 4K, and digital audio and video standards." The EBU's state-of-the-art transmission platform brings premium live sports from stadium to screen – from football to motor racing, from skiing to athletics. For music broadcasters, the EBU transmits more than 4,000 concerts a year, from the classical elegance of the annual New Year's Eve concert by the Vienna Philharmonic Orchestra to jazz, folk, pop and rock.

In news, the EBU delivers all the day's top international news stories on its 24/7 exchange platform from where the news is breaking straight to the radio and television broadcasters who put them on air – more than 50,000 news reports every year. It also provides broadcasters with the technical facilities to allow their correspondents to report live into their news bulletins from top stories around the world.

"The EBU is at the forefront of the news industry," says Deltenre, "transmitting the stories that count – like the Coronation and, indeed, every major royal story since. We are proud to have accompanied the longest serving monarch on her journey. And we will be honoured to continue doing so long into the future."

Thorough expertise

New Zealand Bloodstock

"A preoccupation with horses predated every single other thing we knew," says New Zealand Bloodstock Ltd co-founder, Sir Peter Vela, of his lifelong passion that formed the basis for taking ownership of New Zealand's leading thoroughbred auction business more than 20 years ago.

Celebrating a 90th anniversary of its own this year, the business may be half a world away, but it shares this significant milestone with Her Majesty The Queen. It has provided the focal point of the New Zealand thoroughbred industry since its inception in 1927, conducting auctions every year since then.

The Vela family purchased New Zealand Bloodstock (NZB) in December 1995 and, with the family's business acumen and passion for the New Zealand thoroughbred, the company has grown to a position of global prominence. Sir Peter Vela was knighted for his services to the thoroughbred industry in September 2014.

Located in the lush green countryside of Karaka, just south of Auckland, NZB has experienced phenomenal success from its sale ring. From its origins auctioning the likes of the mighty Phar Lap in 1928, through innumerable champions of the 20th century, NZB benefits from New Zealand's idyllic natural environment and expert horsemen and horsewomen to pack a big punch on the world stage.

With more than 100 Group One winners in the past five seasons alone – more than any other sales company in Australasia – NZB graduates are dominant across the racetracks at home and abroad. NZB's multiple Group One successes include King's Stand Stakes winner Little Bridge, witnessed by The Queen at Royal Ascot in 2012, and New Zealand-bred So You Think winning the Prince of Wales's Stakes in the same year. Other recent top-flight successes include 2015 Melbourne Cup champion Prince of Penzance (Australia), 2015 Takamatsunomiya Kinen winner Aerovelocity (Japan) and 2014 Singapore Guineas winner War Affair (Singapore), all of whom carried the "NZ" suffix.

The company's Karaka Sales Complex was built in 1987 with the first sale conducted in January 1988. Through the mid-1980s the then managing director left New Zealand with his architect to uncover the best design aspects of the leading auction houses around the world. Many of these ideas were combined to produce what is in situ today – one of the best purpose-built equine auction complexes in the world.

These days, NZB offers around 3,500 thoroughbreds at auction each year. Already this year the highlight has been the sale of the yearling colt (bred to Southern Hemisphere time) by world champion sire Frankel to an international group of owners, for NZ$1.3 million. With more than half its auctioned stock bought by international buyers, Karaka regularly attracts buyers from Australia, China, Hong Kong, Macau, Malaysia, Singapore, South Africa, Indonesia, the UK, Ireland, Japan, Korea, the United Arab Emirates, Mongolia and beyond.

With its ongoing commitment to supporting equine excellence around the world, NZB's sponsorships include The Queen's Diamond Jubilee in 2012 and 90th Birthday Celebrations in 2016, and Sir Mark Todd's Olympic bids to Beijing 2008, London 2012 and ahead to Rio 2016..

Racing hearts

Donington Park Racing Ltd

In the world of motor racing, Donington Park has long been considered the spiritual home of the sport. Since it was founded in 1931, it has become a treasured national institution. Its position, near the village of Castle Donington in Leicestershire, places it close to the very heart of England.

Now owned and run by CEO Kevin Wheatcroft, the venue was originally part of the Donington Hall estate. The circuit hosted three legendary Grand Prix races in the 1930s but, with the onset of the Second World War, was requisitioned by the Ministry of Defence and used as a military vehicle depot. It remained over-looked and unloved until 1971 when it was rescued from dereliction by successful local businessman and car collector, the late Tom Wheatcroft, as a place to keep his vast assortment of racing cars. The site became home to the Donington Grand Prix Collection, a showcase of the world's largest collection of Formula One cars and then, in 1977, after a hiatus of almost 30 years, Wheatcroft finally brought racing back to Donington.

Working with his son Kevin, Wheatcroft sponsored and ran countless race teams on both two and four wheels. At one time, the pair even manufactured a racing car under the Wheatcroft name. Kevin inherited his father's love of collecting and accumulated as many tanks, motorcycles and other vehicles as his father owned Grand Prix cars. One of Wheatcroft's seven children, Kevin worked alongside his father for more than 30 years, and the two men formed a friendship that transcended the usual father–son relationship.

"My dad was a tremendous enthusiast and something of a visionary," says Kevin. "Motor vehicles were originally his hobby – he actually made his fortune from constructing houses and factories."

By 1977, Wheatcroft had invested more than £7 million of his own money into resurrecting his beloved Donington Park. At this point, his accountant advised him that he would be wise to stop spending with such enthusiasm and attempt to turn it into a viable business.

Wheatcroft clearly took heed because the next stage of Donington Park's history culminated in the staging of its own Grand Prix in 1993. The winner, Ayrton Senna – regarded by many as the greatest driver of his time – described his victory that year as his greatest ever. And in a report by the Millennium Motorsport team, the race was voted the Grand Prix of the century.

Had Donington not been revived in the 1970s, it is likely it would have reverted to farmland or been developed for housing. But today, the once-sleepy nearby village

is a thriving community filled with shops, restaurants and hotels, which owe much of their prosperity to the success of the park.

It hasn't all been plain sailing however. In 2007, the operational side of Donington Park was leased to an outside company, which went bankrupt after just two years. Sadly, this period of its history coincided with Wheatcroft's death, depriving him of the chance to witness his own son rescue and restore his beloved circuit, in a neat case of history repeating itself.

"We took Donington back, and completely repaired and restored it during a closed season," says Kevin. "We opened for business the next year – and here we are, so soon after, attracting record crowds. It's very sad that my father never lived to see this place rise again," he says. "It's something that I think about all the time. But he would have known that I would put my back into resurrecting it from the ashes – just as he had done."

For many years before his death, Wheatcroft had fantasised about owning a number of rare and iconic cars that were not available to buy. So, in characteristic can-do fashion, he galvanised his son and his team, and set about recreating them.

"My late father often reminisced about witnessing the legendary Mercedes-Benz Silver Arrows that first raced at Donington in 1937," says Kevin. "Since it wasn't possible to acquire one, we decided to build one instead. We made six, sold four and retained two. This was very good news for a few fortunate car collectors."

The team also spent 10 years creating an exact, tool-room copy of the legendary Bugatti Royale. "Once the project was completed,"

says Kevin, "the car's crowning moment was to transport Prince Joachim of Denmark and Princess Marie Cavallier of France at their wedding."

The venue now hosts auctions for classic cars, as well as for heavy industrial equipment and machinery – to which people attend from all over the world. It is also a popular venue for corporate and private events, including weddings and even the occasional funeral, at which the ashes of the deceased – in accordance with last wishes – are scattered around the famous circuit.

Kevin supports a variety of charities including Full Stop, the NSPCC's anti-child abuse campaign, of which he is a patron, and Hope Against Cancer, in honour of his late father. He has also established his own "tank bank" – a British army tank into which visitors can make donations, to be shared among military charities.

Donington's owner is showing no signs of slowing down yet. In addition to hosting the gigantic music festival Download, and the global home of Formula E, he is now making plans to host an annual military history celebration, entitled Armour in the Park.

Kevin attributes his success and that of his father to a passionate love of their projects, above the desire to make money. "I could easily have made a decision to sell this place, or develop it for the money and move on to something else," he says. "But in response to a tremendous campaign to save Donington, I piled money back into something that had been a disaster in 2009. I did that in a very bad economic climate, out of love. Luckily I got it right."

Keeping good council

Wokingham Borough Council

One recent royal visit to Berkshire saw The Earl of Wessex visit Wokingham Borough Council's Duke of Edinburgh Award scheme in March 2016. The scheme has encouraged countless youngsters and served as inspiration for the council, motivating its Head of Strategic Commissioning Brian Grady to create a group of Young Commissioners. This team is charged with helping to change children's services, combat bullying and improve housing and support services for children who care for vulnerable adults. "They themselves have had a tough time in life," says Grady, "but now they are doing remarkable things for the community. They are experts through experience."

Community social work with children and families is a key area of innovation for the council. "Our Early Help and Innovation Programme has been transformative," says Grady. "This evidence-based approach offers high-quality professional support to effect change in order that a child's life chances are enhanced. But it all starts with the families."

"Our aim is to give families who want to settle here well-serviced communities with excellent community support and facilities," says Chief Executive Andy Couldrick. As with any council, this means addressing its share of housing shortages and social deprivation. To this end, in addition to its Early Help and Innovation Programme for families, Wokingham Borough Council is investing in thousands of quality homes. It leads the way in pursuing a growth strategy to meet community needs while proactively supporting local economic development.

The council identified four Strategic Development Locations (SDLs) north and south of Wokingham that could accommodate well-designed new communities with great infrastructure. "We have the advantage of brownfield sites near Wokingham," says Couldrick, "which we are bringing to life with a significant new house-building programme, new schools, roads, green spaces and shops." The aim is to provide some 13,000 homes by 2026, both market and affordable.

It's a long-term approach informed by extensive public consultation. "At the Arborfield site," says Couldrick, "much of the decision making for the new secondary school was done by local parents who met with architects and planners to help design the kind of school they wanted for their children."

Wokingham's ambitious home-building programme promises to address demands in the region. Furthermore, its children's services are safeguarding families in need through positive, early interventions that will allow them, too, to benefit from the region's burgeoning economy.

Creativity in flight

Scottish Ballet

"There is creativity in absolutely everything we do," says Scottish Ballet's Christopher Hampson. "We inspire all who come into contact with the company with our phenomenal dancers. To see dance being performed at such a high level gives our audiences images that stay in the mind forever."

Based in Glasgow, the company combines classical and contemporary ballet with brave new commissions, connecting with audiences across Scotland, the rest of the UK and internationally, through live performances and innovative online content. Since becoming Artistic Director in 2012, Hampson has unified the company's artistic aims with its education and outreach programmes.

"Education is not a bolt-on to everything else you do," he says. "It is about engaging with audiences wherever they are." Scottish Ballet was one of the first UK companies to offer live streaming of rehearsals and is developing its digital presence with BBC Arts Online and website The Space. "In 2017, we launch a digital-only season that will allow us to showcase talent choreographically without geographical limitations."

At Tramway, Scottish Ballet's purpose-built studio complex, the rehearsal programme shifts between Christmas classics, including *The Nutcracker* and *Hansel and Gretel*,

and contemporary pieces such as David Dawson's brand new *Swan Lake* and Matthew Bourne's *Highland Fling*, a feisty reinterpretation of *La Sylphide*.

"It's important that we build up an exciting and broad repertoire," says Hampson. "I feel it's our remit to serve Scotland the best of the dance world." To this end the company tours the country each year. Its Edinburgh International Festival 2016 appearance will feature works by Crystal Pite and Angelin Preljocaj, bringing a raw sensuality, power and brutal energy to the stage in this provocative and exciting double-bill.

The company's patron, The Prince of Wales, had a private preview of a rather different production on an official visit to Tramway. "We were rehearsing a *pas de deux* for the opening of the 2014 Commonwealth Games," recalls Hampson, "which the Prince was attending later that evening, so he was able to see it with us first."

Scottish Ballet offers its audience an inspired repertoire both in the UK and internationally, with tours to the USA and across Europe. "Last year we performed in the Mariinsky Theatre in St Petersburg," says Hampson. "We are a Scottish institution that offers an extreme output of creativity from all corners of the world. Our audiences trust us to produce exciting work."

Northern star

Bolton Council

The town of Bolton stands proud against the distinctive and dramatic backdrop of the west Pennine moors. Up until the 19th century it had been a relatively modest market town. But with the development of steam-powered cotton mills it rapidly expanded into one of the country's most prosperous industrial hubs.

As one of England's largest towns without city status – it has a population of around 280,000 – Bolton has played host to numerous royal visitors over the years. These include King George V and Queen Mary in 1913, their son Edward, Prince of Wales (later King Edward VIII) in 1921 and Her Majesty The Queen, who enjoyed the town's hospitality in 1954, 1968, 1988 and, most recently, in 2009.

Bolton also boasts a disproportionately long roll-call of famous citizens, past and present, who have had influence in a variety of fields. "In the field of manufacturing and commerce, Bolton has been home to such figures as Richard Arkwright and Samuel Crompton, pioneers of industrial cotton spinning," says Cliff Morris, Leader of Bolton Council. "And the international sportswear company, Reebok, grew from a Bolton cobbler's shop that started in 1895."

The town has produced playwrights such as Bill Naughton, writer of *Alfie*, and Jim Cartwright, creator of *The Rise and Fall of Little Voice*, as well as the Booker-shortlisted novelist Monica Ali. The actor Sir Ian McKellen grew up in the town, as did comedian Peter Kay, while Danny Boyle, Oscar-winning film-maker and artistic director of the 2012 Olympics Ceremony, was educated there.

"The world of sport is also proudly represented," says Morris. "Cyclist Jason Kenny, World Champion and Olympic gold medallist, was born in Bolton, as was world champion boxer Amir Khan."

Resourcefulness and innovation are evident in all quarters, and the Egyptology exhibition at Bolton Museum is becoming one of the country's leading tourist attractions. "This is the only one of its kind in the world," says Morris. "We've been generously funded by the National Lottery and we have a fantastic collection. A centrepiece of the display is the sarcophagus – a replica of the tomb of King Thutmose III. The exhibition has toured the Far East, and we're hoping to recreate it in Bolton for permanent show."

Bolton's Octagon Theatre adds further prestige to the town. Opened in 1967 by Princess Margaret, the theatre is internationally renowned for its imaginative productions of established and original works, and attracts talent from the highest echelons of the profession.

Another feather in the town's cap is the University of Bolton, recognised by many as an engine of growth. "One of its crowning achievements is CAPE – the Centre for Advanced Performance Engineering," says Morris. "Having partnered with RLR Msport, Bolton is the first university in Britain to have a fully functioning race team on campus." It is now working with the British racing car builders, Ginetta, on its own Le Mans LMP3 car.

In addition to its many successes, Bolton enjoys a unique reputation for its warmth and consideration. "A survey around a decade ago concluded that Boltonians are the friendliest people in Britain," says Morris, "I'm not sure how you quantify these things, but I'm sure that's entirely true!"

A big thank you

The Patron's Lunch

A street party is an infectious and joyous affair. Coronations, royal weddings and jubilees have for decades provided the opportunity for communities to come together, decking streets with bunting the length and breadth of the UK and throughout the Commonwealth. Sunday 12 June will be no exception, with 10,000 guests due to attend the Patron's Lunch, Her Majesty The Queen's very own street party, which will see flag-draped picnic tables stretching out along The Mall.

The climax to a weekend of celebrations, the Patron's Lunch is an opportunity to applaud The Queen's tireless work as patron of more than 600 charities and organisations. And the vast majority of the 10,000 ticket holders for the event – the largest of its kind ever to be held on The Mall – will be those that work for these organisations.

As for The Queen and The Duke of Edinburgh, they will be able to view the party from a specially constructed platform on the Queen Victoria Memorial in front of Buckingham Palace. The royal couple will be joined on the day by other members of the Royal Family, including her grandsons the Duke of Cambridge and Prince Harry – the event's Joint-Presidents.

Once seated along The Mall, lunch guests will tuck into a summer picnic hamper and will also be treated to a carnival spectacular that will progress from Horse Guards Parade along The Mall, ending up in St James's Park. In addition, two large screens will be put up – in Green Park and St James's Park, respectively – enabling a further 15,000 spectators to watch the day's events unfold.

Part of a weekend of celebration's to mark The Queen's official birthday, the Patron's Lunch will be preceded by the Service of Thanksgiving on the Friday 10 in St Paul's Cathedral. Trooping the Colour will take place on the Saturday on Horse Guards Parade, after which the Royal Family will make their traditional appearance on the balcony of Buckingham Palace.

During the Diamond Jubilee celebrations in 2012, local councils received nearly 10,000 applications to host street parties and, in addition to The Mall's festivities, it is expected that a similar number will be held in celebration of The Queen's 90th birthday, providing the wider public with the chance to join the celebrations while raising money for local charities and community programmes.

Community involvement is at the heart of the Patron's Lunch, the core themes of which are charity, community and celebration. Large or small, the charities and organisations that have The Queen as their patron benefit enormously from her support and her ability to raise their profiles. Indeed, The Queen's countless visits to these groups serve not only as a

PREVIOUS PAGES: THE MALL
(LEFT) AND ROYAL PARKS
(RIGHT) WILL PLAY HOST
TO THE PATRON'S LUNCH.
RIGHT: STREET PARTIES
WILL HELD THE LENGTH
OF BRITAIN TO MARK THE
QUEEN'S 90TH BIRTHDAY

reminder of her ongoing commitment, but also as a means of championing
the often unsung work of those employees and volunteers who staff them.

Such recognition is something of a royal tradition – one that The Queen
has shown unswerving dedication to, as evinced by her sheer number of
patronages. The Queen inherited the patronage of many charities and
organisations from her father King George VI, and some boast royal ties
that predate even his reign, such as the Mother's Union, the first patron
of which was Queen Victoria in 1898. Over the years, The Queen has added
to these, granting her patronage to a diverse spectrum of charities and
organisations across the voluntary sector, embracing the arts, wildlife, sport,
science, the young, the elderly and the environment. She is patron of the
Edinburgh International Festival, national children's charities including
Barnardo's and Action for Children, and Commonwealth organisations
such as the Australian Red Cross.

Sports are widely represented, from international bodies such as the
Commonwealth Games Federation to the smaller scale Royal Nassau Sailing
Club. The Queen's interest in animals is reflected in her patronage of the
Battersea Dogs and Cats Home and The Highland Pony Society, among
many others. Patronage of the Sandringham Cricket Club, whose members
are employees of the Sandringham Estate, is typical of the close connection
The Queen and the Royal Family maintain with their estates and those that
live and work on them.

The Queen's patronage continues to inspire the charities and
organisations that she supports around Britain and the Commonwealth.
Big or small, international or local, these groups are motivated by her interest
and involvement in their work. It seems only fitting, then, that in the year
of her 90th birthday, The Queen's enduring dedication is celebrated in the
company of thousands of the hard-working volunteers and employees
who share in her commitment and enthusiasm.

The health of a nation

The NHS

In the year of Her Majesty The Queen's birth, the vast majority of British people did not have access to quality healthcare. Aside from a small number who could afford private healthcare, in 1926 most people were reliant on hospital charities, funded by the benevolent. Some municipalities tried to run hospitals as well as utilities, but GPs were funded by Friendly Societies that paid them as little as possible. Some bigger teaching hospitals (such as St Bart's, Guy's and St Thomas's) received private investment, while others were developed in conjunction with universities. But each voluntary hospital was a law unto itself, raising funds and deciding its own admission policies. Patients were usually charged and many hospitals were near bankrupt.

Three years after The Queen's birth, the 1929 Local Government Act forced local authorities to take over poor law hospitals that now became municipal hospitals serving ratepayers, not paupers. But quality varied from town to town, and many were in need of huge upgrading and investment. By the 1930s, reports by the British Medical Association,

the King's Fund and the Nuffield Provincial Hospitals Trust attempted to bring about a standardisation of care.

The experience of the Second World War, when an emergency medical service was created as the country came under command and control, provided an example of what could be done. William Beveridge, later a Liberal MP and peer, wrote a report on social welfare in 1942, appealing to Conservatives who might fear a health service by arguing that strong welfare institutions would increase the competitiveness of British industry and create healthier and more motivated workers. After Labour's election victory in 1945, Health Secretary Aneurin Bevan presented to the cabinet a plan that favoured nationalisation of all hospitals, voluntary or council, and a regional framework.

The National Health Service started on 5 July 1948 in a society weary but disciplined by war. In a country that was rebuilding itself from the rubble of war and dealing with austerity, rationing, a dollar crisis and a fuel shortage, the NHS

had to compete for resources with other priorities, and new hospitals had little claim on the few building materials available – housing and schools came first.

This was a time of massive innovation. The pharmaceutical industry was creating a flood of new drugs. Antibiotics, better anaesthetics, cortisone, drugs for the treatment of mental illness such as schizophrenia and depression, good diuretics for heart failure and antihistamines all became available. Ultrasound was built upon wartime electronics expertise. These developments, while improving the lot of the patient, raised the cost of the NHS.

Its funding system was unique. The NHS was almost entirely financed from central taxation. The rich paid more than the poor. Everyone was eligible for care, even people temporarily resident or visiting the country. Initially, care was free at the point of use – when prescription charges of one shilling were suggested, it split the Labour party.

On the Conservative party's return to government in 1951, a commitment to the NHS was maintained. Throughout the 1960s and 1970s, the elderly, the mentally ill and handicapped, children's services and the disabled were the subjects of reports, sometimes following scandals. Changes in abortion law in 1968 led to new pressures on gynaecological services. Medical advances included the increasingly wide application of endoscopy and the advent of CAT scanning. Transplant surgery was becoming increasingly successful and genetic engineering slowly began to influence medicine. Intensive care units were now widely available and new drugs appeared, including non-steroidal anti-inflammatory treatments. Kidney dialysis became more widely available and surgery established a place in the care of coronary heart disease.

By the start of the 1980s, and with Margaret Thatcher's Conservative government cutting public spending, there was greater emphasis on the financial bounds within which the NHS operated. With the introduction of MRI scans, minimal-access surgery, increasing heart and liver transplants, and a huge increase in the number of hip and femur replacements, the NHS could no longer even pretend to do everything medically possible.

Following the 1990 Community Care Act, the Conservatives started to introduce the "internal market" in the NHS. It divided sections of the NHS into "purchasers" (health authorities and some family doctors) who were given budgets to buy healthcare from "providers" (acute hospitals, ambulance services, organisations providing care for the mentally ill, people with learning disabilities and the elderly). That internal market has been maintained under successive changes in government since, with NHS Trusts transforming into Primary Care Trusts and Strategic Health Authorities, which in turn evolved into Clinical Commissioning Groups. Regulation came in the form of the National Institute for Clinical Excellence (NICE), which assessed the cost-effectiveness of new drugs and technologies, and the Healthcare Commission, which looked at the quality, governance and financial management of trusts.

After 68 years, the NHS remains one of the UK's proudest achievements – a healthcare system funded by the nation for the nation. Whatever the future holds for it, one thing remains certain, and was summed up perfectly by Bevan: "We shall never have all we need," he said. "Expectations will always exceed capacity. The service must always be changing, growing and improving – it must always appear inadequate."

Treatment for all

Cipla Ltd

It's not often that multinational pharmaceutical companies stand up for the common man. But Cipla, which began life in Mumbai in 1935 as the Chemical, Industrial & Pharmaceutical Laboratories, has distinguished itself in this field with the pledge that "None shall be denied".

Although Cipla was set up by his father Dr K A Hamied – a champion of Indian independence who is pictured, opposite, with his ally Mahatma Gandhi – Chairman Dr Yusuf Hamied has since revolutionised treatment for the poor across the developing world. Nowhere is this more apparent than in the company's approach to combating HIV, the virus which causes AIDS.

It was the African HIV/AIDS epidemic in the 1990s that convinced Dr Hamied that urgent action was needed. Millions were dying as a result of the virus: there were 8,000 deaths a day in Africa alone. Drugs known as anti-retroviral (ARV) medication were available but priced at more than $12,000 per patient per year. With major drug producers adamant that they would not reduce their ARV pricing, the poor stood no chance of survival. As Dr Hamied says: "What's the use of developing lifesaving medicines if you can't make them affordable to the patient?"

Dr Hamied formed an alliance with a small group of people committed to confronting the disease and finding a solution to this humanitarian disaster. The Cambridge-educated chemist sought the help of William Haddad, a pioneering advocate for generic drugs in the US; Denis Broun of UNAIDS; and former Peace Corps volunteer David Langdon. Also on the team was Robert Weissman, of the corporate accountability organisation Essential Action, and James Love, an intellectual property rights activist.

The men had one thing in common: they were appalled that human beings should be left to die in order to preserve the profits of companies.

In 2000, Dr Hamied told the European Commission in Brussels that there should be no monopolies on vital, lifesaving drugs in the developing world; and that Cipla was prepared to offer its own triple-drug ARV for just $800 per patient per year. This pledge was accompanied by a promise to provide free technology to any country that wanted to make its own ARVs.

Even when no one took up the offer, Dr Hamied was determined to break the barrier to making HIV drugs available at affordable prices. So he offered Cipla's triple-ARV combination in a three-in-one tablet to the humanitarian organisation Médecins Sans Frontières (MSF) for $350 per patient per year, the equivalent of less than a dollar a day. This gesture, says Dr Hamied, "lifted the death sentence from millions across the developing world".

"In our crusade against the disease," says Dr Hamied, "we have developed over 15 single and combination medicines that have revolutionised HIV therapy, not just in India but across the world. It's not surprising that today around 1 million patients in the world are on our antiretrovirals, and with regular therapy they can live for years and lead a near-normal life. Our world-class scientific resources and educational platforms are helping physicians across India and the world manage the disease effectively."

Cipla today employs more than 20,000 staff and is still based in Mumbai. With a turnover of $1.78 billion a year, this pharmaceutical firm has more than 1,500 products all approved by regulatory bodies such as

the US Food and Drug Administration (FDA). Over the past 80 years, Cipla has emerged as one of the most respected pharmaceutical names not just in India, but across the 150 countries in which it operates.

As well as being a market leader in ARV therapies, the company has also pioneered treatments for patients suffering from respiratory disorders, and for urological conditions such as incontinence and issues affecting the kidneys. Respiratory disease is one of the largest killers globally and Cipla has been developing solutions for nearly 50 years. Its products include the largest range of inhaled medications and devices in the world for asthma and chronic obstructive pulmonary disease (COPD).

A new advance is the Autohaler, a breath-actuated inhaler that makes it easier for patients to take their medication than metered dose inhalers (MDIs). MDIs are designed to deliver a specific amount of medication to the lungs, in the form of a short burst of aerosolised medicine. The Autohaler enables the medication to be taken more easily by patients, especially children, and by those who suffer airflow obstruction and arthritis.

As for the future, Cipla will remain committed to ensuring people have access to good quality, affordable healthcare. In 2015, it purchased two US-based companies, InvaGen and Exelan, involved in the manufacture of generic drug treatments. This was part of its vision to meet the needs of patients who struggle to afford medicines. According to Cipla's Managing Director and global CEO Subhanu Saxena, the biggest threat to the development of any economy is the lack of good quality, affordable healthcare. "Without a healthy and energetic population," he says, "an economy cannot thrive."

And it is not just the developing world that is in need of access to affordable medicine. NHS statistics show that generic medicines make up almost 75 per cent of the total medicines consumed by patients using Britain's health service. "At Cipla, we believe our work is not just about making medicines," says Saxena, "it's about making a difference."

There's no doubt that there are thousands of people worldwide who are grateful for the difference that Cipla has made to their health, including HIV patients who were once deprived of lifesaving treatment.

Horse power

The Brooke

In the UK, the original definition of horsepower is confined to the history books. But, for the world's poorest communities, working horses, donkeys and mules are still essential. These working equines are the engines that power the developing world, doing the hardest jobs under the toughest conditions to support the livelihoods of 672 million people. That's 9 per cent of the world's population. Yet, sadly, many of these animals suffer constantly to provide their labour to mankind.

It's these hardest-working of animals that are supported by this London-based charity. "The Brooke protects and improves the welfare of millions of horses, donkeys and mules," says Petra Ingram, the charity's CEO. "These are the animals that the world's poorest people rely on to work their way out of poverty, and build a better future for themselves, their families and their animals."

The animal welfare charity is a cause close to the heart of The Duchess of Cornwall, its President since 2006. She was introduced to the Brooke by her parents – indeed, the Duchess's father Major Bruce Shand was a cavalry officer in Egypt, where the charity was founded in 1934. Set up by Dorothy Brooke, the wife of a then cavalry brigadier, the Old War Horse Memorial Hospital was dedicated to the care of former war horses used as beasts of burden in Cairo. Today the Brooke uses its expertise to train and support owners of horses, donkeys and mules – as well as local vets, farriers and harness makers – to improve understanding and care around the world.

While the charity's name and services have changed during the past eight decades, its respect and compassion towards the animals' owners remains the same. "The people we work with live in some of the most marginalised and unstable places in the world," says Ingram. "Their animal is their lifeline to a better future."

So although emergency intervention and veterinary help are part of the charity's work, the emphasis is on empowering local people. As well as training, the charity encourages owners to bulk buy better-quality food and medicine and even offers insurance policies for their animals. "To create positive, lasting change for working animals," says Ingram, "we focus on building skills and knowledge in people."

Along with showing owners how improved animal welfare can benefit their family and livelihood, the Brooke's field experience and research informs its work with governments, promoting the contribution of working equines and securing them the protection enjoyed by other livestock through vaccination programmes and wider health care.

In 2015, the 1.8 million animals reached by the Brooke supported the lives of 10.8 million people. With more than 112 million working horses, donkeys and mules worldwide, the charity will work wherever the need is greatest, be it construction industries like the brick kilns of India, or the coal mines of Pakistan.

"Poverty is complex," says Ingram. "The Brooke offers part of the answer to a really big problem. You can't eradicate poverty without recognising the huge contribution of working horses, donkeys and mules. Good welfare for one horse, donkey or mule can benefit a family of six, so the outcome is for the animal and the people."

Taking care

The Old Vicarage

Caring for older people is not just about ensuring that their health needs are addressed, according to Annie Sinnott. "It's also about treating them as individuals and performing those acts of kindness that brighten someone's day," she says. Sinnott, with her husband Ian, founded the Old Vicarage Care Home in Leigh, Sherborne, Dorset, with two residents in 1984. In 2007, Her Majesty The Queen recognised Sinnott's commitment to social care by awarding her the MBE.

Treating people with dignity and patience, as well as getting to know them individually, is central to how the Old Vicarage is run. From discovering that someone likes watching *Strictly Come Dancing* to taking time to look at family photographs with a resident, the emphasis is on forming strong relationships with people. A recent innovation has been the introduction of iPads so relatives can send emails and residents can Skype their loved-ones.

"We are very much part of the village community," says Sinnott. "We organise wine tastings, crib evenings, dog shows, garden parties, lunches, church visits and other events with villagers. We are providing a home, not an institution, and people should feel secure in the latter chapters of their life, as well as being treated with affection."

Sinnott is equally dedicated when it comes to the recruiting and nurturing of the home's staff. She chooses to take on young people with a view to unlocking their potential through quality training and mentoring. This emphasis on learning and development ensures that employees grow in confidence and that they in turn "own" the care they deliver.

No more so is this evident than in the example of apprentice carer Jade Facey, who won a 2015 National Care Award in recognition of excellence in the care sector. The 21-year-old now acts as an ambassador in schools, demonstrating to children what they can achieve without necessarily going to university. "Staff need to value themselves to value our residents, and I tell all my young employees that they can reach the top," says Sinnott. "Jade had a difficult time growing up but she's determined to make the best of her life and have a career in care. The award judges said she gave out such a positive message and the Old Vicarage is so proud of her."

Like Jade, all of the staff at the Old Vicarage go the extra mile for the home's residents. As Sinnott says, her job and that of her colleagues is to "make people feel valued", and that comes from those small but important daily deeds that show they care.

Faith, hope and charity

Christian Aid

Each year in May, red envelopes appear on Britain's doormats, encouraging people to give small change to make a big difference. The envelopes hail the beginning of Christian Aid Week, the flagship event of Christian Aid. Working in over 40 countries, Christian Aid is dedicated to tackling the causes and effects of poverty and providing emergency relief.

The humanitarian work of Christian Aid has changed little since the organisation's inception over 70 years ago. "Some things have remained the same at Christian Aid," says director David Pain. "Support for Christian Aid continues to come from churches and communities across the UK, organised by volunteers linking up with local communities in the poorest parts of the world to make both a practical difference and work for long-term change."

Christian Aid Week is an expression of this collaborative effort, and each year more than 100,000 volunteers from around 20,000 churches collect money. Contributing around 13 per cent of the organisation's funding, the event connects the volunteer churches with the local community under the message of "Love Every Neighbour".

"This volunteer movement has evolved somewhat since the inaugural event in 1957," says Jack Dear, head of Christian Aid Week. "There are volunteers who have been collecting envelopes for 40 years, and this active Christian engagement strengthens the message. The money raised by Christian Aid Week has a lasting impact on poverty all around the world. In 2016, we're following the story of Morsheeda in Bangladesh, a young mother living near an area of flooding."

Morsheeda's story is just one example of the work the charity does with its partnership communities. The work of Christian Aid is broad, yet focused. "No-one wants to be dependent on aid so we work with communities to bring about sustainable change," says Pain. "This means working with people to develop businesses, access markets and secure an income; it also means working with communities to ensure they can have access to the healthcare, education and other essential services we all need."

In the pursuit of eradicating the causes of poverty, Christian Aid's focus now encompasses climate change. "We've done a lot to strengthen the voices of the poorest and most marginalised countries in the global climate negotiations," says Pain, "and now we're aiming to step up demand on the ambitions of the Paris Agreement [COP21], and ensuring that all of our international development programmes are addressing this. Ultimately, climate change affects the poorest, as they are the people typically living in vulnerable areas. We want to build resilience – how to plant crops in areas where there is no water from drought or too much water from flooding, for example."

Although the red envelopes appear just once a year, the impact of the UK's generosity is huge. Whether it's tackling disease, providing food and shelter for refugees, or helping fight gender injustice, Christian Aid's work doesn't just achieve sustainable development goals; it gives strength, gives voice; and gives hope to humans in crisis around the world.

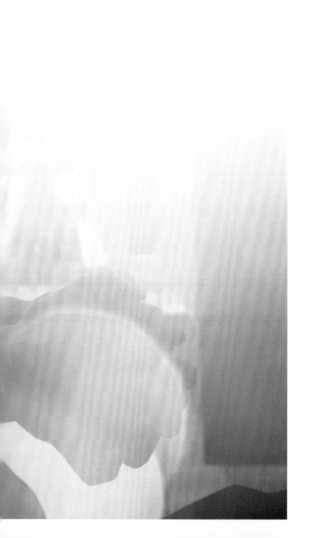

From darkness into light

The Good Shepherd Centre

The enthusiasm and optimism of youth comes easily for some – but, for others, maintaining a sense of hope for the future is a daily challenge. Sometimes, being placed in secure accommodation is the only way to keep these young people safe or stopping them from harming themselves or others.

Comprising an 18-bed secure unit, a six-bed close support unit, and a three-bed semi-independent cottage, the Good Shepherd Centre in Renfrewshire works with some of Scotland's most vulnerable 12- to 18-year-olds, tailoring a holistic package of care to help them achieve their goals and succeed in life. Its good work is recognised by many, and has resulted in an invitation to Buckingham Palace to receive a gold Duke of Edinburgh's Award in May of this year. "We provide a continuum of care," says Maria Harte, Head of Service. "The children accessing our service are likely to have a history of neglect. Some may have experienced physical or sexual abuse and exploitation, and they may have placed themselves or others at risk."

Understanding the complex feelings, needs and behaviours of the young people in its care, the Good Shepherd Centre adopts an eclectic and holistic approach, considering each young person as an individual but also as part of a family and community. Colin is a case in point. He had become stuck in a cycle of offending in the local community – and despite his guilt about the impact of his behaviour on his family, contact with his dad had broken down. He felt he had no hope for the future.

Upon entering the centre, Colin was assessed and an intervention plan was devised to support him. He participated in an alcohol-and-drugs awareness course, completed cognitive behavioural therapy and enjoyed holistic therapies that helped him to control his temper. After a year in the secure accommodation, he became more self-aware and found it easier to manage his emotions. Colin also gained new skills: he attended a barbering course, earning a qualification that could gain him future employment. He is also a keen amateur chef. "He was so pleased with himself when he cooked a three-course meal for the senior managers," says Harte. "That gave him a sense of achievement." Family relationships have improved too, and Colin now has regular contact with both his gran and dad.

By developing Colin's strengths, the centre motivated him to do something positive with his life. He started supporting catering staff to prepare hospitality for visitors to the centre, and started cutting other young people's hair with support from teaching staff. With his level of risk reduced, he moved on to the Close Support Unit and increased contact with his family, enjoying more time in the community. He also embarked on a fitness regime, joining a local gym. Ultimately, Colin was able to move into the centre's semi-independent cottage. He has more responsibility and is now applying to join the Army.

"Promoting young people's hopes, even when faced with adversity, can be a challenge," says Harte. "But by focusing on their interests and strengths, we can support them, helping them remain optimistic through tough times." This is where the Good Shepherd Centre is unwavering in its commitment, giving young people the opportunity to achieve their full potential and seize the love of life they deserve.

Human nature

WWF

WWF – formerly called the World Wildlife Fund – is well known for its work to protect endangered animals. But the world's leading independent conservation organisation has a far wider role: it is creating solutions to the most serious environmental challenges that affect humanity.

"A living planet is vital not only for wildlife but also as our source of food, clean water and livelihoods," says Glyn Davies, Executive Director for Global Programmes. The emphasis is very much on nature *and* people: communities who live off the land and sea, people who are hit by the impacts of climate change and everybody who cares about the health of our one planet.

WWF has been working to create a better world since 1961, when The Duke of Edinburgh was instrumental in the launch of its first national appeal for funds to save wildlife. The Duke is now International President Emeritus. His long-running involvement in the charity's work has included chairing conservation meetings and summits, and playing a key role in WWF's successful drive to protect the Congo Basin. Since 2011, The Prince of Wales has been WWF's UK President. His unwavering support has included strong backing of WWF's efforts to ensure that timber and forest products are sustainably traded. And he hosted a summit for WWF's young environmental champions, known as Green Ambassadors, at Highgrove.

"We support a lot of research and learning," says Davies. "We contract teams of scientists who produce internationally respected reports that show people the evidence, inspire them to act, and educate them about what they can do to help." WWF has an education area at its UK headquarters – the Living Planet Centre in Woking, Surrey. Since it opened two years ago,

more than 10,000 children have visited to learn about our planet. "We teach them about endangered species, about climate change and its impact, and about ways to change the damaging patterns of behaviour that are harming our planet," says Alison Lucas, Executive Director of Communications and Fundraising. This is learning made fun: workshops introduce children to the extraordinary animals, plants and people who live in endangered areas and explain solutions that will help to protect them.

WWF works in more than 100 countries and uses its global connections to influence governments to improve their policies. "We draw strength from our network," says David Nussbaum, Chief Executive. "You could really see that at the UN climate change conference in Paris in 2015. Our strong international team lobbied hard alongside other organisations for an ambitious global deal, and we are pleased with what was achieved. We are now working with governments around the world to make sure real change happens."

Not that WWF rests on its laurels: as soon as the Paris conference finished, the organisation was preparing for its biggest annual public event, Earth Hour, in March. "Last year, people in 172 countries took part, switching off their lights for an hour to show their concern for our planet," says Lucas. "In the UK, 10.4 million people joined in." This year, WWF wants it to be bigger still.

Awareness of the problems is only the first step: WWF also offers solutions, carefully researched and practical to implement. And this is an organisation that knows what it is aiming for. "We want a world with a future," says Davies, "where people and nature can thrive."

Air support

Royal Air Force Benevolent Fund

For almost a century the Royal Air Force has helped defend Britain and provide aid to disaster-hit countries. During that time, the RAF Benevolent Fund (RAFBF), the RAF's leading welfare charity, has made sure that the people who risk their lives for their country are properly looked after.

In 2015 alone, the RAFBF helped almost 40,000 former and current RAF personnel and their families, offering a wide range of assistance across what Group Captain Mike Neville, Director of Strategy and Fundraising, calls the "spectrum of care". "This covers everyone from the youngest dependant of a current serving member to the very oldest person in the RAF family, who, coincidentally, is the oldest person in the UK." The RAFBF will support anyone from an injured airman or woman, to the centenarian widow of a former airman who needs help with the top-up fees for her care home.

The ageing population has given the RAFBF a great deal to focus on. It provides veterans with mobility devices such as wheelchairs and stairlifts; and recently it launched an initiative to tackle social isolation among RAF veterans. "People are living longer and we need to respond to the needs of the RAF family," says Group Captain Neville. "But many are too proud to seek help. We want them to enjoy their golden years in a dignified way."

To alleviate social isolation issues, the RAFBF is about to launch daily lunch clubs at its welfare centre in West Sussex and a community network phone service. The support extends to younger veterans, such as former Senior Aircraftman Mike Goody (pictured, opposite), who was severely injured after his vehicle hit an improvised explosive device on a tour of Afghanistan. After he was discharged from the RAF, the RAFBF helped Goody with adaptations to his home and supported him to retrain as a paramedic.

The RAFBF also looks after the welfare of current serving personnel and their families. Its Airplay initiative provides childcare centres, a youth support programme and play parks on RAF stations; it works with Relate UK to provide counselling advice and support for serving couples; and its Advice and Advocacy Service helps members claim benefits and the support to which they are entitled. It also funds Citizens Advice Bureau sessions on RAF bases to provide wide-ranging advice.

"Welfare cases are becoming far more complex," says Group Captain Neville, "with many inter-related causes such as mobility, social isolation and psychological problems. And families are more remote from each other nowadays, which increases the potential for isolation."

The patron of the RAFBF is Her Majesty The Queen and The Duke of Kent is its President. Group Captain Neville hopes they will attend the RAFBF's centenary celebrations in 2019. "We are an enduring charity, seeking to provide a helping hand, a hand up rather than a hand out," he says. "But in doing so we need support, not only in fundraising but also in spreading the message that the RAF Benevolent Fund is there to help all those in the RAF family who find themselves in need. We are here to ensure the debt we owe to those who have served or are serving in the Royal Air Force is repaid."

Better together

Macmillan Cancer Support

In 1911, a horsehair weaver named William Macmillan was dying of cancer. Knowing he would not see his son's birthday, William gave him an early present: ten pounds, money that young Douglas Macmillan spent founding a charity to fight the illness that killed his father and improve cancer care. Over a century later, Macmillan Cancer Support is still independent – and still fighting for people affected by cancer. Its high-profile champions include The Prince of Wales, a patron since 1997.

"We support people in a whole range of settings," says Lynda Thomas, Chief Executive at Macmillan Cancer Support. "We are really here for people living with cancer." And for Macmillan, the emphasis is on living. "We do offer support for the last days of those with terminal cancer," she explains, "but as more people are surviving the disease and living longer – an estimated 2.5 million people were living with cancer in the UK in 2015, and that's expected to rise to 4 million by 2030 – much of what we do is about giving support at every stage." That may mean medical help, or therapy to boost self-esteem during difficult treatment or recovery. Or it may just mean a place to congregate, or an online community to offer peer support.

Macmillan does all this. "We have 8,000 Macmillan professional posts," says Thomas. "Not just the Macmillan nurses, although those have been providing vital assistance for 40 years now." The charity funds everything from doctors to social care professionals to massage therapists, builds support units such as the Macmillan Cancer Centre at University College London Hospital ("it's an amazing unit, and a gathering place," says Thomas), and partners with local authorities and charities to ensure that they are adapting their offering to suit local needs. It also campaigns to ensure, for example, that carers get the advice and support they need. "We won that one," says Thomas with satisfaction.

Macmillan Cancer Support knows that it can't entirely prevent the suffering of those who have the disease or the impact this has on their loved ones. What it can do, says Thomas, is help to make the process as painless as possible. "We don't want people to be forced to have the same conversation," she says, "explaining their diagnosis and treatment, more times than necessary." By promoting joined-up care, with the right professionals in possession of the right information at the right time, Macmillan is fulfilling its ambition to ensure that no one faces cancer alone.

"We have teams working with the NHS on the local level," says Thomas, "to really get down to the detail of who suffers from which kinds of cancer, where and what investment would most benefit them." It also runs the Macmillan Support Line, a free helpline where nurse specialists can answer questions and offer practical information and support.

Out in the world, volunteers offer their time and experience to support those with cancer, while Information Pharmacists, trained by Macmillan to support cancer sufferers and their relatives, are in branches of Boots to answer questions and signpost people to relevant support in their local area.

Meanwhile, online, a community of 100,000 people affected by cancer provides peer-to-peer support through the Macmillan website, and the charity's The Source website delivers online tips and practical advice for sufferers and their relatives. Everyone at Macmillan is dedicated to finding better ways to join up services, offer easy-to-access support and make sure that no one has to face cancer alone.

Creature comforts

RSPCA

It was in 1840, 16 years after it was set up, that the Society for the Prevention of Cruelty to Animals was granted its "Royal" prefix. "Queen Victoria gave us our royal status in 1840 because she was shocked by the brutal treatment of dogs at that time," says the RSPCA's Assistant Director, Public Affairs, David Bowles. "Every reigning monarch since has been our patron. It's part of what makes the RSPCA special. We have a 98 per cent recognition rate with the public. They see that we're not afraid to get our hands dirty and do the difficult rescue jobs."

The world's oldest and largest animal welfare charity still uses its influence in parliament to campaign for better standards of animal care to this day. Each year it receives some 1.3 million calls reporting animal cruelty, enabling the charity to act as the government's eyes and ears.

In 2016, the RSPCA's focus is on regulating standards in puppy breeding. "People are often being duped into buying sick dogs," says Bowles. "We want clear guidance for people buying dogs so that they know how to treat them. We live in a throwaway society, but puppies aren't like other purchases."

The RSPCA is unique among animal organisations in having officers on the ground who can investigate – and in some cases prosecute – animal maltreatment. In addition, it operates 49 hospitals and clinics in England and Wales as well as treatment centres, in which animals are cared for until they can be released or found a home.

The charity's interventions sometimes brings it into close contact with social services and the NSPCC. "We often get called first so we are able to spot signs of other domestic abuse," says Bowles. "There are cases of abused women refusing to leave their partner because they don't want to abandon their pet. We now foster pets so that a woman being cared for in a shelter knows her pet is safe as well. People often underestimate the profound connections between animals and other social issues. Think how important an animal is to an old person for comfort and company."

The RSPCA also plays an important role in raising consumer awareness of the conditions in which animals raised for food are kept. Its food-labelling scheme, RSPCA Assured (formerly Freedom Foods), assesses the space, light, bedding and shelter provided by a farmer.

"Our labelling shows that animals have had a reasonable life," says Bowles. "More than 50 per cent of eggs sold in Britain are now RSPCA Assured, as is a third of UK-produced pork. People will pay a little more for better welfare. Of course, globalisation means we also need to consider how other countries that produce our imported meat treat their animals."

Many former Commonwealth countries were among the first to introduce animal protection laws because of the culture of care the RSPCA established. "We're now working with the governments of China, South Korea and Malaysia to help them create and enforce animal inspectorates," says Bowles.

Britain is a nation of animal lovers, but the RSPCA still collects or rescues nearly 130,000 animals each year. "We are 192 years old, and in some areas dealing with the same problems, which underlines how slowly change in animal welfare moves," says Bowles. The RSPCA is as relevant today as when Queen Victoria ennobled its work: its voice still heeded in government, its expertise and compassion valued more than ever.

Fighting the good fight

The Salvation Army

In 1865, the levels of poverty, exploitation and misery widespread in the East End of London prompted Methodist preacher William Booth to put his Christian faith into action by working to improve the lives of people who were living in intolerable hardship. The world and the challenges may have changed a great deal over the past 151 years, but today the Salvation Army is one of the largest providers of social care in Britain.

"We are still continuing to meet the social needs of the population," says Lieut-Colonel Melvin Fincham, the Salvation Army's Secretary for Communications, "be it poverty, homelessness, loneliness, alcohol and drug addiction or domestic abuse."

From its 100 centres across the UK, the army has been a pioneer in the treatment and rehabilitation of drug addicts and has been a leader in supporting homeless people and in working to help unemployed people find their way back into work. Its Employment Plus Service has supported more than 22,000 people with unemployment and skills issues since it began in 2011. Last year alone, every week more than 6,800 people came to its 264 luncheon clubs, 8,100 attended its drop-in centres and 1,352 children joined its 27 playgroups.

Most recently its officers were in action in the floods in the North of England where Salvation Army emergency mobile units helped keep both the emergency services and evacuees fed and watered. After the 7 July 2005 terrorist attacks on the transport system in London, more than 500 volunteers helped provide support at incident sites with mobile canteens, some staying in one location for 17 days and nights.

"Where there is a need or a crisis, the Salvation Army is there to help and we've done that down the years," says Lieut-Col Fincham. "We are always keen to work in partnership with other churches and local agencies." As a church and a charity, the Salvation Army has also been involved with some of the global problems affecting Britain: since 2011 it has worked with the UK government to help more than 3,000 men and women who have been the victims of human trafficking.

The Salvation Army has always maintained strong links with the Royal Family. During her reign, Her Majesty The Queen has supported its work on many occasions, including opening support and accommodation centres for homeless people – Hopetown in East London, in 1980, and Edward Alsop Court near Westminster Abbey, in 1996. Her Majesty also wrote a foreword to a 2012 book that marked the 100th anniversary of the death of William Booth.

While the Salvation Army would be delighted if it were no longer needed to provide help with social needs, it is almost certain that society will need to draw on its fighting spirit to tackle the crises that the future will bring.

"Sadly, from 1865 right up to 2016, those needs are still prominent and relevant today and the Salvation Army will continue to meet those needs in the future," says Lieut-Col Fincham. "We are always innovating and looking for new opportunities and locations where we can offer help so we can meet needs effectively and efficiently. We do what we do because we believe in people, and we are mindful that everything we do is about promoting social justice for all races and faiths."

Transforming medicine

AbbVie

"As a biopharmaceutical company, we are guided by the needs of the patients we serve and the role we play in bringing significant innovation to the market," says Greg Miley, Vice President of Corporate Communications for Chicago-based multinational AbbVie. Miley has seen a transformative change in medical science in the past decade, with his company working as a leading entrepreneur and innovator. "When you think about the pharmaceutical industry's contribution to healthcare, the industry continually strives to meet the evolving needs of patients with new and innovative medicines."

AbbVie began life as Abbott in 1888, named after founder Dr Wallace Abbott. It is a speciality biopharmaceutical company producing medicines to tackle major diseases such as cancer, Crohn's disease, cystic fibrosis, hepatitis C, HIV, psoriasis, rheumatoid arthritis and ulcerative colitis. AbbVie's success in bringing these medicines to patients is due to its focus on research and development (R&D). With more than $4 billion of investment in 2015, R&D accounted for more than 18 per cent of the company's revenues.

"Out of a global workforce of 28,000, around 8,000 are dedicated to researching and developing new medicines," says Miley. "We prioritise our R&D portfolio into four pillars of innovation: immunology, oncology, virology and neurology." In the case of virology, developments in the treatment of hepatitis C have transformed care. "For years it was a devastating disease. Many treatments used interferon, with side effects that meant patients often stopped using them. AbbVie now has a therapy without interferon that was clinically proven to cure 95 to 100 per cent of people who took the therapy."

At the heart of AbbVie's mission is the patient experience. "We believe that the world needs new approaches to address today's health challenges,"

says Miley. "We go beyond medicine to deliver innovative, holistic solutions to patients and the healthcare system." AbbVie has programmes that are designed to help patients start on therapy and adhere to it. For dermatology patients in certain countries, AbbVie offers access to patient ambassadors and nursing support to help with their therapy. The company also offers patient programmes that can increase access to necessary treatments, help improve patient outcomes and address local healthcare challenges.

On a broader level, AbbVie is engaged in initiatives that are aimed at building a sustainable healthcare system. "For example," says Miley, "we work with healthcare stakeholders from around Europe to address how healthcare systems can become more sustainable and meet the challenges of managing long-term conditions." Lifelong prevention, early diagnosis and effective intervention are all important measures in improving the sustainability of healthcare systems. Governments, private sector companies, social insurers, healthcare providers, and people living with chronic conditions each have a role to play. "We all need to work in partnership to change and transform our healthcare systems to fit the future," says Miley.

For the past three years, AbbVie has been ranked in the top 10 of Fortune's World's Most Admired Companies in the pharmaceutical industry. Peer recognition aside, however, patient experiences and outcomes continue to motivate AbbVie. "We have scientific capabilities that are beyond what we had 10 years ago," says Miley. "Our focus as a biopharmaceutical company is to deliver a consistent stream of innovative medicines that solve serious health issues and have a remarkable impact on people's lives."

Stable mates

Redwings Horse Sanctuary

"It all started with one pony," says Nicola Knight of Redwings Horse Sanctuary. "Sheba was rescued from a dealer in 1978 and her recovery inspired the formation of a sanctuary dedicated to saving horses from a life of fear and neglect. We now care for more than 1,500 horses, ponies, donkeys and mules every day."

Now the largest horse sanctuary in the UK, Redwings has grown from its founding in Norfolk in 1984 to have over 250 staff at ten centres across the country. As a charity it is entirely reliant on its growing band of supporters. "Everyone works towards one goal – to provide and promote the care and protection of horses and donkeys," says Knight. "We believe that every horse, pony, donkey and mule has the right to a happy and healthy life." The charity's admirers include The Princess Royal, who wrote to thank Redwings after a particularly large rescue.

With help from dedicated care staff to the eight specialist vets treating the charity's rescued animals, both donkeys and horses find a permanent sanctuary at the centres, especially those needing lifelong special care. As well as ensuring the animals' welfare and offering a safe home, the charity's third focus is a rehoming programme that has provided new "Guardians" who look after 500 more of Redwings' horses, many of whom have recovered from terrible neglect and even cruelty.

"We've all heard the saying, 'an elephant never forgets'," says Knight. "Well, this is the same for horses. We strive to be leaders in ethical training techniques for our horses, to train them in the most humane way possible so they never have to be afraid of humans again."

Involved in a string of large-scale rescues over the past 30 years, the reward is seeing ill-treated animals recover although sadly not every story has a happy ending. But, for many, Redwings quite simply transforms their lives, such as the "M25 group" of eight horses rescued from London by Redwings and the RSPCA, which were brought to the charity for rehabilitation.

Weighing the same as a small pony when he came to Redwings, two-and-a-half-year-old Kensington was so emaciated that staff had never seen a skinnier horse. In his first six months at the sanctuary, he almost doubled his weight to make a full recovery. "It is a delicate job," says Knight, "supporting and nurturing a fragile body without doing too much, too quickly, which could have fatal consequences."

A horse called Finchley, also 2 when he arrived with Kensington, could never be ridden again even after making his own slow recovery. Laid-back and easy-going despite his early neglect, the bay gelding now has a new home as a companion horse as part of the rehoming programme.

Perhaps the happiest ending was for Victoria whose mother, Mayfair, was rescued along with Kensington and Finchley while heavily in foal. Born at Redwings, Victoria has gained a legion of fans who now await her twice-yearly letters and birthday party as part of the £12.50 annual adoption scheme.

With more than 150 horses, ponies, donkeys and mules still being rescued every year, Redwings always needs support. A handful of its benefactors make a life-changing difference by, for instance, funding vital veterinary equipment for the operating theatre and intensive care stables, field shelters, stable blocks, paddocks and horseboxes. "Sadly our rescue teams are still needed and that means we still need support too," says Knight. "Together we can help even more horses in need."

Life support

Royal Trinity Hospice

"People don't understand what we do, and they're scared," says Dallas Pounds, CEO of Royal Trinity Hospice. The irony is, of course, that what this hospice does best is to help with the fear and the incomprehension that so often accompany terminal illness. It's why Britain's oldest hospice has attracted the patronage of the Royal Family – Queen Elizabeth The Queen Mother served as Trinity's Royal patron for 76 years, with The Duchess of Cornwall taking up the role in July 2006. Last year, just ahead of its 125th anniversary, it was awarded Royal status.

Royal Trinity Hospice is housed on the edge of Clapham Common, where a light-filled Georgian building with 28 beds overlooks beautiful gardens. It was set up in 1891 by William Hoare, a member of the Hoare banking family.

"He was concerned that people had nowhere to go to die comfortably," says Pounds. "That is an important service that Trinity still provides, but we also offer all sorts of outpatient and community care: doctors, nurses, therapists and social workers."

Patients would rather stay put at this difficult time, and Trinity Hospice facilitates that. "We can send nurses or specialists to people wherever they call home," says Pounds, "whether that's a care home, a hostel or even prison." Less than a third of the £11 million annual cost comes from public funding. "The rest is split between income from our 24 shops and fundraising.

We rely on the generosity of the community. Some people don't understand what hospices do: they think of them as somewhere dreary and scary, somewhere to die."

The hospice turns 125 this year. "We want to open an outpatient and community-based centre in central London," says Pounds "A place the healthy can come to find information on helping loved ones with life-limiting illnesses. Somewhere to plan for death and dying, with a café – a place that will be a resource for the whole community. There's a real need for more community services."

Hospices don't replace hospital treatment, says Pounds – they supplement it. "We address the physical, emotional, spiritual and psychological issues that a hospital may not have the time or expertise to look at," she says. The earlier Trinity becomes involved, the more it can do, helping people to navigate their way through a sometimes bewildering health and social care system.

"We support people to live the way they want to, insofar as that is possible, and to make informed choices until they die," says Pounds. "Then we support those close to that person in whichever way suits them." That is a vital part of what she sees as Trinity's main responsibility: helping people with life-limiting illnesses to live every moment.

"As I dedicate myself anew
to your service, I hope we will
all be reminded of the power of
togetherness and the convening
strength of family, friendship and
good neighbourliness, examples
of which I have been fortunate
to see throughout my reign"

Her Majesty The Queen, Diamond Jubilee message, 5 June 2012

Schooled in excellence

Ninety years of British education

Throughout her 90 years, Her Majesty The Queen has seen significant changes in the realm of education. From the introduction of compulsory education for over-14s to the abolition of corporal punishment and the founding of a standardised National Curriculum, the past nine decades have seen the UK continually breaking new ground. The result is an education system, from early years to adult provision, that is internationally respected and admired.

The country has come a long way. While in 2016, free, universal education for all is a given, at the time of The Queen's birth in 1926, this was a new concept. In what was then a progressive and bold step, the 1918 Education Act introduced state-funded compulsory education for all five- to 14-year-olds. But while this was an example to the world, there remained no compulsory education for older teenagers in the UK for many years. Younger children, meanwhile, received a chalk-and-talk style of education, offered on an ad-hoc basis, without a standardised curriculum or school inspections. Students primarily learnt by rote, studying the "three r's". Discipline was brutal, physical education was rigorous and stereotypical gender roles were enforced, with girls studying needlework while boys were kept busy with woodwork. For all, Christianity was at the core of the school experience, with daily assemblies including hymns, bible readings and prayers.

Things continued in this vein until the 1944 Education Act, which brought academic selection. While free education was still available throughout the UK, children were now streamed at the age of 11. Those deemed the brightest attended grammar schools, and the rest either went to a secondary modern or a technical school. This Act also raised the leaving age to 15, and formalised the concept of educating "the whole child", outlining that schools should cater for spiritual, physical and vocational needs, as well as academic prowess.

It wasn't until the 1960 that the systems that are so familiar today started to emerge. Government spending on education increased, and attitudes turned against the elitism of the grammars – which were by now accused of creating a two-tier system. By the early 1970s, most secondary schools were mixed-ability comprehensives. The school leaving age was raised to 16, and teachers began to experiment with child-centred learning, encouraging creativity and empowering children through debate. Their parents also gained a voice when, in 1976, Labour Prime Minister James Callaghan delivered a speech that prompted a national "Great Debate", inviting families and industry to play their part in shaping the future of education. Shortly after, new tests were introduced for children, new guidelines were set for teachers, and schools saw their performance monitored.

Because of this, by the 1980s, a market had emerged in which parents could choose which school they preferred for their children – aided, in some cases, by publicly published test results. Parents were also invited to join governing bodies, where they could have a say in the running of their school. "Political indoctrination" was banned from schools by the 1986 Education Act, a standardised National Curriculum was introduced by the 1988 Education Reform Act, and Ofsted – the schools inspectorate – was set up in 1992. Conditions improved for children too, with corporal punishment banned in 1986 in the state sector, and in 1998 in private schools.

Today, state schools educate around 93 per cent of all children in England and Wales. Formats include both non-denominational and faith schools, those that cater specifically for children with special needs and, since 2000, Academies and Free Schools. The latter are publicly funded independent schools, set up by a collaboration between business, faith, education or voluntary groups, together with the Department for Education and the local authority. Academies and Free

PREVIOUS PAGES: KING'S COLLEGE CAMBRIDGE. OPPOSITE: THE PRINCE OF WALES – THE FIRST HEIR APPARENT TO EARN A UNIVERSITY DEGREE – DURING HIS STUDENT DAYS AT THE UNIVERSITY OF CAMBRIDGE. RIGHT: BRITISH EDUCATORS HAVE RECOGNISED THE NEED TO TEACH MORE THAN THE "THREE R'S" FOR MANY YEARS NOW

LEFT: THE QUEEN MAKES
A SCHOOL VISIT IN 2015.
OPPOSITE: THE UK'S WORLD-
RENOWNED EDUCATION
SYSTEM IS A PRIME EXPORT

Schools needn't follow the National Curriculum and can set their own hours and term dates. But the newest kid on the UK education block is the University Technical College (UTC). These are government-funded schools for 14- to 18-years-olds that work with local universities and employers to deliver technical and practical education. Between 2010 and 2016, 35 UTCs were launched with over 55 more due to open by 2017.

Of course, in addition to these state-funded schools, the UK boasts some of the most famous and respected independent schools in the world, drawing students from all corners of the global. Some count royalty among their alumni. While The Queen herself was tutored at home, The Prince of Wales attended Gordonstoun school in north-east Scotland, and The Duke of Cambridge and Prince Harry both attended Eton College in Windsor. Private schools set their own curriculum and admissions policies and, like state schools, are regularly inspected to ensure high standards. Indeed, due to their exceptionally high quality, the global popularity of these schools render them a key British export.

As for non-compulsory post-16 education, the UK's FE colleges have a strong history, and their apprenticeship programmes in particular – which see young people earning a wage as they learn vocational skills – have been a focus for recent governments. The country's world-renowned universities, meanwhile, are oversubscribed and thriving. It isn't hard to see why, in the 2015/16 QS World University Rankings, England alone bagged four of the top ten spots. Britain also boasts the three oldest universities in the English-speaking world: the University of Oxford pre-dates 1167; the University of Cambridge can trace its origins to 1209; and the University of St Andrews in Scotland – from where The Queen saw the now-Duke and Duchess of Cambridge graduate in 2005 – was founded around 1410.

Today, the spectrum of education establishments continues to develop and the nation's teaching priorities remain much debated. It's this spirit of debate that has allowed the country's education system to grow and it's global reputation to flourish throughout The Queen's lifetime. Never faltering in its ambitions for academic excellence, the UK remains keen to learn lessons from its past and nurture a range of environments to prepare young people for the challenges of the future.

Flawless foundations

Benenden School

In 1923, three female teachers left their employment at Wycombe Abbey to establish a new school that would provide academic excellence but also a breadth of education to its girls. As it approaches its 95th anniversary in 2018, Benenden School still maintains that ethos in the way it educates the 550 pupils at the school that is set in the beautiful surroundings of the Kent countryside.

Benenden School has many illustrious alumnae, including former MI5 Director General Baroness Eliza Manningham-Buller, actress Rachel Weisz, former *London Evening Standard* editor Veronica Wadley and, most famous of all, The Princess Royal, who last year accepted an invitation to become the school's Founders' Patron.

Headmistress Samantha Price says that Benenden is far from many people's understanding of a traditional girls' school, offering a strong extracurricular programme as well as a dynamic and rigorous academic education. It is the only girls' school to be based wholly on boarding, which means that every girl has the same opportunities and educational experience.

"We can offer what we call a complete education: an education in the classroom as well as pastoral and co-curricular excellence," says Price. "What we do at weekends and outside the teaching time is part of the personal development for each girl that gives them the well-rounded education that we pride ourselves on." These extracurricular activities include music, with the vast majority of girls learning an instrument throughout their time at Benenden. In 2015 it launched the Benenden Arts Festival, a three-day celebration of music and drama over one weekend in April.

The school achieves very strong academic results. The most recent year saw its best ever A Level results, with 31 per cent of all grades at A* and 90 per cent of all grades at A* to B. For September 2016, Benenden girls have already received 13 offers of Oxbridge places and two have secured places at US universities. Benenden Seniors, as former pupils are known, leave the school with both strong qualifications and a strong individual identity. "We want all the girls to achieve their potential academically and identify subject areas that they feel really passionate about," says Price.

After a recent visit, an independent inspector described the girls at Benenden as being "stretched without being stressed". "We want the girls to be aspirational but to retain a balance in their lives and a sense of responsibility to their community," says Price. "One of our values is that every girl should be confident without being arrogant, to put herself forward, and be compassionate and look after others."

As Benenden approaches its centenary in 2023, the school has an ambitious programme. Its innovative curriculum, which will include a professional skills qualification, will be supported by enhanced facilities, including a new music school and teaching facility with a business centre. "We are very keen on the possibilities offered by science, design and business to help move the girls forward into the world of work," says Price.

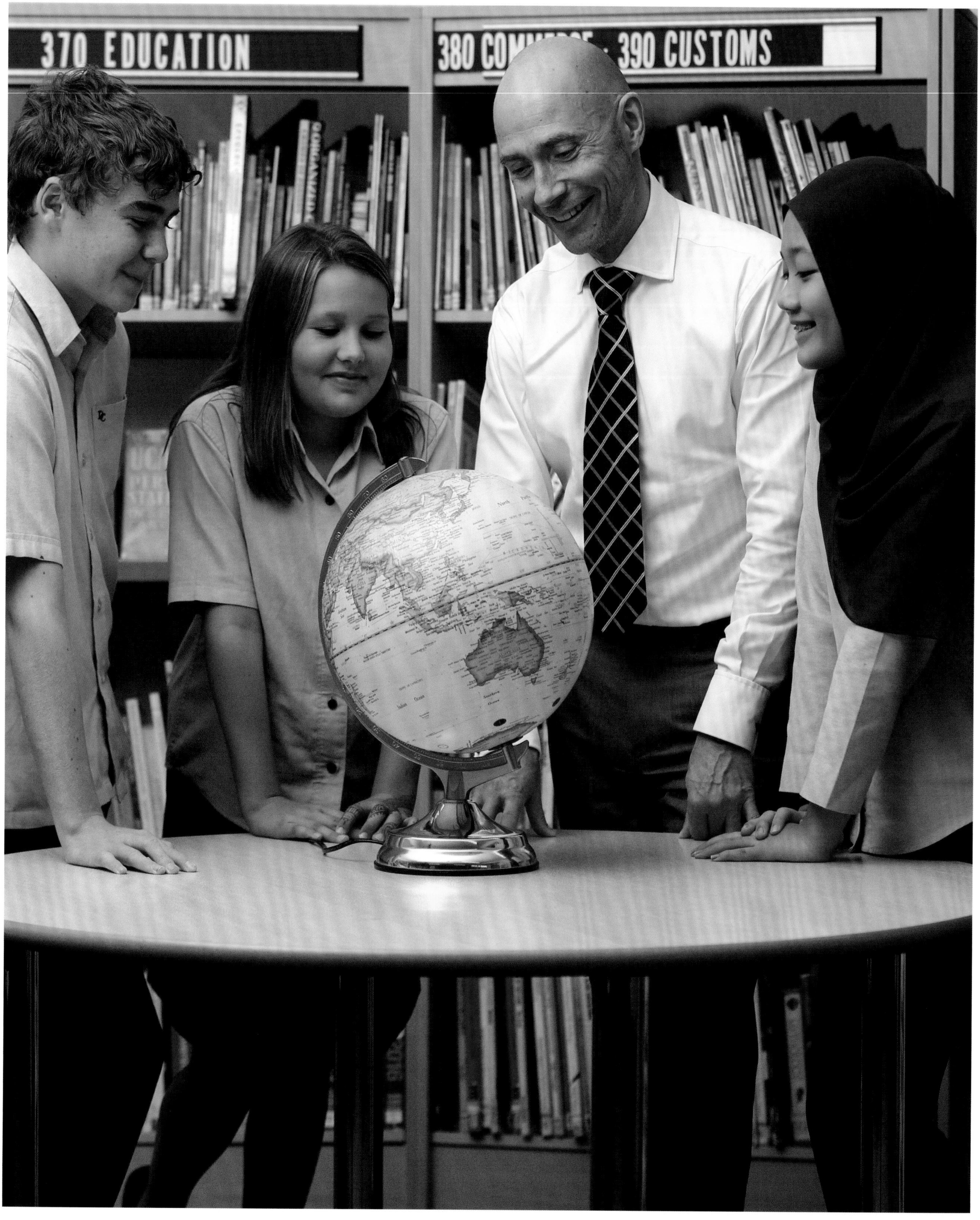
370 EDUCATION
390 CUSTOMS

The best of British

Doha College

For many years, received wisdom among British expat parents was to send children home for their schooling. In the far-flung corners of empire, there were rarely sufficient facilities to provide the kind of education that parents sought for their children. These days, the picture is very different, with a network of high-performing British international schools spread around the globe providing a more-than-viable alternative for parents living and working overseas.

Doha College – a British international school in Qatar – is a case in point. Examination results place it within the top 10 per cent of schools in the UK, while some 95 per cent of Doha College leavers are accepted into their first-choice universities across the world. As a result, the school has become the first choice for many Qatar-based parents of all nationalities seeking the best possible education for their children.

It's not just in the classroom that Doha College students have the chance to excel. Alongside its academic credentials, the school boasts impressive sports facilities with its own athletics academy offering a broad range of pursuits, including netball, football, swimming, rugby and basketball. Added to this is the extensive list of extracurricular activities offering students the opportunity to explore a broad range of hobbies and pursuits.

Of course, like any top-performing school, the competition for places is high. "Here in Qatar if you say the word 'school' then the first that will be mentioned is Doha College," says Principal, Dr Steffen Sommer. "There are only a few other schools in the Middle East that are of the same calibre, which makes us a popular choice among students of all backgrounds."

The school's well-earned reputation made it a natural choice for The Countess of Wessex to visit when on a tour of Qatar last year. The Countess took time to praise the efforts of students taking part in the Duke of Edinburgh's International Award. "Doha College was the first school in Qatar to introduce the programme and we have had more than 2,500 students complete it to date," says Dr Sommer. "We are extremely proud of our students' achievements and honoured to have Her Royal Highness recognise their efforts."

Despite its enormous student body, with some 1,900 pupils between the ages of 3 and 18 enrolled for the current year, there is a strong sense of community on the Doha College campus.

"Many of our students are expatriates away from their homes," says Dr Sommer. "Doha College acts as an extended family providing a holistic learning environment supporting their education, health and social life. Our alumni feel a very strong affinity to the school which is more commonly found at university level rather than school level."

Soon, the school will take up its place on a new and larger campus in Doha's prestigious Education City. Designed to provide a bespoke academic environment based on learning pavilions, the new campus will be built on Doha College's tradition of providing students with the very best educational and recreational resources to prepare them for entry into British and international universities. As Dr Sommer concludes: "We hope each student leaves Doha College with the confidence to excel, the passion to continue to learn and the empathy to be a global citizen."

Keep on trucking

DAF Trucks

DAF Trucks is one of the largest HGV manufacturers in Europe, with one in every four trucks on British roads being produced by the company. To maintain this market-leading profile, DAF has run one of the country's most prestigious apprenticeship programmes for more than 20 years. "We continually develop and enhance the programme," says Tony Shepherd, Business Services Manager. "We work closely with the dealer network and we have regular governors' meetings with all partners in the programme – our managing agent Skillnet, City of Bristol College and the dealers who employ the apprentices. The meetings allow all parties to discuss the programme and how we can improve it."

This includes making sure that the programme is regularly updated to reflect current industry requirements, such as investing in additional equipment so that the apprentice technicians can work with the latest product range. This priority is made possible by DAF's highly successful partnership with its 131 dealerships that offer servicing, repair and maintenance. "We as an organisation firmly believe in the 'DAF difference'," says Shepherd, "What that means to us is that our relationship with our dealers and customers is hugely important."

Some 80 young people pass through the DAF Trucks apprenticeship programme every year – that's 1,500 young people to date who have had their working lives launched by this highly successful programme. Every year their achievements are celebrated at the Graduation and Apprentice of the Year event, a real highlight in the DAF Trucks calendar. "It's hugely rewarding to watch parents seeing their son or daughter achieve something pretty

phenomenal," says Shepherd. The National Apprenticeship Service has also recognised DAF Trucks for four out of the last five years as one of the country's top 100 apprentice employers. "That's really special," says Shepherd. "We are proud to be recognised for the amount of work that's going into the programme and the commitment from our dealers."

By the end of the programme, the apprentices are ready to enter the world of work. "Not only do we develop some highly skilled technicians but also some genuinely nice people," says Shepherd. "The programme is not limited to technical skills: we include life skills in as well, such as road safety, first aid and customer service – all skills that make a difference to our apprentices. In the commercial vehicle industry, customer skills are vital; customers need their trucks to be working and everyone needs to understand the importance of minimising downtime." The investment in DAF apprentices doesn't stop at graduation. There is ongoing training tailored to suit their individual skills and ambitions.

DAF Trucks is part of PACCAR, a global leader in the design, manufacture and customer support of high-quality premium trucks, which means that opportunities for apprentices are spread globally. "We say that the apprenticeship programme can offer you either a job or a career," says Shepherd. "Not everyone wants to become MD – some do and will be in the future, but many aspire to be master technicians giving an excellent service day after day. Whatever they do, the programme gives them a fantastic grounding and leaves them feeling part of the DAF family, with a great deal of DAF loyalty."

Bright futures

St Margaret's Anfield CE Primary School

"There's something very special about this school," says Lesley Hughes, Head Teacher of St Margaret's Anfield, a primary school in central Liverpool. "I'm biased, of course, but it's what other people say, time and again, when they visit the school."

Academic success and good behaviour are crucial to creating this environment, of course – but ever since it was established in 1879, the co-ed school has maintained close ties with the church and this has nurtured a strong ethos. "We offer a warm and loving environment," says Hughes. "We're also sporty and creative, among so many other things – there's truly a place for every child and interest here."

In recent years, the school has fully embraced technology. "We have a broad and balanced curriculum, but schools need to move with the times," says Hughes. "As such, we've also brought in a range of state-of-the-art technology and equipment to support and extend our children's learning."

One notable example is its creative technology club, which has enabled pupils to learn animation. "It's a real stimulus," says Hughes. "The film clips can be a starting point for discussion or for getting the children to write their own stories."

The school's creativity was seen in its First World War Centenary commemorations in 2014. "We decided to host an exhibition," says Hughes. "The initial idea was just to show a few pictures – but, as a school, we don't tend to keep things small. Our efforts always reach to extraordinary lengths."

True to form, the result was anything but. "The whole school was decorated – absolutely everywhere," says Hughes. "We had displays, tea parties and an afternoon tea dance with distinguished guests present. The Lord Mayor and representatives from the Royal British Legion were invited, as well as some troops from the army who built a trench on the school's sports field. We'd planted poppies beforehand, too, which were growing by the time of the celebrations."

The following year saw pupils from Year 3 enjoy a similarly less-than-ordinary history lesson, this time at the World Museum in Liverpool. There the school's children formed an enthusiastic welcoming committee for The Prince of Wales and The Duchess of Cornwall on their visit to the museum's exhibition of Mayan culture.

As for the future, Hughes is keen to keep pushing the creative agenda at St Margaret's Anfield. "We're a musical school," she says. "We teach brass, woodwind and the guitar, and we've just started a musical theatre group. I want us to produce an end-of-year musical extravaganza." Some of the school's teachers even take music lessons alongside pupils, to encourage the concept of learning together.

"Our teachers are lifelong learners," says Hughes. "They're always thinking about how to further their abilities and that flows through the school. It's catching – we're all pushing ourselves to be the very best that we can be, and each person is looked after in the best possible way." This investment in people breeds stability and job satisfaction. "We rarely recruit new teachers, because when people come here they stay," adds Hughes.

Nurturing and creative, St Margaret's Anfield is a school where teachers and students are dedicated to making a difference – together.

Learned friends

Cothill Educational Trust

Some things are changing in the world of private preparatory education. The stand-alone independent school is starting to become less and less economically viable. Instead, Britain's venerable educational institutions are starting to team together, to share a governing body with financial security, centralised resources and the many benefits of being part of a team.

"This doesn't mean schools have to relinquish their individuality," says Eddy Newton, Principal of the Cothill Educational Trust (CET), which he describes as a "commonwealth" of schools. "Costs, compliance and increasingly burdensome regulations are challenging private schools and making it difficult to 'go it alone'. We had four enquiries from schools last term alone."

CET currently has five schools under its umbrella, each an outstanding facility in its own right. While a firm commitment to each school retaining its own identity is stressed, membership of the trust brings opportunities for collegiality and the chance for joint ventures between students.

"We want our pupils to experience different challenges and opportunities, developing resilience, independence and an inquisitive spirit," says Newton. "Too many schools are too rigid in their approach – the CET schools are willing to break the mould and spend time doing other things."

One example of this is the term abroad at the Château de Sauveterre school in France, which is open to all Year 7 pupils, while younger students can opt to spend a week at La Chaumière exploring the countryside around Toulouse. "As total an immersion as possible is the very best way to learn a new language and culture, and this is exactly what Sauveterre sets out to achieve," says Duncan Bailey, Head of Cothill House School.

Established in 1870, the school is the oldest member of the trust and exemplifies the best of the British boys' boarding school tradition. Reportedly one of The Prince of Wales's schools of choice for the young Prince William and Prince Harry, Latin is part of the syllabus and Sundays include trips to the village church in tweed jackets. "In the boys' free time, yard cricket is popular – often played in pyjamas on balmy summer evenings," says Bailey. "Cothill boys can also retreat to the woods to build dens and catch crayfish in the stream; with no handheld electronic devices permitted during the week, traditional play is at the heart of school life. All trust schools are committed to the children being active on the sports field and regularly outside, with freedom to roam."

In the past 10 years, the trust has doubled in size. It has added Kitebrook House in Gloucestershire, Mowden Hall in Northumberland and Ashdown House in East Sussex to its portfolio alongside Cothill House and Chandlings in Oxfordshire, the Old Malthouse in Dorset and its two French schools. In the next five years, Newton hopes to increase this yet further, with another overseas venture in China or Hong Kong also on the horizon.

"Each new school must both complement the trust and bring something to the table," he says. "We want schools that are willing to think outside of the box and not be bound by 'narrow' education. Growing up at school is about far more than academic results, although those are very important too!"

School Britannia

The British School In The Netherlands

The British School In The Netherlands (BSN) began from humble origins when, in 1931, half a dozen children gathered in a single room in The Hague. The school's commitment to British educational values is as strong as ever but today it occupies four sites on more than 50 acres.

Educating over 2,250 students from 85 nations, it is the largest British international school in Europe and has hosted numerous royal visits over the years. Her Majesty The Queen visited in 1958, and other royal guests have included Princess Margaret, The Princess Royal and The Earl of Wessex. The British Ambassador, Sir Geoffrey Adams, chairs the School Association and the latest Junior School was opened in 2010 by Princess Máxima, the current Queen of the Netherlands.

However, for all of its focus on Britain, the school is anything but insular, priding itself on introducing different cultures to one another – to the benefit of everyone. "It offers a wonderful opportunity to interact with the world," says CEO and Principal Kieran Earley. "The children discover different outlooks and leave more tolerant and broader in vision."

Lessons are in English but the stand-alone language school offers mother-tongue programmes, while anglophone students learn other languages, too. "It is absolutely not about indoctrination," says Earley. "We want students to value and share their cultural connections – everyone here has something to offer."

This inclusive attitude is replicated everywhere. "We want to educate the whole child," says Earley, "not at the expense of academic achievement but in addition to it. We want our young people to be able to apply creativity

and thought to the world's problems rather than just remembering answers." To this end, students are encouraged to participate in all kinds of activities, from sports to debating to public service and creative pursuits. "In my 20 years' experience," says Earley, "it's the active students who achieve the best academically – not those who are never allowed to look up from their books."

The school's British label can be misleading: only a quarter of BSN students are in fact British. "The concept of British education has changed," says Earley. "These days it's about combining rigour, understanding, tolerance and fun – it's a unique system. And it works. The market is choosing a British curriculum and British standards."

The students' creativity and independent thought is particularly visible in their commitment to sustainability. "Young people here have a real sense of their place in the world and their responsibility to it," says Earley. There are student-led eco committees, organising waste and energy management, and Forest Schools, where younger children learn outdoors. They camp with their parents in the school grounds. "There are even beehives here," says Earley, "where we produce our own BSN honey!" No wonder the school was awarded the prestigious Eco Schools mark.

The BSN continues to grow. "We are not acquisitive but we are ambitious for our young people and our staff," says Earley. "That's what makes British education so attractive – it's innovative, flexible, future-facing. We have always served the international community in this part of world and we will continue to do that. We have a moral responsibility to provide the very best for those who want to learn here."

A winning formula

St Joseph's College

When St Joseph's College, Reading was named 2015 Independent School of The Year at a ceremony in London last November it was, says Headmaster Andrew Colpus, a tribute to the whole school. "I told the pupils in assembly that they can now say they are at the school of the year," he says. "They can wear that badge with pride. It's an award for staff, pupils and parents. It's recognition of everybody's contribution towards developing the school."

It comes as St Joseph's, located in the Royal County of Berkshire, continues a process of innovation and re-invention that began in 2010, when the school, founded in 1894 as a Catholic convent for girls, went co-educational. The school caters for pupils aged 3 to 18 and over the last five years it has grown from 300 to around 480, with an eventual target of 600. It has managed to do all of this whilst cutting fees – 17 per cent over four years – and increasing investment.

"It's a new business model," says Colpus. "We want to make it possible for more people to send their children to an independent school by making fees more affordable." St Joseph's has achieved this while remaining rooted in the Catholic ethos in which it was founded. Although the school has not been run by a religious order since the late 1970s, it still places Christian values at its heart. "We are open to those of any faith, or those of no faith," says Colpus. "We have a mixed population but we very much hope to promote the ideas of respect and tolerance, care for others, people looking out for each other. The values that the order put in place are still as important today as when the school first opened. Visitors often comment on our ethos and atmosphere."

Since arriving as headmaster in 2012, Colpus has focused on four values that he believes vital for a modern school. "We looked at our aims and identified four attributes that we want our pupils to develop," he says. "These are: commitment, collaboration, confidence and communication, and each one is a thread that runs through each child's spiritual, academic, extracurricular and pastoral education. It's not just about getting them into university, it's about developing characteristics that will serve pupils 20 or 30 years into their working lives."

The school offers bursaries to help parents who may not otherwise be able to meet the fees. And it recently restructured its scholarship system – the focus is now very much on the prestige and honour of being a scholar, rather than any monetary award. "Previously, the scholarship might go to a family that didn't need reduced fees," says Colpus. "Now we hope it will reward and reinforce a love of learning."

While the school is strong academically and is investing in its facilities, Colpus is firm in his belief that education is about much more than impressive buildings and league tables. "As a team with the governors we look at everything we do and ask if we can do it differently or better, and sometimes that involves thinking out of the box," he says. "I want the pupils to think the same. The world is continually changing and some of them will be doing jobs that don't even exist now. Results are important but the qualities they'll learn to be successful in life are more important still."

School of thought

St Andrew's International High School

Visible from the classroom windows at St Andrew's International High School in Blantyre, Malawi is the west face of the magnificent Ndirande mountain. Despite the challenges facing the township adjacent to the school, the community is vibrant and friendly, reinforcing the reputation of Malawi as "the warm heart of Africa".

"The need of the people here is huge, and students see it on their journey into school every day," says Head Teacher Kieron Smith. For this reason, fundraising activities and social projects play a central role in a SAIntS education. Students engage with their local communities and take part in the school's effort to make life better for those living far below the poverty line. One group of students is working with an orphanage for street children, while others are helping an older group learn vocational skills like tailoring and carpentry.

A recent project saw students join forces with pupils at a partner school in the UK to raise funds for an ambulance. With no means of transport, people struggle for miles across the mountain to receive medical attention, often pushing infirm relatives in wheelbarrows. The ambulance will serve the clinic just outside Blantyre, where the Queen Elizabeth Central Hospital – Malawi's largest, opened by Queen Elizabeth The Queen Mother in 1957 – is also situated.

"Parents are attracted to our British curriculum and value our blend of British and international cultures," says Smith. "We believe in educating the whole child. One element of that is teaching them to help others, particularly in this environment, where you're in the developing world. It's easy to get fixated on examinations and we do have excellent results here. However, our students are able to proudly assert themselves as confident, global citizens who progress on to universities and careers worldwide."

The school also makes good use of the Malawian landscape in its outdoor education, running the Duke of Edinburgh Award at bronze, silver and gold levels. Students at SAIntS engage with a varied programme of extracurricular activities, including a wide range of sports and creative pursuits alongside community assistance. The school stays busy well into the evening with members of the wider community coming in to use its swimming pool, climbing wall, IT rooms and football pitches.

For many students, participation in school and community life continues at weekends. Many volunteer for house social projects. "A lot of them carry on this work after leaving school too," says Smith, who regularly bumps into former students in the close-knit Blantyre community. "Part of our mission statement is to encourage our students to be globally aware and, in Malawi, there really is no better place to start than on your own doorstep."

Broad horizons

The British International School

In the entrance lobby of the British International School (BISU) in Kiev, a portrait of Her Majesty The Queen takes pride of place. The portrait alongside that of the current President of Ukraine, Petro Poroshenko, epitomises the philosophy of the school – that of offering the highly prized British system of education while respecting its host nation.

The school was founded in 1997 by Olga Zastavna and was the first to offer a British-style education in Ukraine. "As a passionate educationalist my vision was simple – to create a world class school that we could all be proud of," says Zastavna. This dream has been achieved and continues to flourish. Standards are assured by combining the International Baccalaureate (IB) Primary Years Programme, with a keen focus on high standards of numeracy and literacy that you would expect in a high-quality British school. This allows the children to progress effortlessly on to the English National Curriculum offered in the secondary school, which prepares students for their IGSCE examinations at age 16. Post IGSCE, students follow the IB Diploma and Ukrainian Atestat, giving parents the very best choice of a bilingual education.

Despite being rooted in the traditions of a British school, BISU ensures that students have a global view of the world. "The concept of being a world citizen is central to what we do," explains Keith Jackson, Director. "We're very British in our approach; in both atmosphere and ethos, while recognising that we are international citizens. The school community, made up of 30 different nationalities, reflects a variety of cultural, ethnic and religious backgrounds, allowing students to learn from each other and develop their wider understanding of the world."

Popularity has seen the school grow from a single Kiev-based campus to three, with a fourth in the city of Dnipropetrovsk, serving a total of 600 children. All seek to serve the needs of a growing population of Ukrainian parents who want a British international education for their children, often leading to enrolment in leading British universities, as well as the needs of a growing expatriate population.

"We've taken our place on the European stage," says Jackson. "People know us now, teachers seek us out as an exemplary place to work, and our ambition will drive us on to an even bigger and better future."

BISU is accredited as an examination centre by the University of Cambridge International Examinations Organisation, and is a member of the Council of British International Schools, who work closely with the UK government to ensure that quality remains high. Further to this, the school is also registered with the Ministry of Education in Ukraine, which has recently marked the school as A*, in recognition of its achievement in bringing the best education possible for Ukrainian children, both academically and pastorally.

"My aim was to build a school that children love to come to and we have done it," says Zastavna. "It's a real community and this is the source of our strength. The Queen's portrait hangs over us because we are a British school and we are proud of all it stands for."

Lessons in life

The Kingsley School

When it was founded in 1884, the aim of the Kingsley School was to offer a well-rounded education for girls. At a time when gender equality was not as it is now, this was a revolutionary sentiment. The modern landscape may be different, but today this independent day school in Royal Leamington Spa remains a bastion of high academic achievement.

Currently educating 340 girls, aged three to 18, with boys welcome in the Preparatory School, Kingsley is large enough to respond to every pupil's academic and pastoral requirements, yet small enough to address every individual need. What makes Kingsley so special is its caring ethos and ability to inspire every pupil to become their very best self in every area of school life.

"Our ethos is one of positivity and we promote a love of learning and a can-do attitude," says Heather Owens, Headteacher. "We have a broad curriculum built on the backbone of sound academic rigour. One of our core beliefs is that everyone possesses a talent or gift and our aim is to allow these to flourish. We celebrate when our girls succeed and this is how they grow, develop and gain lifelong confidence."

One Year 7 pupil is a talented rhythmic gymnast who, with the full support of the school, maintains academic excellence in tandem with pursuing her Olympic dream. A Year 12 pupil is on the cusp of becoming a professional skier: she manages to juggle this with her education thanks to the extra care and commitment given to her by the whole school community.

As well as striving for their academic best, girls leave Kingsley thoroughly prepared for the modern world. An annual trip to Balliol College Oxford inspires them to aim for top universities. Talks and presentations from global employers encourage them to learn about leadership, while girls also learn real-world employability skills by undertaking an annual work-experience week. They are also involved in charity projects.

Kingsley is proud of its history and heritage and can also boast some royal connections. The Preparatory School presented a cornflower posy to Her Majesty The Queen when she visited Royal Leamington Spa. The school was honoured to receive a letter from The Duke and Duchess of Cambridge in 2011 thanking staff and children for their Royal Wedding celebrations, while Kingsley's playing fields have recently been used as a landing ground for The Earl of Wessex's helicopter.

Kingsley girls become strong, independent young women with a balanced outlook on life and learning. Confident, capable and resilient, they become the very best version of themselves that they can be.

Straight talking

The Manchester College

As an exceptional provider of opportunities for learners of all ages, the Manchester College played host to a visit from The Duke of York in 2012. The college's ESOL course, whose students include young people on the Prince's Trust scheme, is no exception. With an approach that goes far beyond its brief of teaching English for Speakers of Other Languages, its inspirational project-based teaching method has been deemed "Outstanding" by OFSTED.

At the head of the ESOL department is Hilda Koon, who displays an irrepressible enthusiasm for embracing innovation and incorporating ideas that can improve the life chances of those in her charge. "We embed a number of soft skills into our courses," she says, "including employability, citizenship skills, personal presentation and social interaction."

The ESOL department teaches a wide range of students, from young people looking to improve their prospects to elderly people seeking to gain invaluable life skills. The course also works with employers, and students referred by the Department for Work and Pensions, as well as hospital trusts.

Koon is keen to promote the idea that total fluency in English is not the only priority, stressing the usefulness of areas such as protocol, etiquette and presentation skills for those entering the job market. "Something as simple as personal space is very different in every country, so we teach the subtleties of these things in a way that is fun," she says. "We also deal with how you listen, and acknowledge that you have listened. We even teach our teenagers personal hygiene! We tackle everything we do using English as a vehicle. We find teaching opportunities in everything, rather than just in the classroom."

Some of her students recently adapted Charles Dickens's *A Christmas Carol* for a performance in English, with original music composed by one of the college's teachers. "The story lends itself well to learning English," says Koon. "It has, for example, the past, the present and the future tenses!" To tie in with the production, some entrepreneurial students set up and ran a Christmas craft market, which entailed learning about recycling, finances and sales.

"We are very open to new projects and new ideas," says Koon. "My team says: 'If it's possible, Hilda will always say yes!' If there's a chance to improve my learners' future prospects, I'm going to give it a go. We won't know until we try it out!"

International vision

Greengates School

When in 1964, The Duke of Edinburgh, visited Mexico, a group of students from Greengates School had the opportunity to meet him. He found an expat community being prepared for their future studies in the UK.

Located just ten minutes from the centre of Mexico City, Greengates School is a prime example of that most sought-after of British exports: an institution that provides excellence in education. Offering the University of Cambridge's IGCSE certificate, the International Baccalaureate (IB) and the International Primary Curriculum (IPC) at primary-school level, Greengates School caters to around 1,300 students aged three to 18. However, when it was founded in 1951, the setting was somewhat more intimate.

"Initially, we had eight pupils who were taught in a small house," says Dr Clarisa Desouches, who attended the school and is now its CEO. "Today, we're based on a leafy purpose-built campus with computer and science labs, a garden with a lab for biology classes, rugby and football pitches, basketball courts, a gym and a covered swimming pool."

Two things that haven't changed, however, are the co-educational school's international outlook and its first-class learning environment. "Greengates was set up by British expats who wanted to prepare their children for sixth form in the UK," says Dr Desouches. "These days, we still insist on small class sizes, and most of our students are from outside Mexico, with 50 different nationalities creating a stimulating multinational setting."

Parents choose Greengates because, as the leading British international school in Mexico's capital, it consistently outperforms most schools around the world, in both IGCSE and IB exams. "We've had links with the University of Cambridge since the 1970s," says Dr Desouches, "and its examining body's positive assessment of our teaching is a source of great pride."

Since the school's language of instruction is English, its teachers are recruited mainly from the UK and chosen because their individual specialisms help provide a comprehensive education. As part of the IB programme, Greengates also offers an unusually high total of more than 40 courses, some of which count towards university degrees.

"It's the type of offering that foreign parents look for when they move to Mexico," says Dr Desouches. "And our students can also sit exams in their mother tongues here on campus, even if we don't teach those particular languages."

Catering for day students only, Greengates offers an extensive range of extracurricular activities, such as drama, photography and art classes, and orchestras in both the primary and secondary schools, as well as many sports. "But, above all," concludes Dr Desouches, "we offer a high-quality education that enables our students to go to university anywhere they like, whether it's top British institutions or a university closer to home."

A fluent delivery

St Anne's School

Set in the elegant Avenida Alfonso XIII, in one of Madrid's more exclusive areas, St Anne's School has been providing a first-class British education for more than 40 years. The school was established in 1969 by educationalist Margaret Jean Raines to fulfil her dream of sharing British culture with children in Spain. To this end, the teaching follows the UK's National Curriculum, and pupils benefit from the opportunity to attain fluency in one of the world's most spoken languages.

Pupils can enrol at the age of three and study up to A levels at the age of 18. Relatively small in scale – with a headcount of no more than 400 – St Anne's provides a happy and harmonious environment, in which children benefit from close relationships with staff. They are encouraged to develop self-reliance, independence and the leadership skills to equip them for adult life. Emphasis is also placed on problem solving, decision making and becoming independent learners.

Religious and moral education is central to the school's ethos, and all faiths are welcome. However, the official denomination is Roman Catholic, and pupils are offered preparation through the Parents' Association for First Holy Communion and confirmation in the local parish church. Discipline is also important, but it is approached in a friendly way, through reason and the promotion of self-control. Pupils are encouraged to take personal responsibility, and are able to make contributions at staff meetings through their representatives, led by a head boy, a head girl and school prefects.

St Anne's is divided into primary and secondary sections. Primary pupils learn in much the same way as children in British schools, and are also taught Spanish language and social studies.

In this way the secondary section successfully fulfils the requirements of both the Spanish Ministry of Education and the UK's Department for Education, and is subject to regular inspection by both. The statutory requirements of Spanish language and literature, Sociales and Conocimiento del Medio are taken care of, and the rest of the curriculum is taught in English by qualified British teachers.

On completion of the IGCSE exams at the end of Year 11, pupils follow the Spanish Bachillerato syllabus, which enables them to take the national university entrance examinations Prueba de Acceso a la Universidad (PAU). At the same time, they prepare for the University of Cambridge Advanced and Proficiency exams and the Cambridge Business English exams, at Vantage and Higher levels. This equips them with the fluency and sophistication necessary for high-level study and professional employment.

Students are prepared for London University GCSE examinations and Cambridge University IGCSEs, and consistently achieve impressive results. Indeed, the range of qualifications this system generates offers school leavers an unusually wide choice of universities worldwide, with most opting to study in the UK, the US or Spain. It seems only appropriate for a centre of learning that promotes such an international mindset.

United nations

The British School Manila

As Her Majesty The Queen celebrates her 90th birthday, the British School Manila (BSM) is marking its 40th anniversary, looking back on four decades at the heart of the British community in the Philippines. Each year, the school celebrates The Queen's birthday with a huge party, attended by 2,000 guests and held in partnership with the British Embassy.

It's just one highlight in a packed calendar of events hosted by the school for its students and the wider community. BSM epitomises a holistic, international approach to student development. "We provide a challenging, personalised and fun educational programme that equips our students with 21st-century skills and offers authentic, real-life learning opportunities," says Simon Mann, Head of School. "An important part of this is playing an active role in the local and international community. We also place high value on respect, honesty, kindness, integrity and taking responsibility for one's actions."

Mann is particularly proud of the school's student-led service programme which forms a central part of the curriculum starting in Nursery (age 3) and continuing to Year 13 (age 18). "BSM ensures that all our students fulfill their potential and become truly global citizens, contributing positively to making the world more peaceful, fair and sustainable."

He describes the school's approach as "hands-on". "We engage students to be a direct part of the experience of making life better for others in the Philippines," says Mann. He recalls the devastation wreaked by Typhoon Haiyan in 2013. "As the UK raised funds for those affected by the typhoon, and became the greatest single contributor of relief, BSM was galvanising not only our own community but also the British community across Southeast Asia, raising over £100,000 and distributing this directly to areas that had yet to be reached by major aid agencies."

The British School Manila offers a multicultural environment for students of all backgrounds to pursue a British-based education in the Philippines. "We have over 900 English-speaking students," says Mann, "representing 36 nationalities, including British, Commonwealth and Filipinos. But it is still a smaller school, with a warm family atmosphere and strong sense of community."

The school was founded by a group of British parents in Manila, and the initial focus was on educating expat children to prepare them to return to life in the UK. Today, BSM students attend top universities around the world, thanks in large part to their strong academic performance and wide base of extracurricular pursuits, which includes the Duke of Edinburgh Awards, Model United Nations, art, music, drama, sport and service.

It's a source of pride that BSM played host to a visit from The Princess Royal in 2015. "When the visit was announced, we discussed what we thought Her Royal Highness might most enjoy and what it was we wanted to showcase," says Mann. "Unsurprisingly it was our students, staff and families, their learning and our sense of community."

Raising aspirations

Sunderland College

"We're about changing lives and mindsets, as well as raising aspirations and attainment," says Ellen Thinnesen, Chief Executive and Principal of Sunderland College. With more than 15,000 students passing through the college's doors every year, Thinnesen's 650-strong staff play a major role in shaping the future lives of young people and adults of all ages.

Their dedication to providing quality academic, professional and technical education across the college's four campuses has yielded impressive results. Performance tables show that Sunderland College students achieve higher grades than any other further education college in the area for both A-level and vocational courses. In 2015, the college achieved a 99 per cent A-level pass rate for the seventh year in a row, with 970 students progressing to higher education. With success has come recognition: The Prince of Wales met several of the college's National Citizen Service students in person in 2015, as part of his ongoing commitment to social-action projects.

As well as contributing to its students' success, the college is also contributing to the regeneration of Sunderland and the wider region. At the heart of this vision for growth is a new £29 million city campus. "The new campus will support Sunderland's growing economy," says Thinnesen. "It will give students access to state-of-the-art resources and high-quality learning that will equip them for the challenges of a changing economy and a high-skilled and entrepreneurial workforce. As a hub for stakeholder engagement in the development of skills and future prosperity, the campus will provide new opportunities for employers to invest in their

workforce and broader business strategies. Our governors, staff, students, the city and our wider communities will be immensely proud when this campus opens in September 2016."

Accommodating 2,000 students and offering more than 100 courses, the new campus will be pioneering in its approach to learning. "The focus is very much on providing a real-life working environment," says Nigel Harrett, Deputy Principal. "Alongside classrooms, there will be workshops for advanced manufacturing and engineering, motor vehicle maintenance and construction skills, which will be of the professional standard found in leading companies. A realistic aeroplane cabin will enhance the learning of travel and tourism students; and two hi-tech teaching kitchens will be on campus for catering and hospitality courses. Many students will be involved in running commercial ventures such as a restaurant, a bakery, a luxury spa, or a hair salon, and all these are accessed directly by the public."

To ensure courses are relevant to the workplace, the college continues to work alongside leading employers. Sony and other industry leaders have been instrumental in creating a digital technology skills academy with the college, where students benefit from a course in computer games design, run in association with NextGen, including training in animation and visual effects.

Thinnesen and her team at Sunderland College are passionate about raising students' ambitions and inspiring them to progress in their chosen careers. They know that equipping them with enterprise and employability skills will provide them with a strong foundation to succeed in the future.

Bede Building

↖ Reception

THIS STONE
WAS LAID BY
...D. M. SWAIN, J.P.
CHAIRMAN OF THE
...UCATION COMMITTEE
...APR 7ᵗʰ 1932

Making the grade

The British International School

International Day is a major event at the British International School of Moscow (BIS). Every year, before the October half-term holiday, pupils and staff gather together to celebrate cultural diversity by wearing national costumes, learning about national foods and contributing to a debate on global issues of the day. The festivities culminate in a major concert, which represents a highlight of the school's social calendar for many who take part.

The event recognises the importance of multiculturalism, in the wider world but also in the school itself, where more than 65 nationalities are represented in a student body of more than 800 children aged between 3 and 18 years. "One of the major contributory factors to our success as an international school is the way in which we celebrate our cultural diversity," says Academic Director Denis Kelly.

Each week, school assemblies focus on a difference aspect of this diversity, which feeds into all aspects of school life, from academic interaction in the classroom to artistic, athletic and social pursuits in the extracurricular programmes. "Our students enjoy their academic successes in a highly diverse community and an atmosphere where they can comfortably mingle with their peers from so many nationalities and cultures," says Kelly.

While academic excellence is at the forefront of the daily agenda, BIS schools also offer students the opportunity to engage in a broad range of extracurricular activities, including art, music, drama and sports. The daily programme as a whole is designed to challenge students and enhance their personal development, the benefits of which are evident in their attitudes and in their outlooks on life.

"I think our students really appreciate and value the rewards they gain for their endeavours, both personally and academically," Kelly explains, adding, "Students who attend BIS feel they are special because they have the opportunity to develop as a valued member of the school community." They also make a contribution towards supporting the wider local community with regular fundraising activities held throughout the year, including the autumn and summer fairs, to support disadvantaged groups in Moscow society, such as young people affected by disability and families living below the poverty line.

Since it was founded in 1994, the underlying principle of BIS has been to provide a first-class education to a multicultural student body. The opening of the school came during a milestone year for British–Russian relations when, just a few months after BIS opened its doors, Her Majesty The Queen made an official state visit to the country, marking the first state visit by a British monarch to Russia since the establishment of the Soviet Union.

BIS is made up of seven schools with separate campuses spread across Moscow. Six of the schools follow a programme based on the English National Curriculum with one offering teaching based on the Russian Federal state system. Both A levels and the International Baccalaureate are offered, giving students a range of routes to achieve their higher education goals.

The coming years will see BIS, in partnership with Cambridge Education UK, pursue the completion of its accreditation as a British School Overseas, which it expects to achieve by the end of 2017, further establishing its status as a top institution for British-style learning in the Russian capital.

Teaching for life

St Andrews (Barnsbury) C of E Primary School

After taking over as Head Teacher of St Andrew's School in Barnsbury, North London, Felicity Djerehe decided to collaborate with the parents, governors and pupils to devise a new motto. Between them, they came up with the phrase: "Realising potential through faith, hope and love".

"This is intended to reflect the values of the school," says Djerehe, "and acknowledge the importance of its life as a Church of England school."

St Andrew's is a single-form entry school with around 200 children. It is located in an area near King's Cross that is economically and culturally diverse, with both The Prince of Wales and The Duchess of Cambridge visiting the area in recent months to support local regeneration schemes. Djerehe is keen to encourage aspiration in all her charges, and for them to carry its values into their next schools and beyond.

St Andrew's is blessed with unusually attractive grounds, of which it increasingly makes good use. "We now have a member of staff in charge of the Forest School project, a system of outdoor learning," says Djerehe. "We have lots of cagoules and boots, so we go out in all weathers! These days we actually use the outside learning environment as much as the inside."

The school also hopes to raise funding to enable the children to keep chickens, beehives and raised beds as part of a sustainable and community-based project.

Djerehe is keen that her pupils, first and foremost, are happy. "We aim to promote their mental health, and instil in them a sense of spiritual and physical wholeness," she says. "We also want our children to become independent, and develop a love of learning. Fortunately, we have a very positive, focused group of teachers and support staff, who really understand that learning never ends."

Learning through teaching is an important component of the St Andrew's approach. Children are given responsibilities throughout the school, in different areas – including as playground friends, dinner hall helpers, digital leaders and participants in school council.

"We try to instil a sense of resilience in everyone," says Djerehe. "We recognise that life can be hard, and they need to be able to bounce back. We want our children to understand that things aren't always going to go according to plan – so we do our best to give them the resources to cope once they leave St Andrew's."

Values added

St Michael's Church of England School

As a happy gathering of mini, would-be Her Majesties recently went to show, St Michael's Church of England School in Maidstone, Kent is no ordinary primary school. "We recently held a royal banquet where the children dressed as princes and princesses," says Executive Head Teacher Lisa Dicker. "Those kinds of experiences help create a special, safe environment where children can be themselves."

Articulating the values of a school can be tricky for some, but at St Michael's they've nailed it. "Four values – respect, friendship, perseverance and happiness – describe the essence of everything we do," says Dicker.

With just 120 children, St Michael's is a small co-ed at the heart of its local community. It is perhaps the school's ethos that really places it, however, and those four crucial words. Respect, for example, is both taught and modelled. "Our aim is to produce polite, well-rounded children who can face the world with confidence," says Dicker. "Our topic-based curriculum is all about working together. But teachers work together too. I'm often in the lunch hall, serving dinners and scraping plates, so the children see that no job is too big or too small for anybody."

As for friendship, the school's 2014 Ofsted report – which deemed it "Outstanding" – notes that St Michael's pupils "love learning and care for each other". "That's paramount," says Dicker. "You've got to care!"

Perseverance, on the other hand, is about determination. "Getting something wrong isn't a bad thing here," she says. "We don't talk about 'failure', we talk about a 'first attempt'." With a rigorous new national curriculum introduced in 2015, this has been crucial to maintaining enthusiasm and confidence.

"Happiness is about children wanting to come to school and leaving with a smile on their face," says Dicker. "I see it as my job to make sure that staff, children and parents are happy."

In this way, St Michael's nurtures not only the whole child, but the whole community. Reflecting its strong ethos beyond the school gates, it works with The Vine Church, fundraising to support homeless people, and is also linked with a children's home in Grenada.

"This Christmas, we sent presents for every child at the orphanage," says Dicker, with a smile. This typifies St Michael's, and it's the four pillars of respect, friendship, perseverance and happiness that give this small school such a big heart.

A palace of learning

The Whitgift Foundation

Nestled in the heart of Croydon's Old Town sits an extraordinary palace, a former summer residence of the Archbishops of Canterbury, and an incredible site of historical significance frequented by royalty and the Church over the centuries. The palace boasts one of the finest medieval great halls in southern England, a Guard Room, Long Gallery, chapel and even a bed chamber used by Queen Elizabeth I, and now provides a unique place of learning for girls at Old Palace of John Whitgift School.

Students relish studying in an historical setting where Henry III and Edward I have resided, King James I of Scotland was held prisoner, Catherine of Aragon and Mary Tudor visited and, most recently in 1996, Her Majesty The Queen and The Duke of Edinburgh were entertained to lunch in the Guard Room to celebrate the 400th anniversary of the Whitgift Foundation.

One of the palace's regular visitors, Archbishop John Whitgift, forged a strong attachment to Croydon. He believed in supporting the vulnerable sections of society and so, in 1596, he laid the foundation stones at the Hospital of the Holy Trinity (now known as the Whitgift Almshouses). This saw the founding of the Whitgift Foundation, a charity with a mission to support the Croydon community, providing education for the young and care for the elderly.

"Archbishop Whitgift started by educating the boys of the town so that they, in turn, could grow up and give back to the local community," says Martin Corney, Chief Executive of the Whitgift Foundation. "He purchased land with a view to using the income it generated to subsidise the schools and care homes."

Today, the foundation's property portfolio, including the freehold of the Whitgift Shopping Centre, provides income to support the education of 3,000 students at Whitgift School, Trinity School and Old Palace School, and look after 100 older people at Whitgift Care. More recently, this has been extended to supporting carers in Croydon through the Carers' Information Service. This long-term commitment to the town is manifested in other ways too, through the organisation of the Croydon Heritage Festival. Support also comes from students at the foundation's schools who are given the opportunity to engage with the needs of their local community through a broad programme of social development activities such as volunteering in local schools and care homes.

"We place great emphasis on developing a distinguished sense of social responsibility in students and encouraging them to think beyond their own ends and channel their energies into working towards the greater good," explains Old Palace Head, Carol Jewell. "And the history of the buildings has inspired generations who have passed through them."

Around £5 million a year is channelled into fee support; 46 per cent of students at the foundation's schools are supported by the charity's generous bursary scheme, a higher number than nearly any independent school in the country, enabling students to benefit from learning in a richly diverse environment – a first-class education for pupils from all social, cultural and ethnic backgrounds.

A culture of respect

St Mary's Church of England Primary School

A great deal has changed at St Mary's Church of England Primary School over the past three years – and, judging by the smiles at the school gates, its students, parents and teachers approve. This is a school that welcomes children from diverse backgrounds, and builds unity through its strong ethos and its creative curriculum. "Our school population used to be mainly white British with about 30 per cent Afro-Caribbean children," explains Lynn Thorne, Head of this primary school, based in the Walkley area of Sheffield. "Now, it's incredibly diverse. We've got children from all over Europe and the Middle East – and that's brought a cultural richness."

Life isn't easy for many, however, so St Mary's works hard to support incoming families. "We make sure they have vouchers for food banks and we provide uniforms," says Thorne. "We care for our children and, because of that, they thrive and blossom." And, with St Mary's having only single-form entry, it still has the feel of a village school. "Not only do I know every child by name," says Thorne, "but I know every child's attendance and ability."

The school has seen structural change too, joining the Diocese of Sheffield Academies Trust in 2013. A skills-based curriculum was brought in, nurturing children's creative strengths through music and the arts. "For example, Year 1 children are studying outer space, so they're building spaceships in the classroom." Children in Year 6, meanwhile, have enjoyed learning about the history of the Royal Family, making portraits of Henry VIII and his six wives and other monarchs.

New expertise has been brought in too. "I've now got teachers who specialise in maths, in literacy and in creativity," says Thorne. "And I'm a national trainer in philosophy for children. It's a programme that is about developing democracy, respecting British values and being socially responsible citizens, but it also gives children the tools with which to reason and be reasoned with. Because of that, we have very few behaviour issues."

Children engage with charitable work too. Last year pupils from the school even met Her Majesty The Queen when she visited Sheffield Cathedral for the Royal Maundy service. The school also supports the Cathedral Archer Project, which works with homeless people, and contributes to Sheffield Children's Hospital's project, Herd of Sheffield. St Mary's will also be decorating a model elephant to be displayed in the city. Regular commitments, meanwhile, include concerts at old people's homes and care homes. "We've got a very active choir," says Thorne, "and are also part of the Archbishop of York's Youth Trust, to develop young leaders.

But it's perhaps St Mary's links with the local parish church that most strongly reflect its ethos. "We work closely to develop spirituality," says Thorne. "That can be difficult because the children come from a range of faiths – so we focus on respect for each other, respect for ourselves and respect for the environment. This culture is key for us all. And the children are so happy. They really do skip into school every morning."

World class

Chartwell International School

With its spacious, bright classrooms, park-like gardens, sports fields and swimming pool, Chartwell International School, situated in a beautiful residential area of Belgrade, Serbia, has for the past 15 years more than lived up to its international title.

Providing education to pupils aged two to 19 across four premises, the school currently encompasses 36 nationalities. A little world of its own, the unifying factor of this tightly knit and culturally diverse establishment is accreditation from Cambridge International Examinations (CIE), recognising Chartwell as a Cambridge International School, as well as the registration by the Serbian Ministry of Education.

The school follows the CIE programme, which is based on the English national curriculum. Academic standards are monitored keenly, with classes tailored to suit the needs, interests and potential of each child and including additional personalised tuition if required.

Contemporary learning methods and an interdisciplinary approach are applied at Chartwell. The school's teachers are highly qualified and come from a variety of backgrounds, but they all share a common passion for teaching, and a commitment to the students and their education.

Lessons are taught in English but a variety of languages are on the curriculum. Indeed, cultural diversity plays a vital role at the school, which celebrates United Nations Day each year, promoting tolerance and respect. Children also perform at regular poetry and music evenings in their mother tongues and in the languages taught at school, and Chartwell International School marks a host of British traditions, including St Patrick's Day and Mother's Day. It is also the only school in Serbia to celebrate Bonfire Night.

Chartwell fosters a strong family atmosphere that is not governed by rules, but rather by respect for others and common sense. This makes for a unique, tension-free environment where, regardless of cultural differences, students and teachers are encouraged to respect each other and work closely to achieve the best possible results.

"Our graduating students leave us to go to universities around the globe and achieve good results," says the school's founder Nenad Gazikalovic. "We are, of course, very proud of them but most importantly, we are proud that they have become good people – people with the right values, who respect themselves and who have learned to respect others regardless of differences."

Understanding that education is about a lot more than the academic programme alone, an emphasis is placed on extracurricular activities, ranging from sports to dance and drama. Chartwell's students are also involved in community life and regularly attend workshops, exhibitions and plays. They also take part in humanitarian activities through the school's Something for Everyone – Children to Children project.

Growing up alongside fellow pupils from around the world, Chartwell's students have a heightened understanding of what the world at large has to offer. This ensures that when they leave their "little world" in Belgrade, they do so equipped to meet the challenges of an increasingly globalised and competitive world.

Community champ

St Thomas Church of England Primary School

Her Majesty The Queen and The Duke of Edinburgh have visited Greater Manchester on countless occasions, for instance, at the opening ceremony of the Commonwealth Games in 2002, to present the University of Manchester with its Royal Charter two years later and to inaugurate the region's vibrant MediaCityUK as part of the Diamond Jubilee celebrations.

On a different scale to these grand occasions, but no less worthy of credit, is St Thomas Church of England Primary School in Werneth, Greater Manchester. On first sight, the school looks much as it did when it was built in 1847. But, although the Grade II-listed building's facade has been preserved, a great deal has changed within. "People think we're a small school," says Headteacher Angela Knowles, "but it's like a Tardis."

Founded as a Sunday School, St Thomas was set up by the local community with money raised by public subscription. It has served the area ever since – which, in 2004, called for expansion when another local primary closed. Twelve new classrooms, a nursery, music room, art room and all-weather pitch were added to the back of the building, followed, in 2010, with a further four classrooms, studio and parents' room and, in 2015, nursery facilities. The school recently added a peace garden and an immature forest to its grounds.

Bricks and mortar aren't the only changes at St Thomas. The school initially educated predominantly white British children living in Oldham's "Grand West End" – a prosperous district that thrived during the Industrial Revolution. In contrast, the vast majority of today's students belong to an ethnic minority group, with 80 per cent from deprived backgrounds, and 98 per cent speaking English as an additional language. "Our Christian ethos has remained," says Knowles, "although we're now serving a predominantly Muslim community."

St Thomas was recently rated "Outstanding" by the Statutory Inspection of Anglican and Methodist Schools. Year 5 teacher Laura Carruthers believes this success is down to strong leadership. "That's the driving force," she says. "We're all on the same page, from teachers to cooks to cleaning staff. That brings consistency for the children." Managing a school that's more than doubled in size in the past decade requires staff training, and the school offers continuous professional development. Parents and the community benefit too, with St Thomas running a number of courses in conjunction with Oldham College.

It's this kind of approach that illustrates the school's lifelong commitment to serving its local area, and makes this seemingly small outfit a big hitter in the Greater Manchester community.

"We know, everyone of us,
that in the end all will be well;
for God will care for us and give us
victory and peace. And when peace
comes, remember it will be for us,
the children of today, to make
the world of tomorrow a better
and happier place"

Princess Elizabeth, wartime speech, 13 October 1940

Royal Windsor

A history to celebrate

"If it wasn't for the castle, I don't think we'd be here," says Councillor Eileen Quick, Mayor of the Royal Borough of Windsor and Maidenhead. "Windsor itself wouldn't be here: Old Windsor is a few miles down the road and Windsor is officially New Windsor, which was built up around the castle. We are very proud of our royal connections."

Those royal connections stretch back for hundreds of years to the Norman Conquest. While Edward the Confessor held his Great Councils of the Realm at Old Windsor, the current town's history begins with William the Conqueror, who established a fortification on a bend in the River Thames in 1070.

Within a few decades, the imposing castle had become a royal residence as King Henry I moved his court from Old Windsor, before marrying in the chapel and crowning his queen there. Over the centuries, the site has witnessed the birth of The Most Noble Order of the Garter under King Edward III and the creation of the medieval St George's Chapel by King Edward IV.

In total, 10 sovereigns are buried in the chapel – a Royal Peculiar, which does not come under the jurisdiction of a bishop or archbishop – and Windsor is still a royal residence to this day. The largest occupied castle in the world, Her Majesty The Queen still takes up residence at various times during the court calendar, as well as using it as a private home.

The town's history is closely entwined with that of the Royal Family. Granted its first charter in 1276 by King Edward I, many firms display their Royal Warrants in the windows of Windsor's streets to this day, while the historic streets have one of the highest concentrations of listed buildings in the country.

"Many of the families that have been here for several generations include family members who have served the Royal Household in the past," says Councillor Quick. "Whether that's working in the castle or on the estate, they're very proud of this fact. Local people do feel that association with the Royal Family, a personal connection."

It seems fitting, then, that Windsor should take centre stage for Her Majesty's birthday celebrations. The private grounds of Windsor Castle will host The Queen's 90th Birthday Celebration, where some 900 horses and more than 1,500 participants will tell the story of her life and reign in four spectacular nightly events.

Created by the team that organised the Diamond Jubilee Pageant in Windsor in 2012, it's the latest in a string of royal events to take place in the town. "It does take some organisation," says Councillor Quick. "We are lucky to have had so many events over the years, so officers are very well practised. There's a good relationship between the Crown Estate and the local authority."

While tickets sold out instantly for the evening events held in the purpose-build arena used for the Royal Windsor

OPPOSITE: THE ANNUAL ORDER OF THE GARTER SERVICE, WHICH TAKES PLACE AT ST GEORGE'S CHAPEL, IS JUST ONE OF WINDSOR'S ROYAL OCCASIONS. RIGHT: THE QUEEN ATTENDS THE DIAMOND JUBILEE PAGEANT IN THE GROUNDS OF WINDSOR CASTLE

Horse Show, there is also a special ballot for The Celebration on The Long Walk, where 5,000 winners and their guests can watch the celebration on large screens situated at the top of the castle's impressive approach.

It's important to everyone that the castle is an integral part of the town, says Councillor Quick. "There are very strong connections between the town and castle. Local residents have free access when the castle is open to enjoy the grounds, as well as the services at St George's chapel. It's a lovely gift from Her Majesty to us."

With new tourism markets including China, Windsor has also been working hard to persuade those visitors attracted by its royal history to stay in the town, rather than visiting on a day trip from London.

"Tourism does now bring quite a lot of money to the local economy," says Councillor Quick. "We are very lucky that we have beautiful attractions as well as the castle. The Thames at Windsor is a lovely stretch of river, people come to walk in

the hundreds of acres of the Great Park. We have the race course too and Ascot in the borough, so there's something for everyone."

One of the town's biggest challenges stems from the same historic charm that draws visitors in the first place. "Like many old towns, it's very difficult to provide enough parking," observes Councillor Quick. "But there are plans to create a rail link between Windsor and Heathrow to reduce the need to travel by car."

If visitors can't expect quite the same red carpet treatment as that delivered to Queen Victoria, who was provided with a Royal Waiting Room at both of Windsor's stations when the railway was built, it's enough for many to walk in the footsteps of Britain's monarchy, in a town where royalty has been born, lived and celebrated for well over 900 years.

Just the ticket

Bath Bus Company

The Berkshire towns of Windsor and Eton are always thronging with royal sightseers, no more so than in Her Majesty The Queen's 90th year. And, as ever, Bath Bus Company offers a relaxing, informative and convenient way to visit them.

Bath Bus Company provides historically rich recorded tours of the two towns, as well as Bath and Cardiff, on its modern, open-top, hop-on, hop-off service. In 2013, the company won City Sightseeing Operator of the Year against competition from 100 cities around the world.

"We offer highly popular multilingual tours as well as tours with live guides in Bath and Cardiff," says Victoria Annett, the company's Marketing Manager. "The guides add their own personal flair and local expertise."

Bath Bus Company recognises the value of personal engagement on its tours. "Even if visitors opt for the taped multilingual commentary, their driver will also have great local knowledge," says Annett. "We choose our live guides for Bath and Cardiff not just because they know all there is to know about their city, but because of their natural delivery, which keeps the tours fresh."

Each tour is scripted in house and is then translated into 10 languages. As Annett explains, this keeps the recordings personal and engaging rather than formulaic. "We are also seeing ever greater numbers of Chinese tourists," she says, "so we now offer both Mandarin and Cantonese tours."

Complementing these tours, Bath Bus Company operates Air Decker, a bus service connecting Bath and Bristol Airport, which launched in 2013 and which has seen passenger numbers double.

"The service runs pretty much around the clock and takes in local stops along the route," says Annett, "so it works for business travellers as well as tourists and shoppers." Realising that its welcoming and helpful staff are key to the success of its tour buses, Bath Bus Company drivers were enlisted to train the new Air Decker drivers when the service launched. "For many people arriving at Bristol Airport, their first impression of England is through our drivers," says Annett, "so being friendly and approachable is essential."

Bath Bus Company's fleet, which has been decorated especially for Her Majesty's celebrations, is playing a lead role in the tourist experience in Windsor during 2016, proving that a refreshing, engaging and fact-packed bus tour is a winning business formula whatever language it's in.

A right royal feast

Windsor Grill

It is only a short stroll from the magnificent Windsor Castle, but the first thing that strikes a new visitor to David Wilby's Windsor Grill is its relaxed and understated glamour.

"It's the sort of restaurant that I like to eat in myself," says Wilby. "It is important to me that people feel comfortable when they visit us. As a local independent restaurant, we have a great relationship with our customers and they know that they will always receive a warm welcome, as well as an unpretentious meal, using quality produce."

Good produce is key for Wilby. Menus are based largely around steaks and rare-breed meat, but also include fresh seafood dishes, classic cocktails and carefully selected wines.

Most of the beef on the menu – including steaks such as 35-day dry aged rib-eye – come from selected farms in Aberdeenshire, most of which Wilby has visited in person. It is also no secret that Windsor Grill uses the same butcher as a certain close neighbour who is celebrating a significant birthday this year.

"Good produce doesn't need to be manipulated", he says. "Once we receive our ingredients, we season them well and treat them with respect."

Wilby's distinguished background as a chef and restaurateur spans more than 30 years. He has worked and trained in some of the top restaurants in Britain and the United States, with a CV including spells at The Mirabelle in Mayfair and Menage a Trois in Knightsbridge. He also launched Fifty-One Fifty-One in Chelsea, London's first Cajun Creole restaurant.

These broad influences are evident in his menus. Customer favourites include blackened prawns, chateaubriand steak, pork five ways, and a famous take on the Eton mess pudding, this one with a Windsor twist.

In addition to Windsor Grill's loyal local following, it is a popular venue for small corporate events. From time to time, leading figures from the worlds of sport and entertainment can be sighted taking advantage of its laid-back, discreet atmosphere.

"While we might be based in central Windsor, we are hidden away from the hustle and bustle of the town centre," says Wilby. "It makes us very popular with locals and those who are keen to enjoy a more relaxed evening with good food and wine."

Acknowledgements

PUBLISHER

Custom publisher St James's House is the official publishing partner to The Queen's 90th Birthday Celebration.

St James's House
(Regal Press Limited)
298 Regents Park Road
London
N3 2SZ

+44 (0) 20 8371 4000
www.stjamess.org

Richard Freed
Director
richard.freed@stjamess.org

Richard Golbourne
Director of Sales
r.golbourne@stjamess.org

Stephen van der Merwe
Business Development Director
stephen.vdm@stjamess.org

Stephen Mitchell
Head of Editorial
stephen.mitchell@stjamess.org

Anna Danby
Head of Creative
anna.danby@stjamess.org

PHOTOGRAPHY

Khalil Al-Zadjali (pp. 356 and 357), Snowdon/Camera Press London (p. 5), Cipla Archives (p. 389), John Donat & RIBA Collections (p. 193), David Eustace (p. 375), Getty Images, Harrie-art (p. 312), Gareth Jones (p. 427), John McCann & RIBA Collections (p. 192), Mirrorpix, naturepl.com/Anup Shah/WWF (p. 398), Network Rail (pp. 264–5), Press Association, Rex Features, Ken Spence (p. 150), Richard Stonehouse/WWF-UK (p. 399), TEAS/Eldar Akberov (p. 229), TEAS/Andrew Wiard (p. 228), Alister Thorpe/Sims Images (pp. 194 and 195).

Other images are the copyright of individual organisations.

A special thank you to the Royal Mail Group for providing the cover image of the Machin bust created by Arnold Machin and to the Trinity Mirror Group for allowing access to its extensive picture archive Mirrorpix.

ORDERS

To purchase additional copies of *The Queen at 90*, visit www.hmq90books.com

Index